Mum,

Thank you for coming to visit. It has been an absolute pleasure to see you again, and I hope that you have enjoyed your time down-under.

I wish it wasn't so long between visits. Hopefully I will get over to Scotland in about three years time!

lots of love

Julie

25 May 1998.

Steve Parish

CELEBRATING AUSTRALIA

VICTORIA

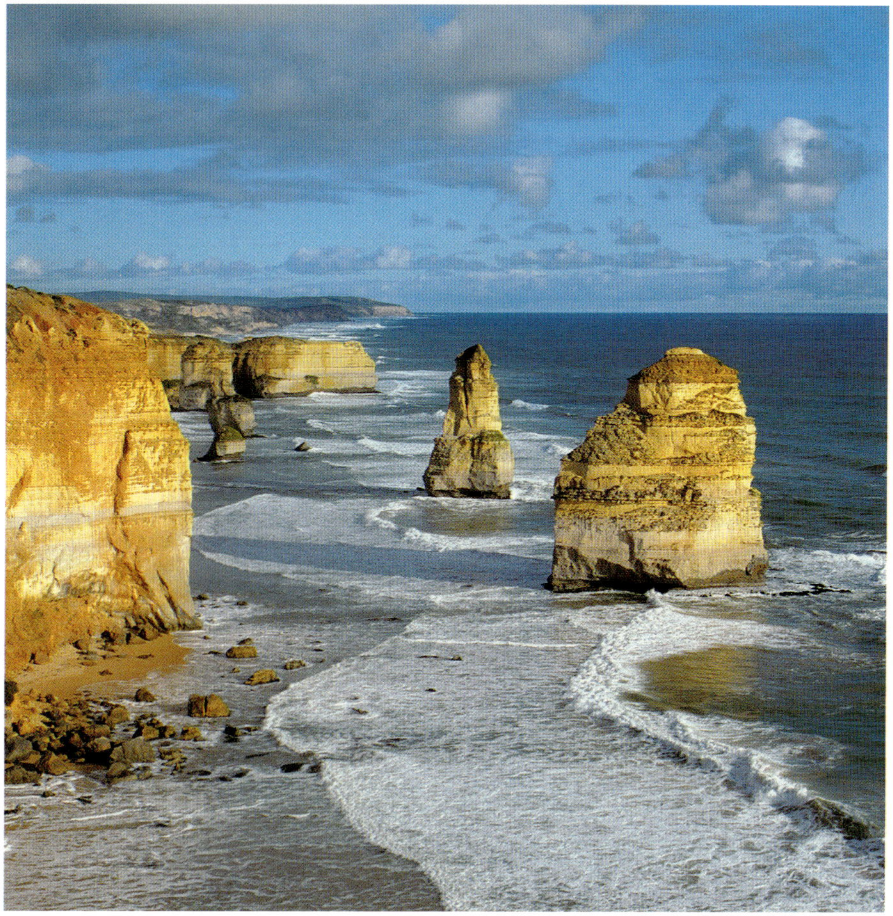

Steve Parish
PUBLISHING

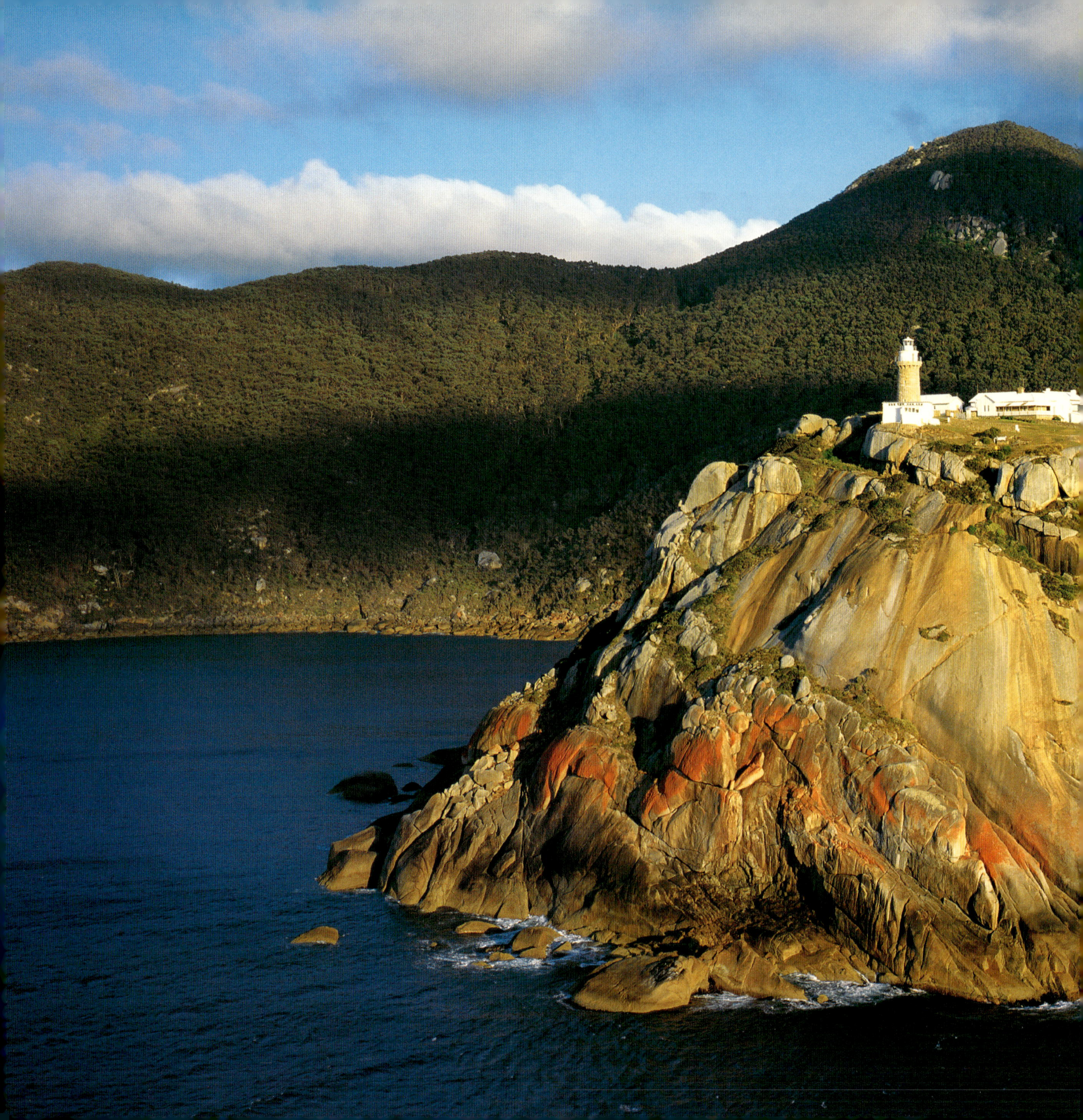

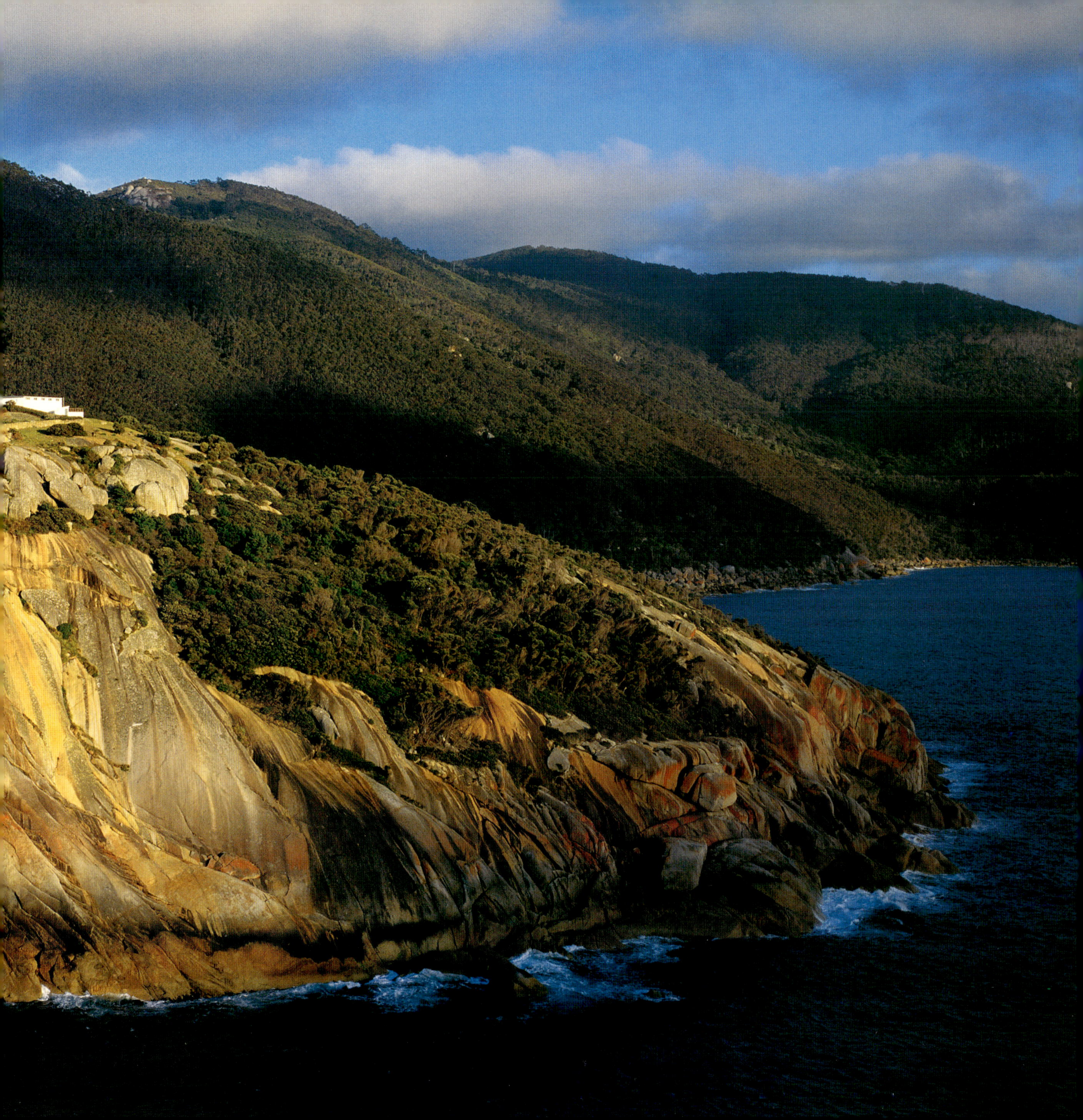

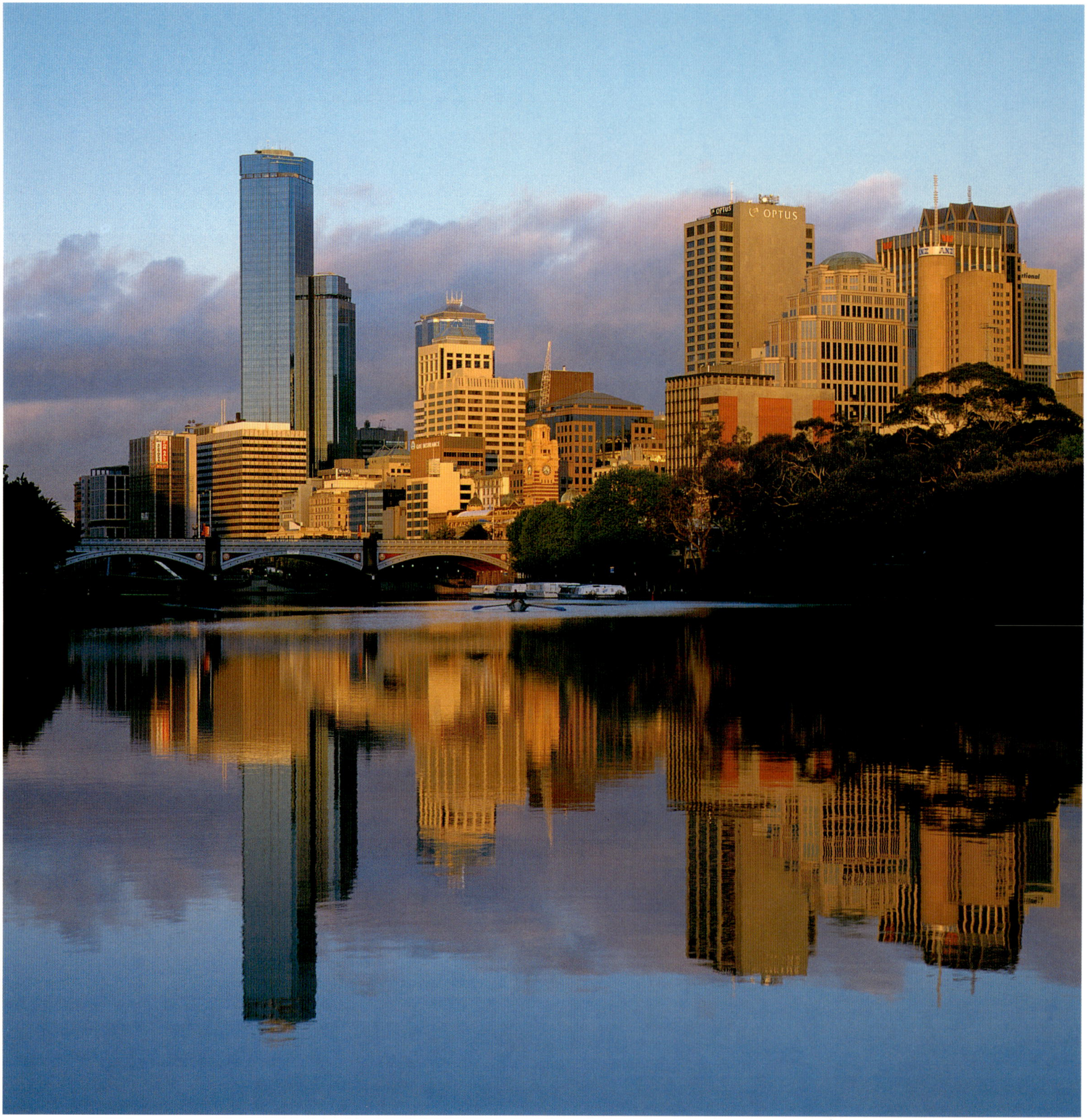

Title page: The Twelve Apostles stand sentinel on the Shipwreck Coast.
Preceding pages: The stone lighthouse on Wilsons Promontory's South East Point.

Above: The buildings of Melbourne city lit by the morning sun and reflected in the Yarra.

Introduction

The thought of Melbourne conjures up a series of visual images of remarkable beauty: the Yarra River at dawn with a solitary racing shell leaving a v-shaped wake in its silver surface; Flinders Street Station in the magic twilight moment when lighting turns it into an oriental palace; a green and gold tram rolling past the National Gallery; the splendour of the Royal Exhibition Building; the Hotel Windsor in all its stately glory; the soft brown eyes of a gorilla at Melbourne Zoo, gazing thoughtfully back at his adoring public. There is Cook's Cottage, the sophistication of Southgate, the charm of Port Phillip Bay and so much more.

Touring Victoria reveals a richness of scenic variety, including even the most-often-pictured landscapes, for they constantly change as, in these southern latitudes, the natural light varies from moment to moment. A gully in the Dandenong Ranges or a stretch of water in the Gippsland Lakes can become a vision of delight as the sun filters through the forest canopy or slants down through storm clouds. The Great Ocean Road, that miracle of engineering, is a favourite route to adventure, winding beside spectacular coastline with sheer cliffs and rolling surf, through holiday townships, State Park reserves and the rainforest of the Otway National Park, to the Shipwreck Coast and the magnificent Twelve Apostles. Around May each year, in the waters off Warrnambool, unofficial capital of the Shipwreck Coast, whales arrive from Antarctic seas to give birth.

To me, the essence of Victoria is that *this time* it is wonderful, but there is so much to see and so much to capture on film that the moment I leave it beckons me back, promising that *next time* even more of its wonders will be revealed to me. This book offers some of my favourite Victorian places, in a State where I have spent some of my happiest and most productive photographic hours.

Steve Parish

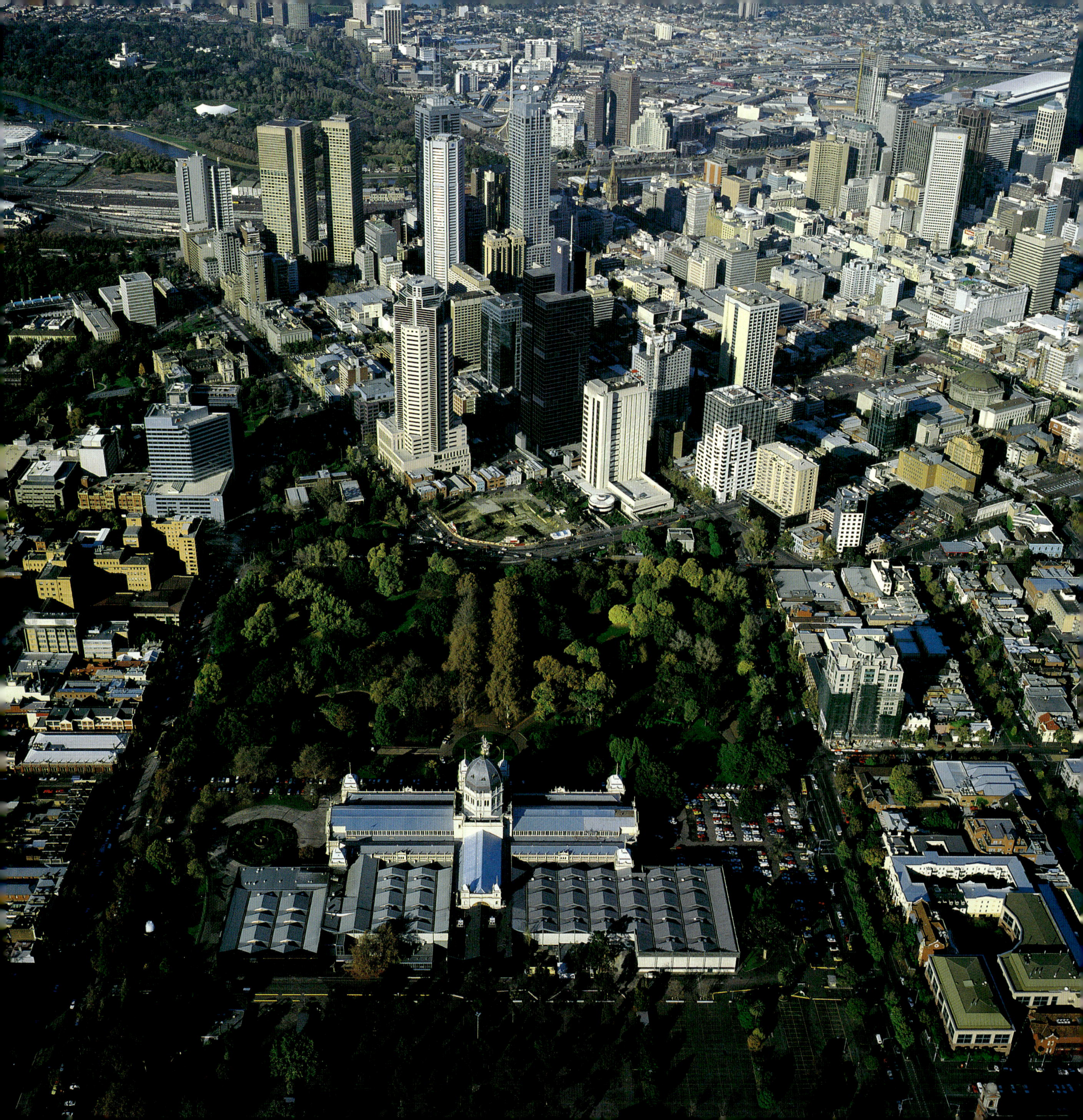

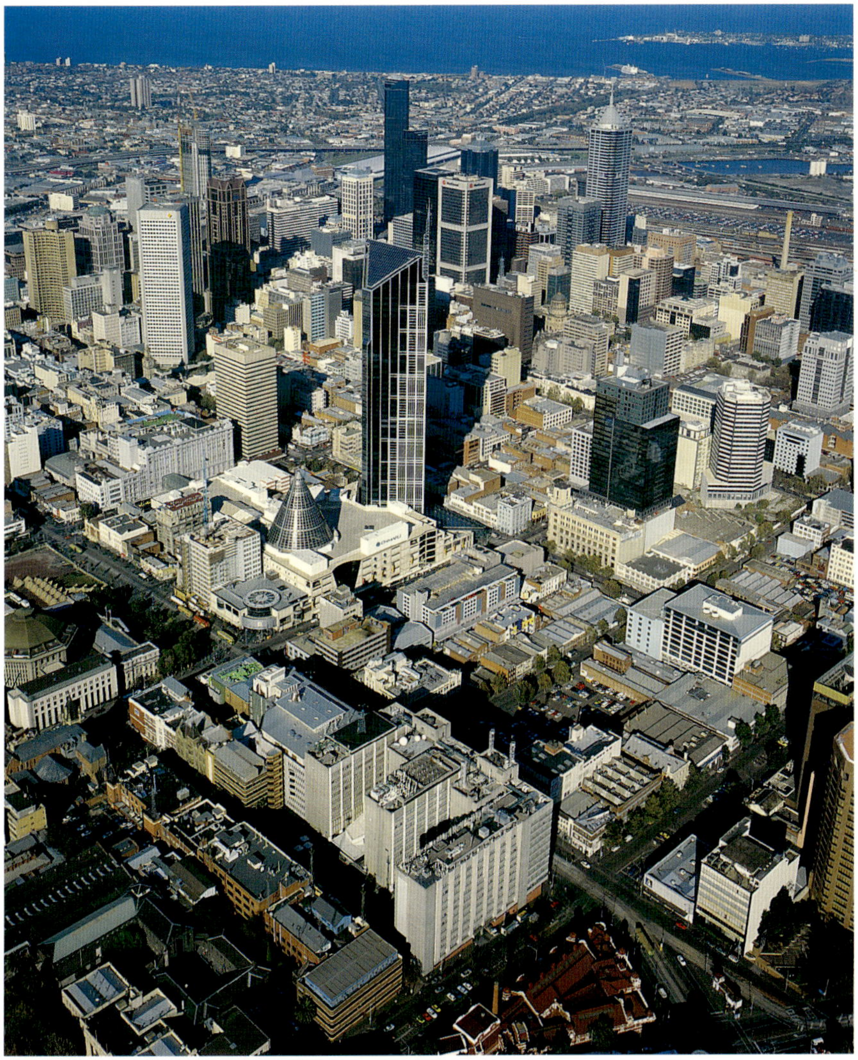

Above: Melbourne city centre and, in the distance, Port Phillip Bay.
Opposite: A view of the city over Carlton Gardens and the Royal Exhibition Building, erected for the Great Exhibition of 1888.

Melbourne

Melbourne is one of the world's great cities, a sophisticated centre of culture, commerce and government, the capital of a State of about 4 500 000 million people and still growing. A handsome, energetic city, Melbourne is home to a multicultural population – a home which retains among its exciting modern architecture the grace and charm of fine nineteenth century buildings.

In 1835, John Batman, born in Australia and the son of convicts, sailed from Launceston to port Phillip Bay and declared "the place for a village" on the Yarra River. By the year 1851, when the independent colony of Victoria was created, Melbourne was a thriving township bidding fair to become the beautiful city it is today.

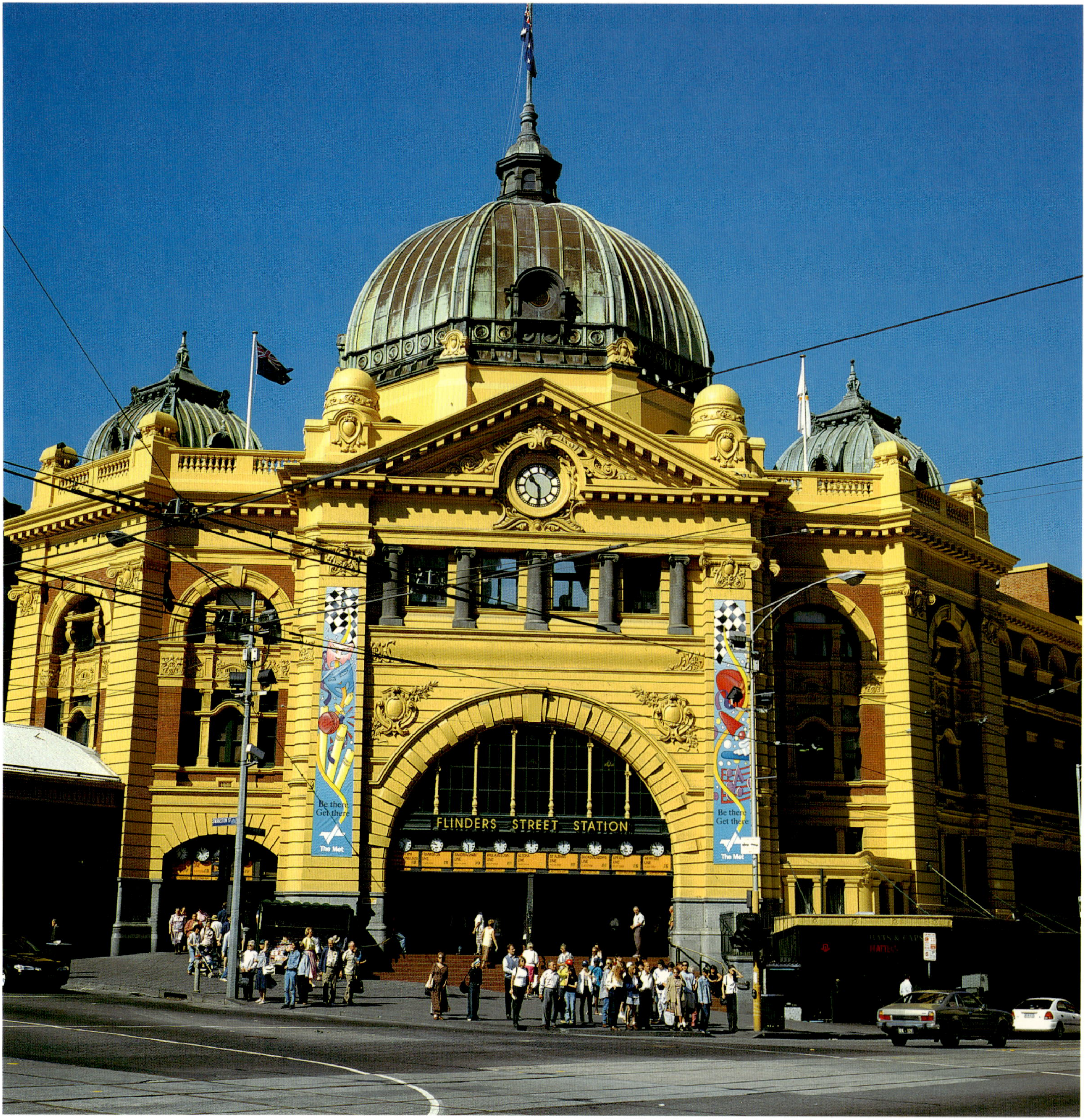

The main entrance to Flinders Street Station, hub of an efficient metropolitan rail service and Melbourne landmark, is on the corner of Flinders and Swanston Streets.

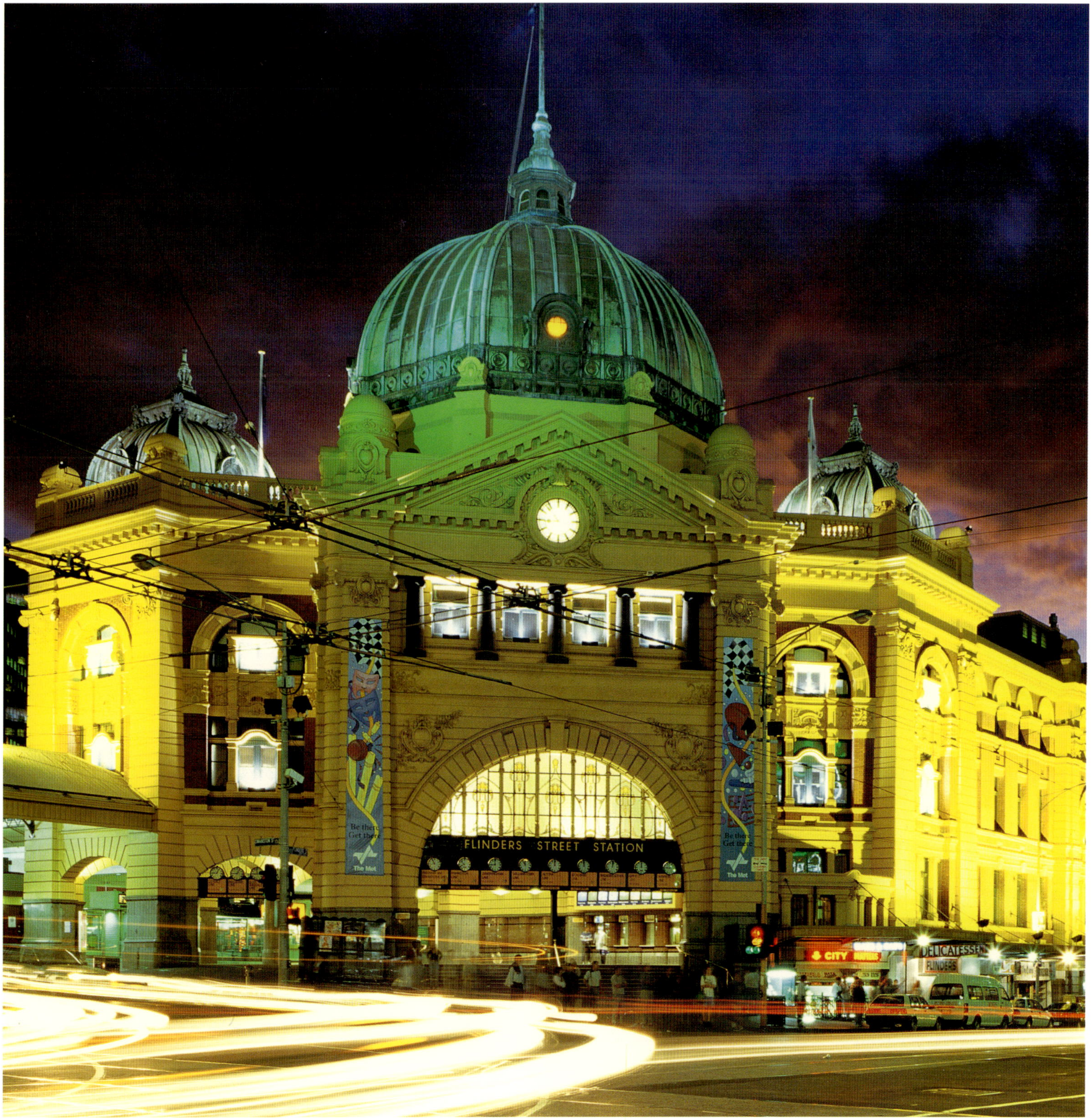

Flinders Street Station is splendidly lit at night. This impressive building, with its domes, towers and clocks, was erected in 1899 on the site of Melbourne's first fish market.

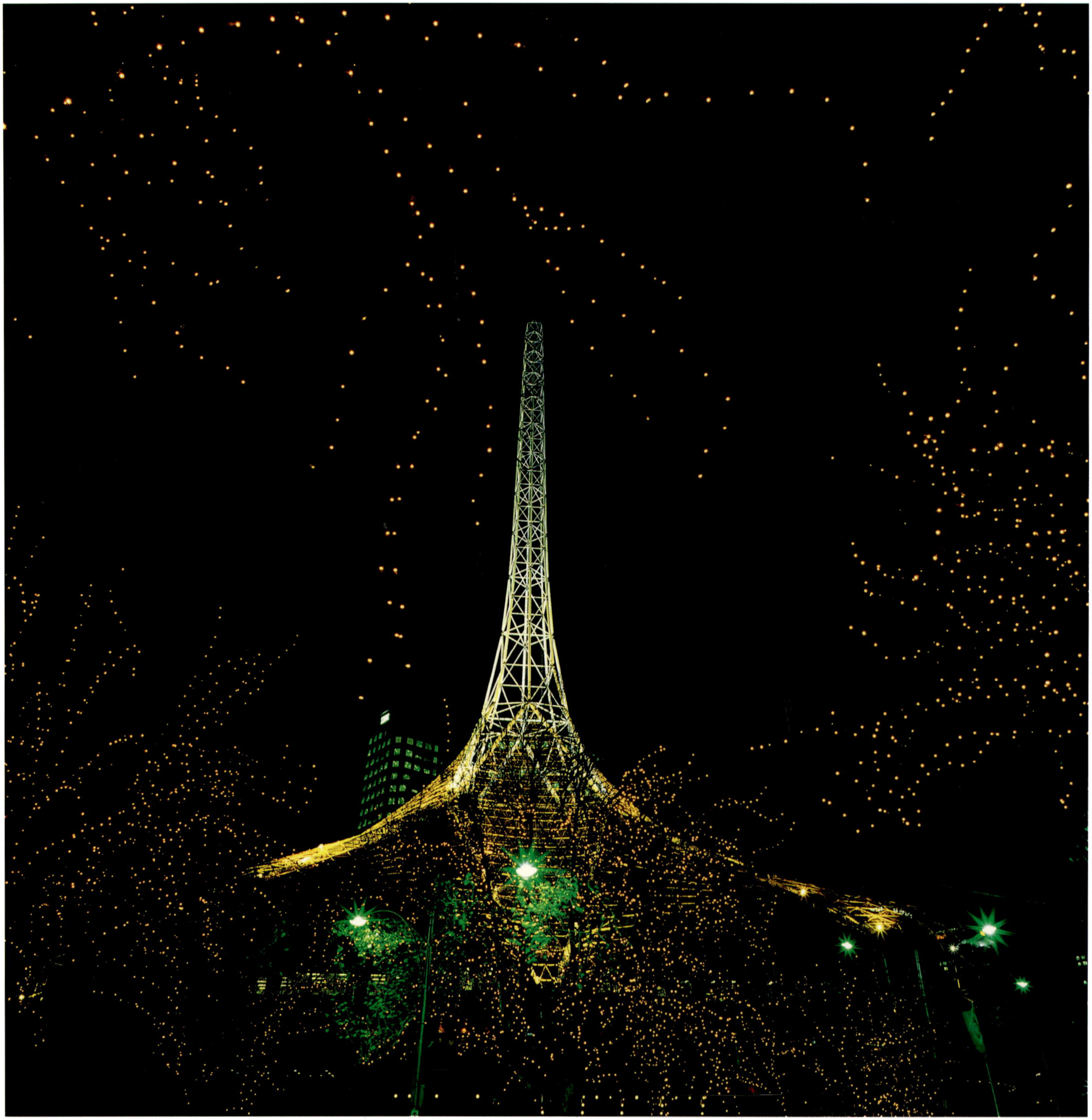

The spire of the theatre complex of the Victorian Arts Centre on St Kilda Road which also contains the National Gallery of Victoria and the Concert Hall.

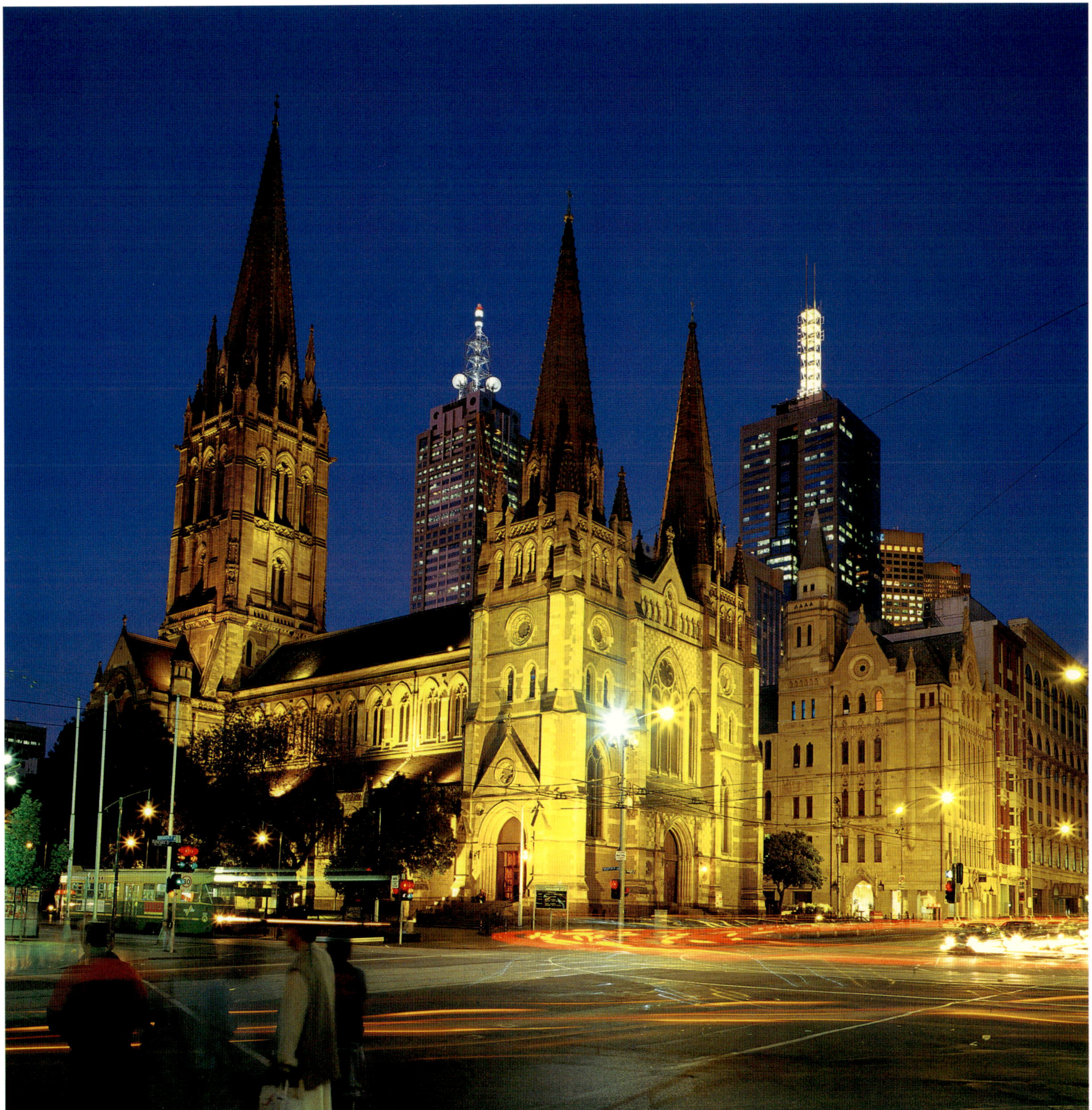

St Paul's Cathedral was built between 1877 and 1891 and its towers added in 1931. It stands on the opposite corner of Swanston and Flinders Streets to the domed Flinders Street Station.

Melbourne, a wonderful place to shop

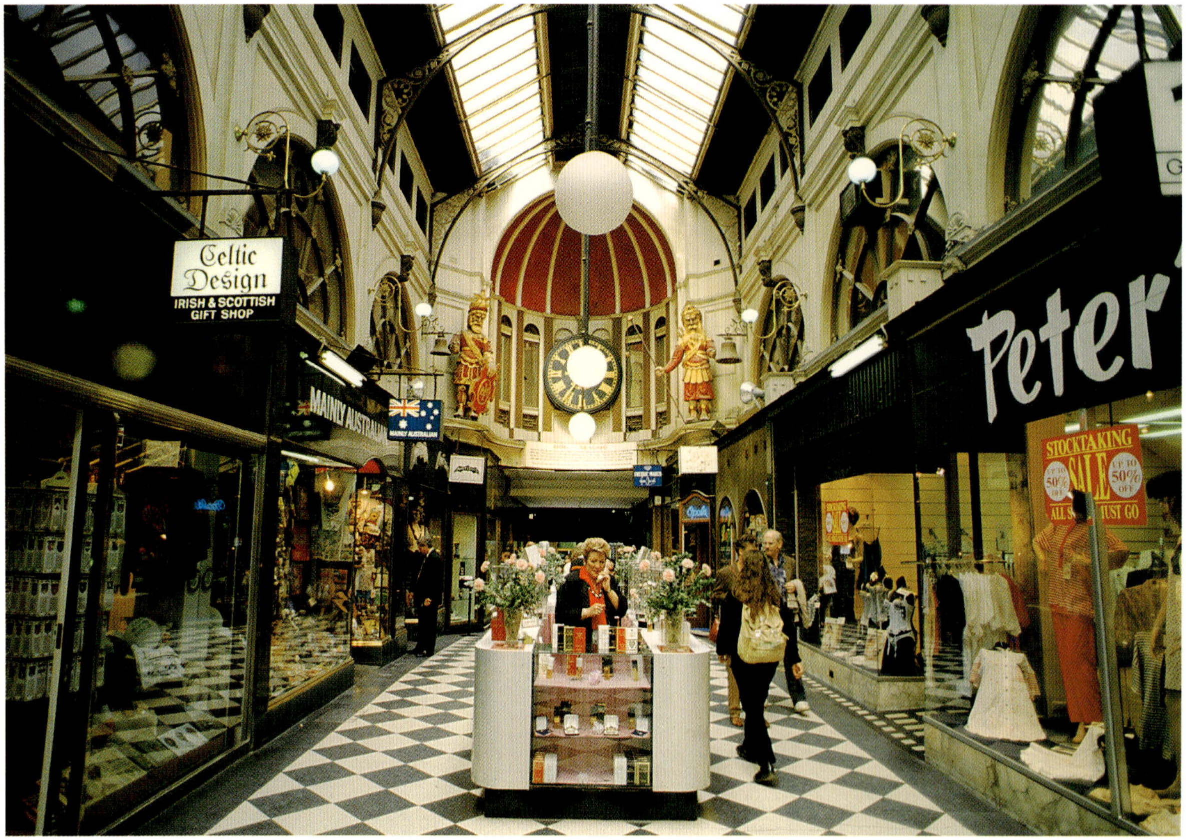

Above: Gilded figures, Gog and Magog, above an entrance of the Royal Arcade. *Opposite:* One of the famous Melbourne trams passes Melbourne Central.

Melbourne has a wealth of shopping venues which offer international wares as well as Australian-made goods. The Royal Arcade is one of many elegant paved pedestrian ways, lined with exclusive boutiques and tempting coffee shops. Those who enjoy the best the world can offer may spend many happy hours at Melbourne Central, a shopping and office complex on La Trobe Street. The complex features a 20-storey-high conical glass tower which houses an historic Shot Tower built in 1889, and contains a branch of the famous Daimaru Department Store.

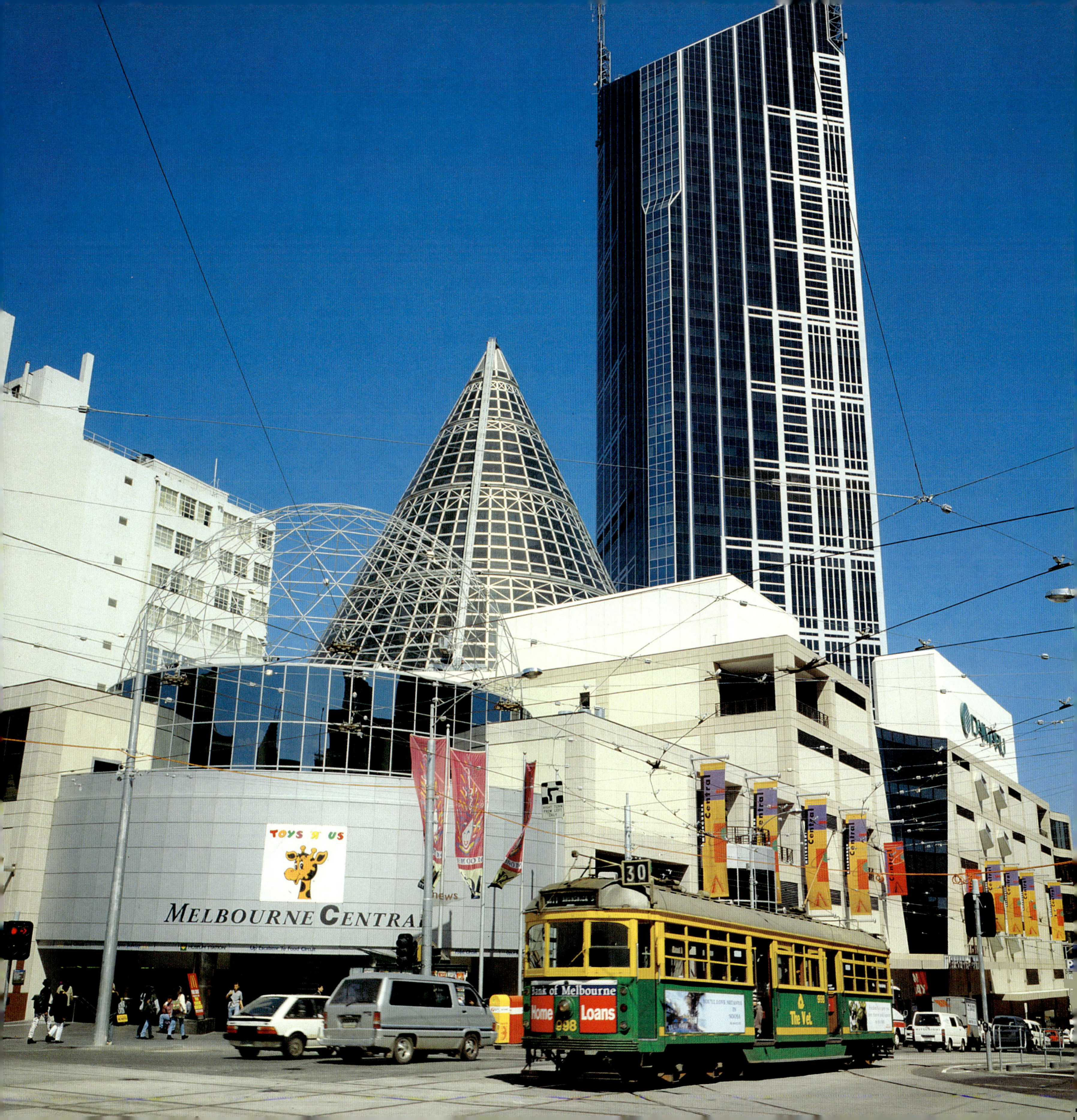

TOYS "R" US
MELBOURNE CENTRAL
30
Bank of Melbourne
Home
Loans
The Vet.

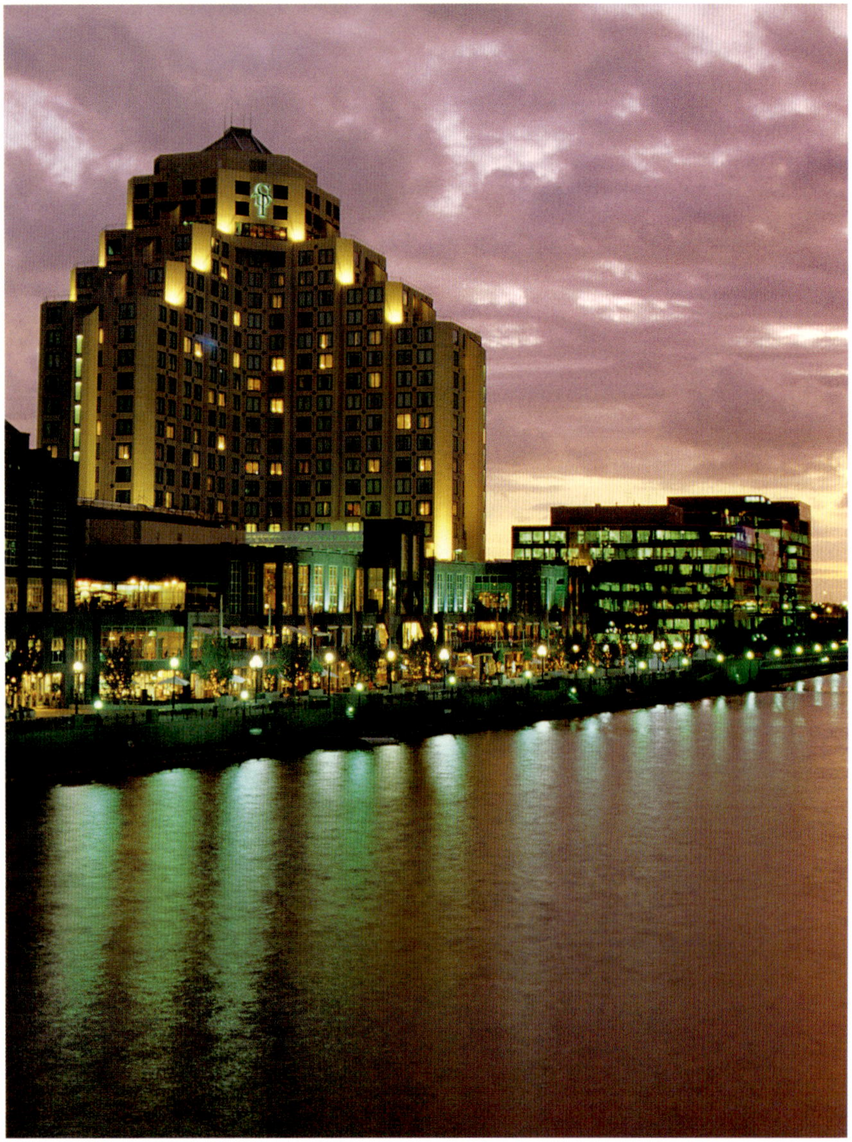

Above: The Southgate complex extends along the south bank of the Yarra River.

Southgate on Yarra

The magnificent Southgate complex is very central and very accessible, making it one of Melbourne's most popular places to promenade, shop, dine or simply relax, take light refreshment and watch the Yarra slide practically past. On the three levels of this very modern development are restaurants, speciality boutiques, an international food hall and galleries. The public art, such as sculptures and performance art, are great attractions. After refreshments at Southgate, it's a short stroll to the Victorian Arts Centre and the National Gallery of Victoria around the corner on St Kilda Road.

Opposite: A charming footbridge stretches across the Yarra at Southgate.

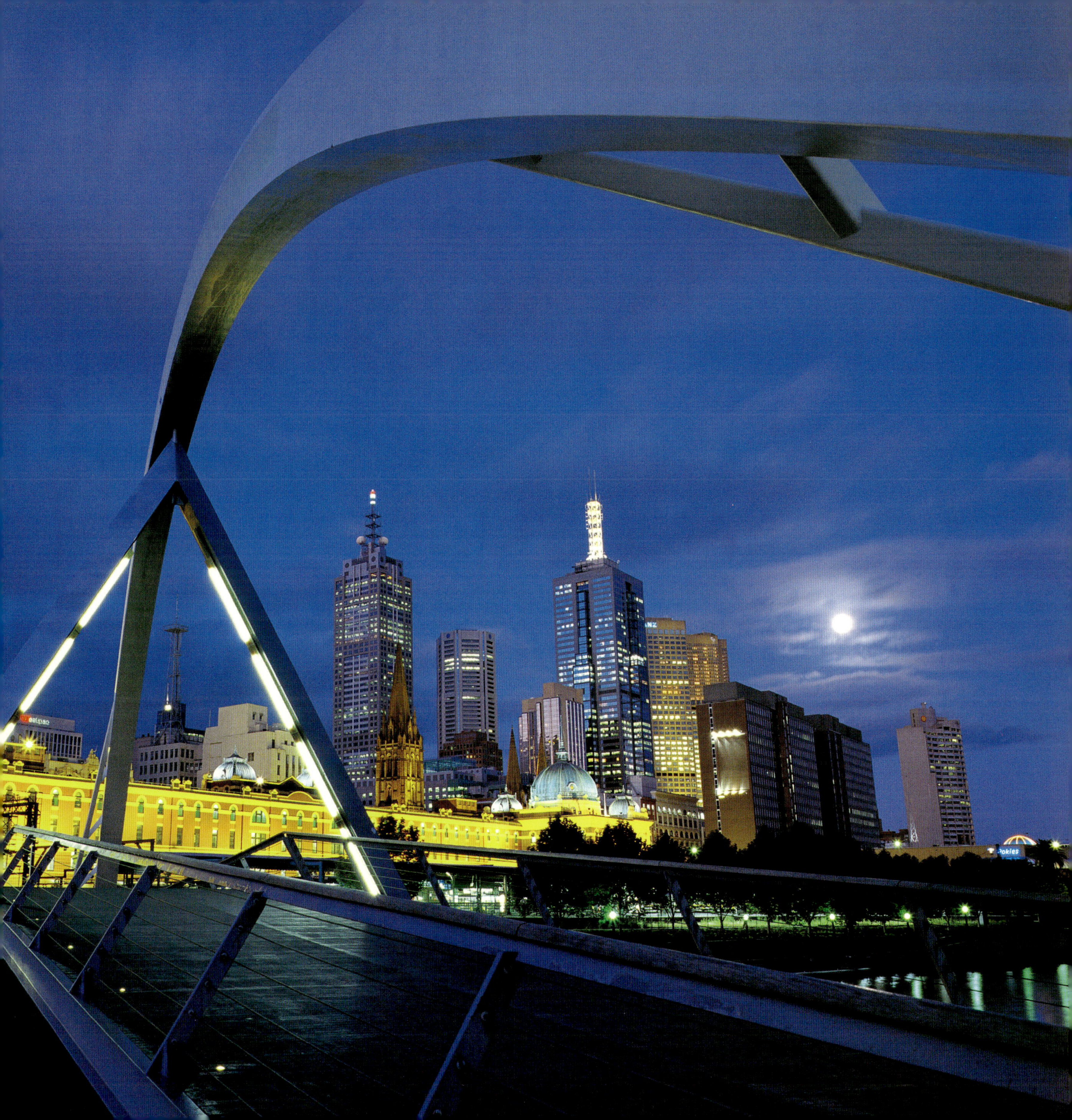

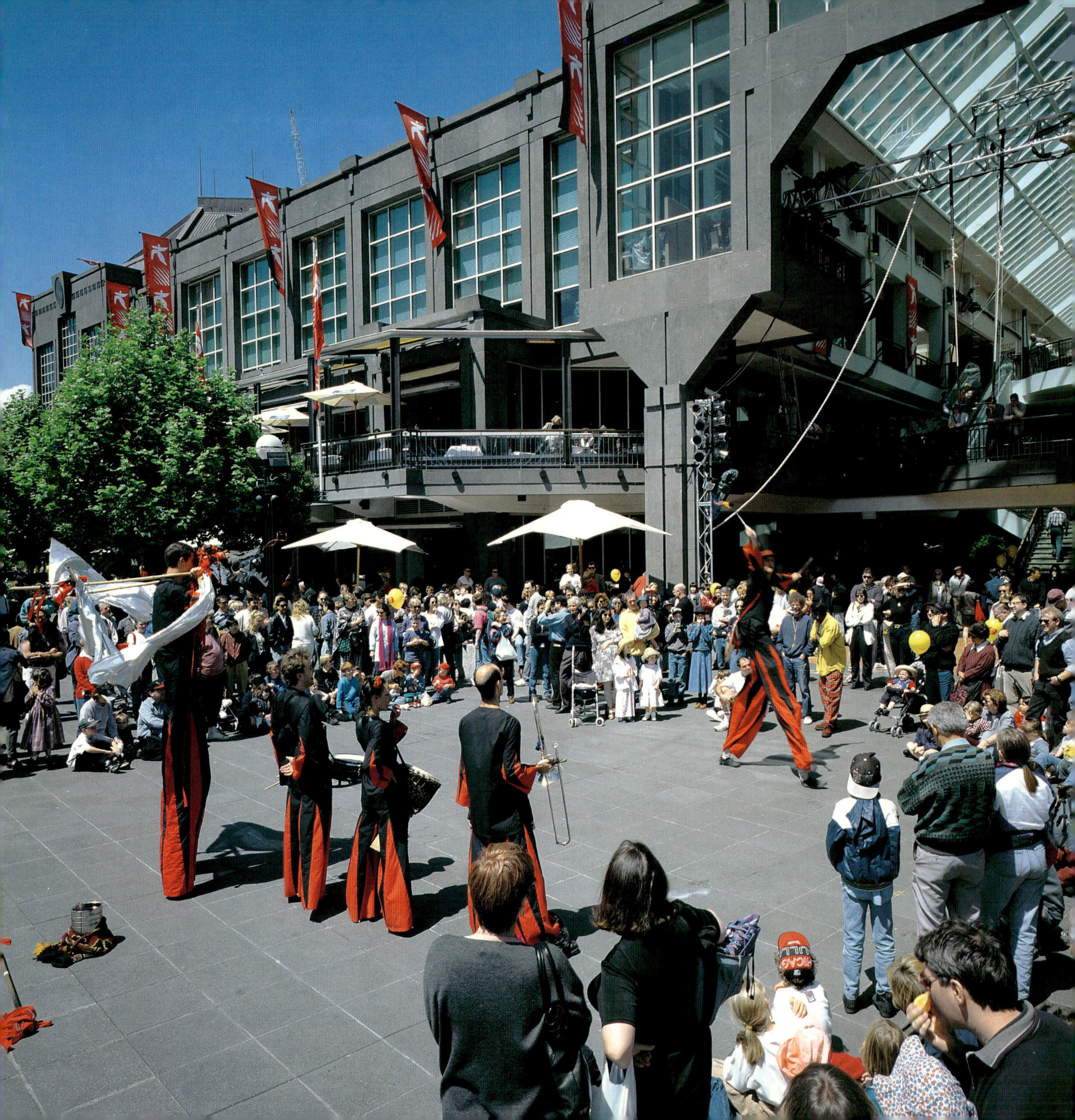

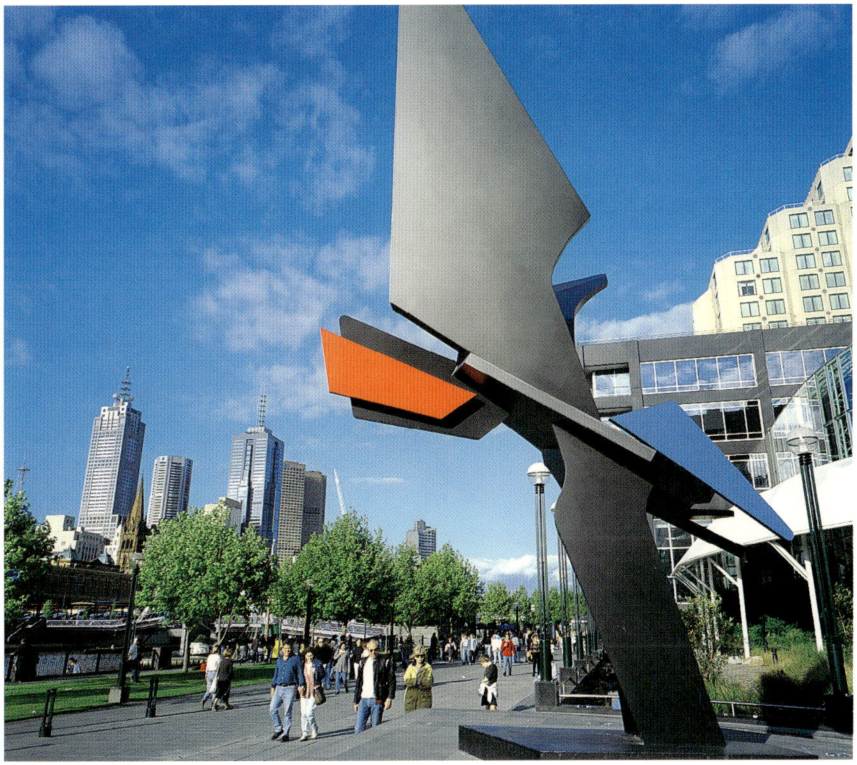

Above: A sculpture at Southgate.

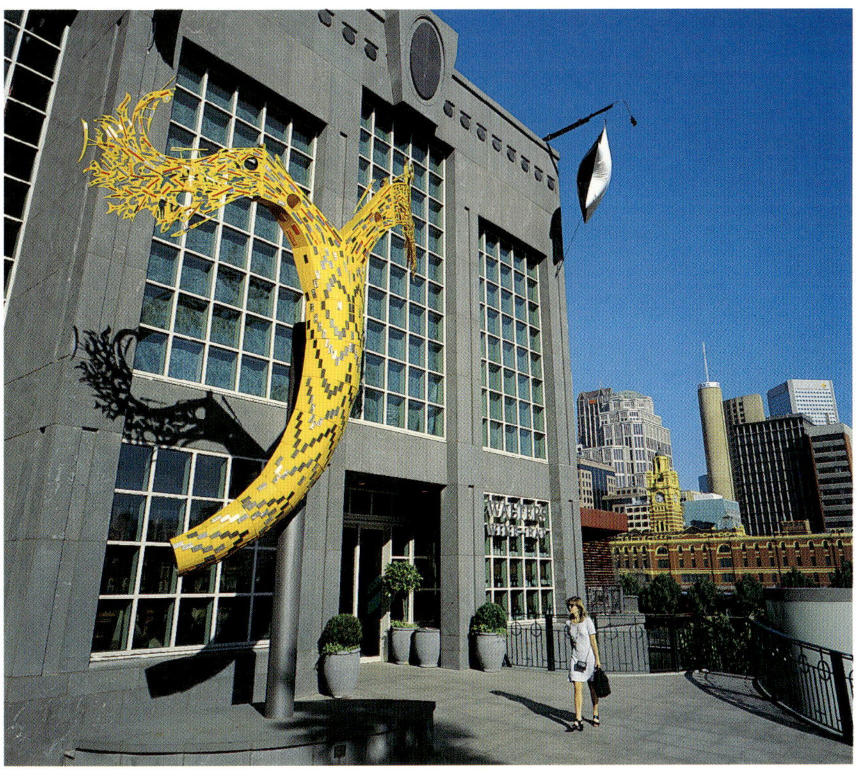

Opposite: Theatre in the round, Southgate. *Above:* Melbourne offers art in public places.

A city for culture

The gold rushes of the 1850s and 60s made Melbourne a rich city and brought a surge of immigrants who had a taste for theatre, opera and other cultural pursuits. Melbourne's reputation as a city of culture has continued to this day: its splendid Arts complex is only part of the story. The city and suburbs contain many art galleries and theatres of all sizes and Melburnians take for granted the place of outdoor performances, sculptures and other, less permanent creations such as pavement artworks, in their everyday lives.

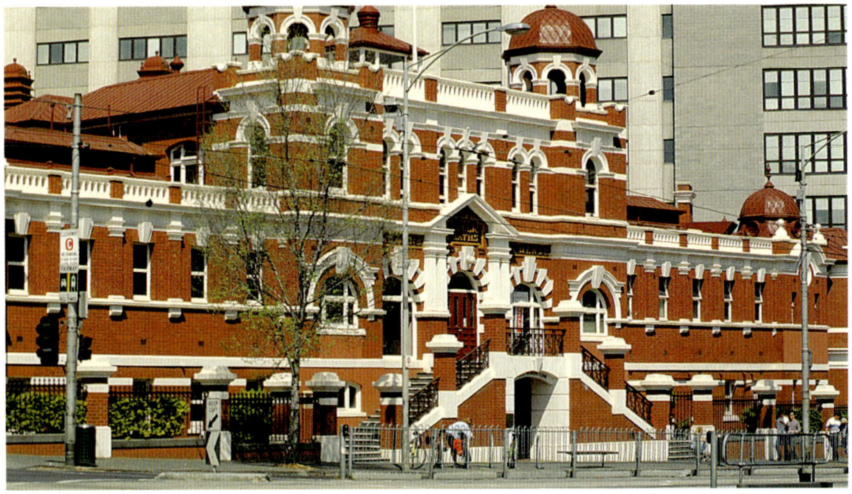

Above: Melbourne's imposing red brick Public Baths, on the corner of Victoria and Swanston Streets.

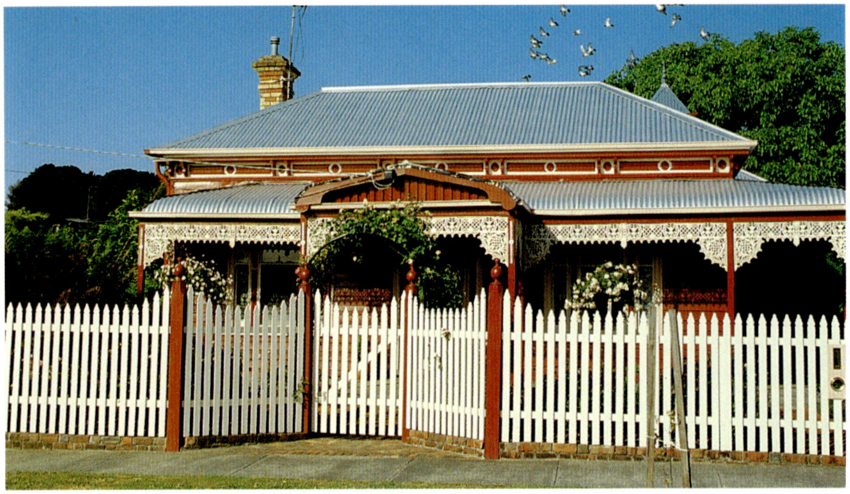

Above: Many inner suburban homes built in Victorian or Edwardian times have been lovingly restored.

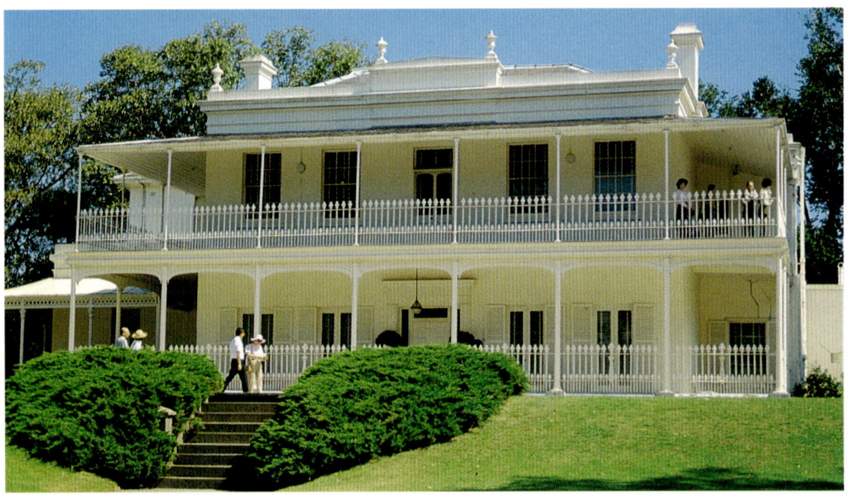

Above: Como House in South Yarra was built in 1847 and has remained substantially unaltered since 1875.

A fine Victorian city

Melbourne's city streets, laid out in a formal grid plan, offer many piquant contrasts between historic stone buildings and modern, multi-storeyed, glass-encased constructions. It has many fine hotels, but the Windsor, in Spring Street, is a city landmark. The National Trust of Australia (Victoria) which administers properties such as Como House in South Yarra, preserves Melbourne's historic buildings and makes them accessible to the public. The wrought-iron lace which adorns the home shown at centre left became popular in the 1880s when it was cast by foundries in England and imported to Australia as ship's ballast.

Opposite: The sumptuous facade of the Hotel Windsor in Spring Street on the eastern edge of the city.

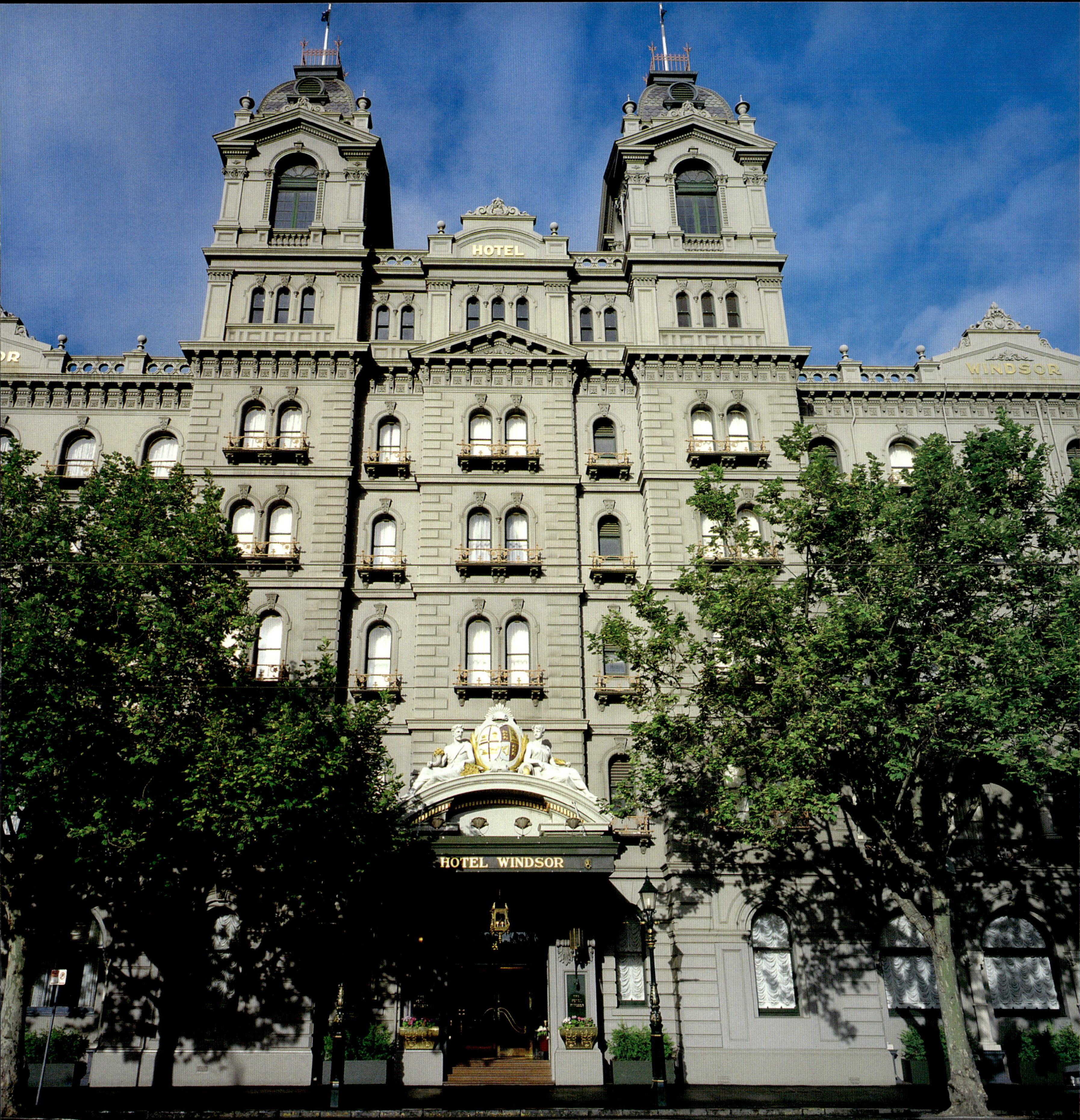
HOTEL
WINDSOR
HOTEL WINDSOR

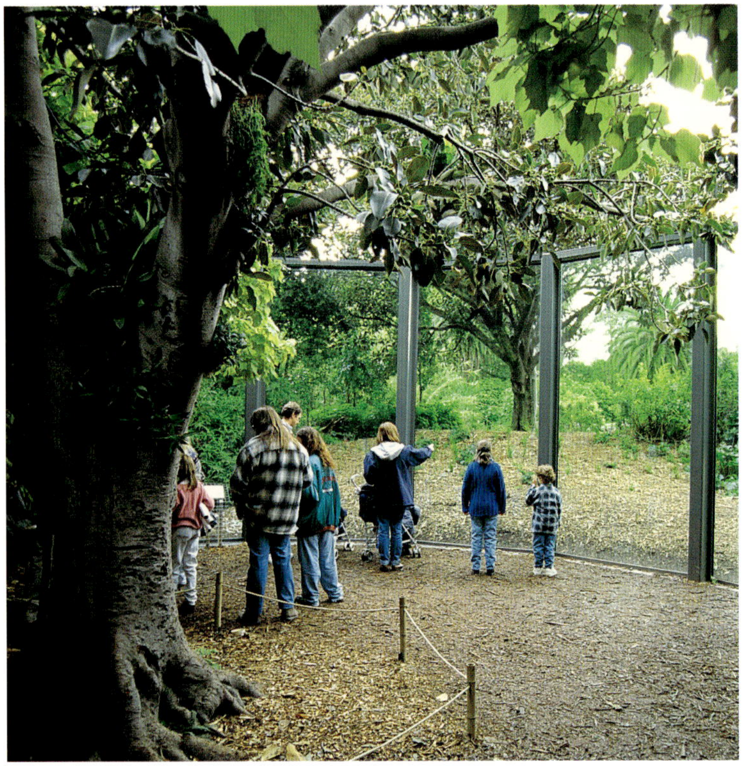

Admiring the outdoor enclosure for the zoo's famed gorilla family.

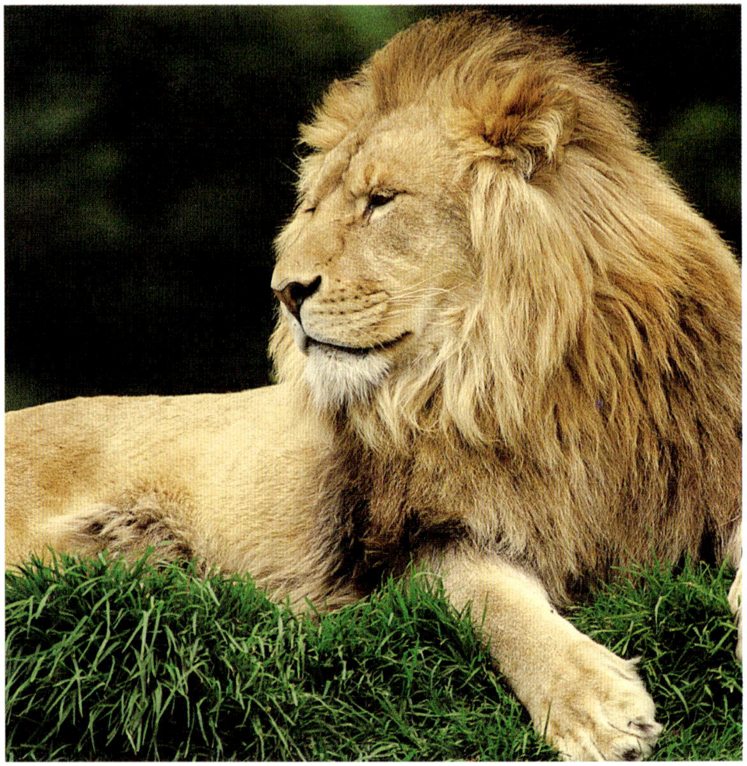

A male African Lion drowses in the pride's large, grassy recreational area.

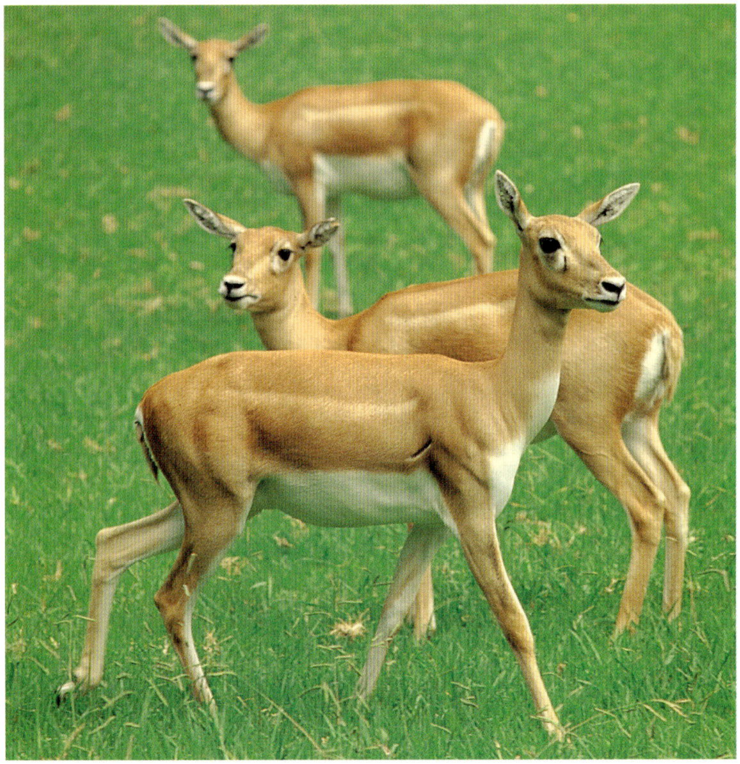

Hoofed animals like these Springbok live in park-like surroundings.

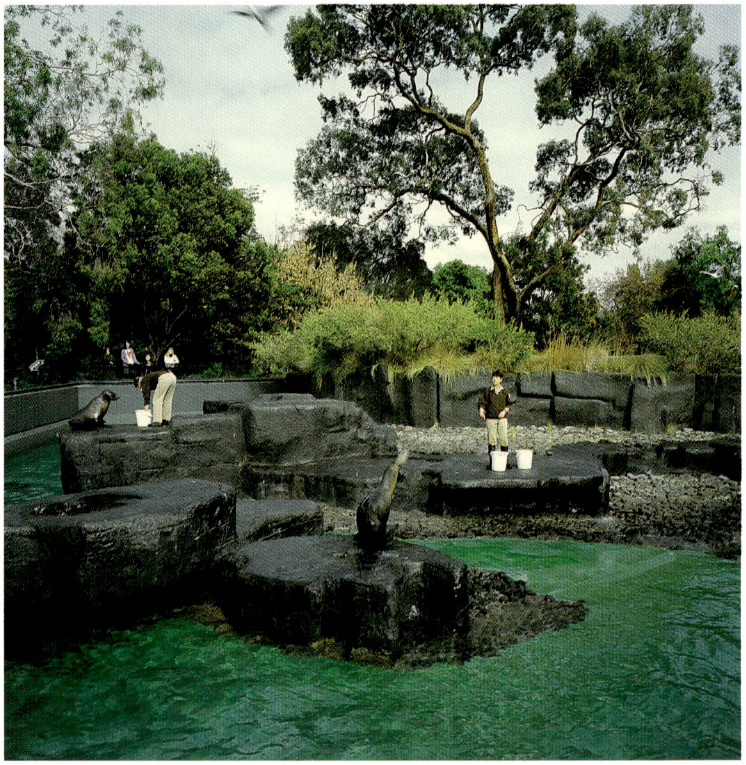

Feeding the seals, which can exercise in a large pool.

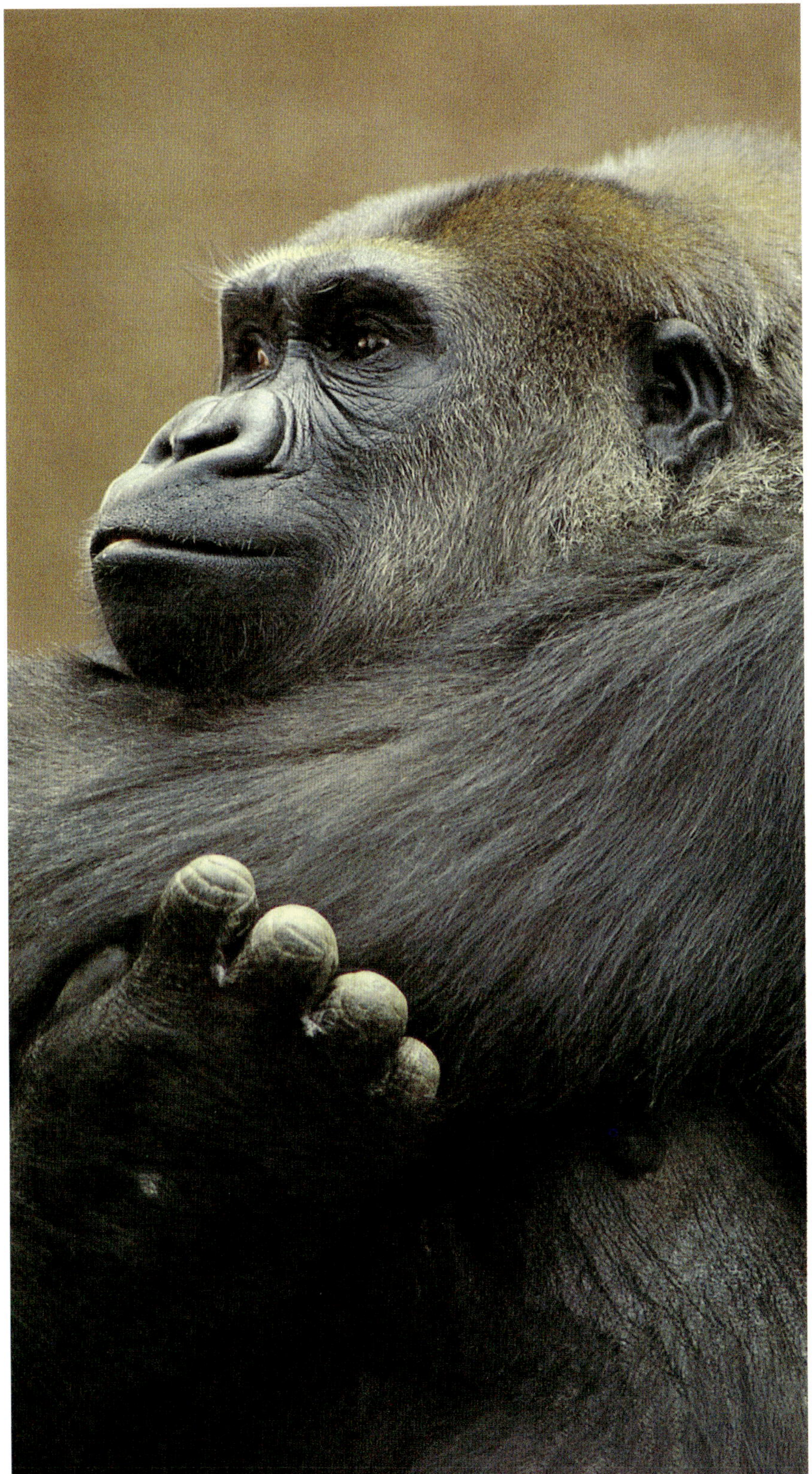

Melbourne Zoo has had success in breeding the endangered Lowland Gorilla.

Melbourne Zoo

Melbourne Zoo was opened in 1862 and was the first zoological gardens established in Australia. Originally it was near the Yarra River, but was moved to Royal Park.

This splendid zoo is home to more than 350 different sorts of animals. While it has had great success in breeding some of the world's endangered species, such as the Lowland Gorilla, it concentrates on the study and preservation of Australia's native fauna. A visit to the zoo offers highlights such as the Gorilla Rainforest, the Butterfly House, the Sumatran Tiger habitat and close viewings of Australia's remarkable Platypus and the appealing Koala.

Gardens of delight

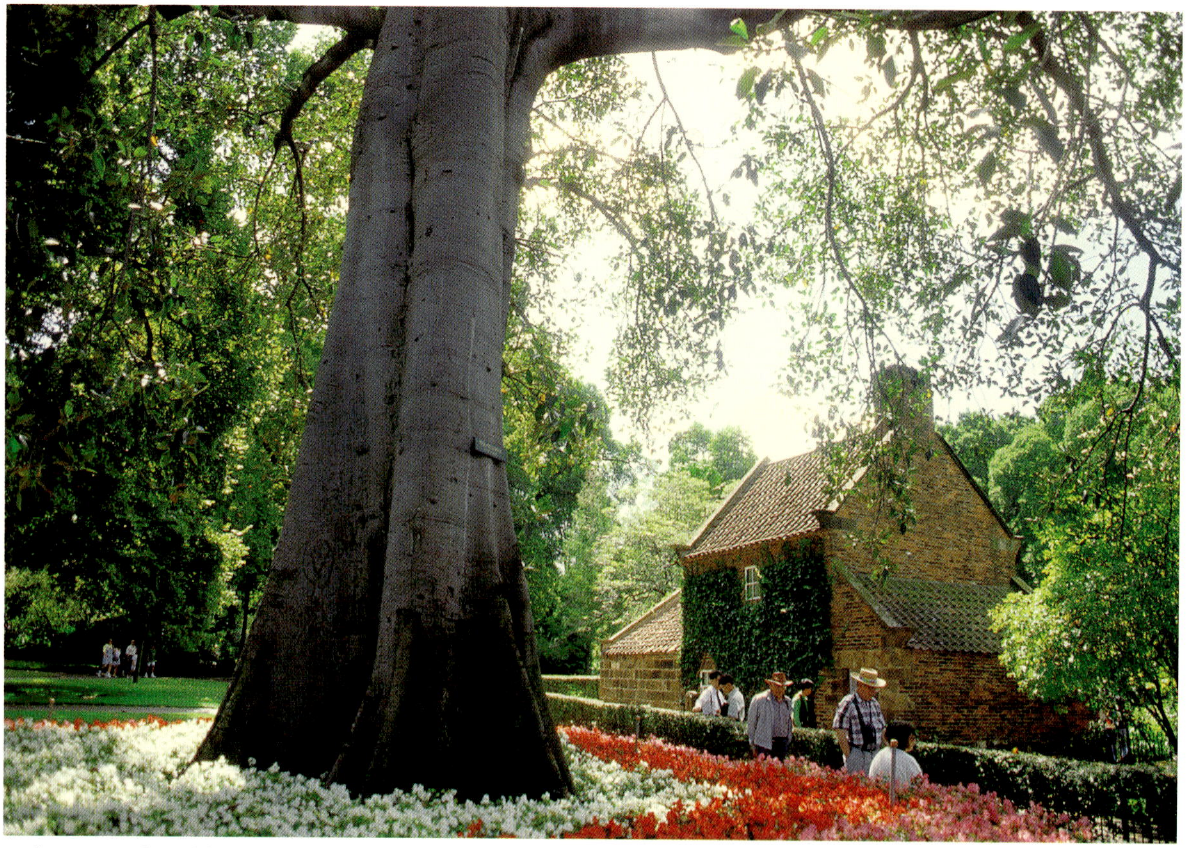

Cook's Cottage, relocated from England, stands in Fitzroy Gardens.

Victoria's early inhabitants reserved large areas of ground for parks and public gardens. Today, the gardens are a glory, especially in springtime. Near the heart of Melbourne city, the Royal Botanic Gardens covers more than 35 hectares and contains at least 10 000 species of plants. Kings Domain is a huge parkland surrounding Government House. Most charming for many visitors is Fitzroy Gardens, in which may be found the English cottage which was the home of Captain Cook's parents, and a magnificent Conservatory. In spring and summer, garden lovers flock to the Dandenong Ranges, where the cooler climate has produced spectacular displays of azaleas, rhododendrons and other floral beauties.

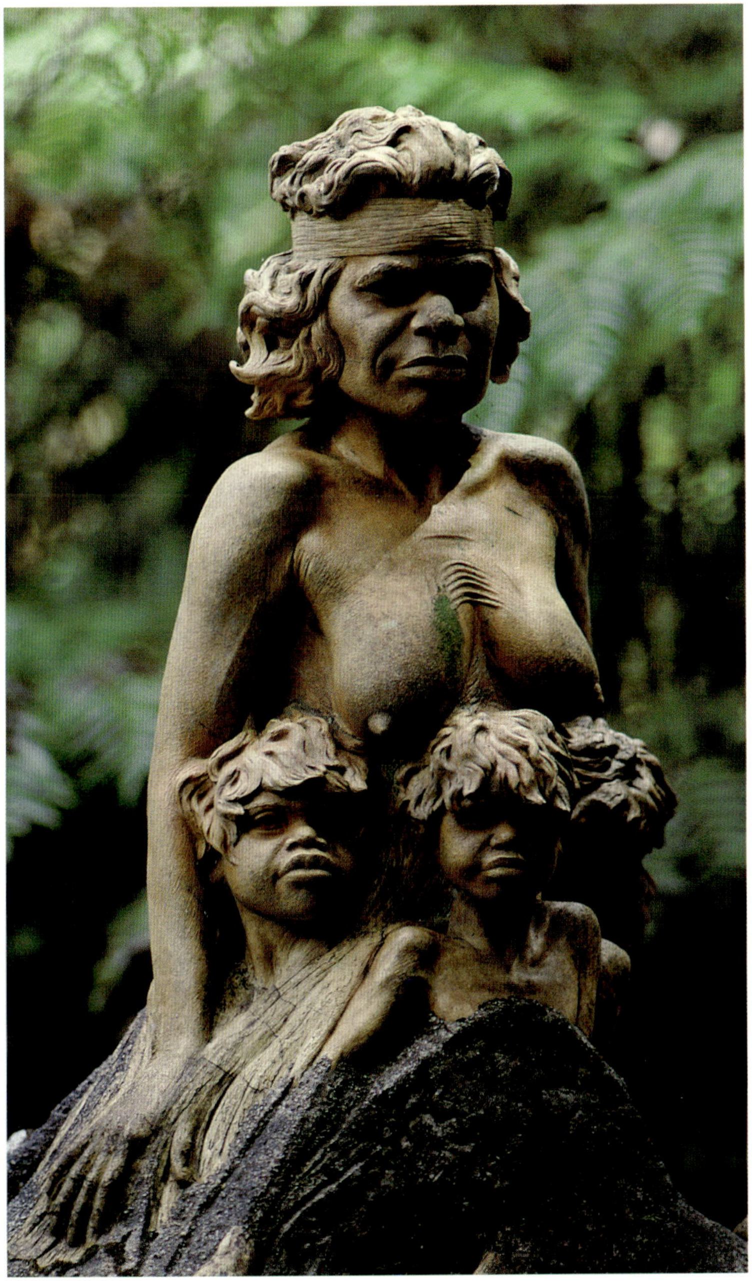

William Ricketts Sanctuary, in the Dandenong Ranges, displays this artist's sculptures.

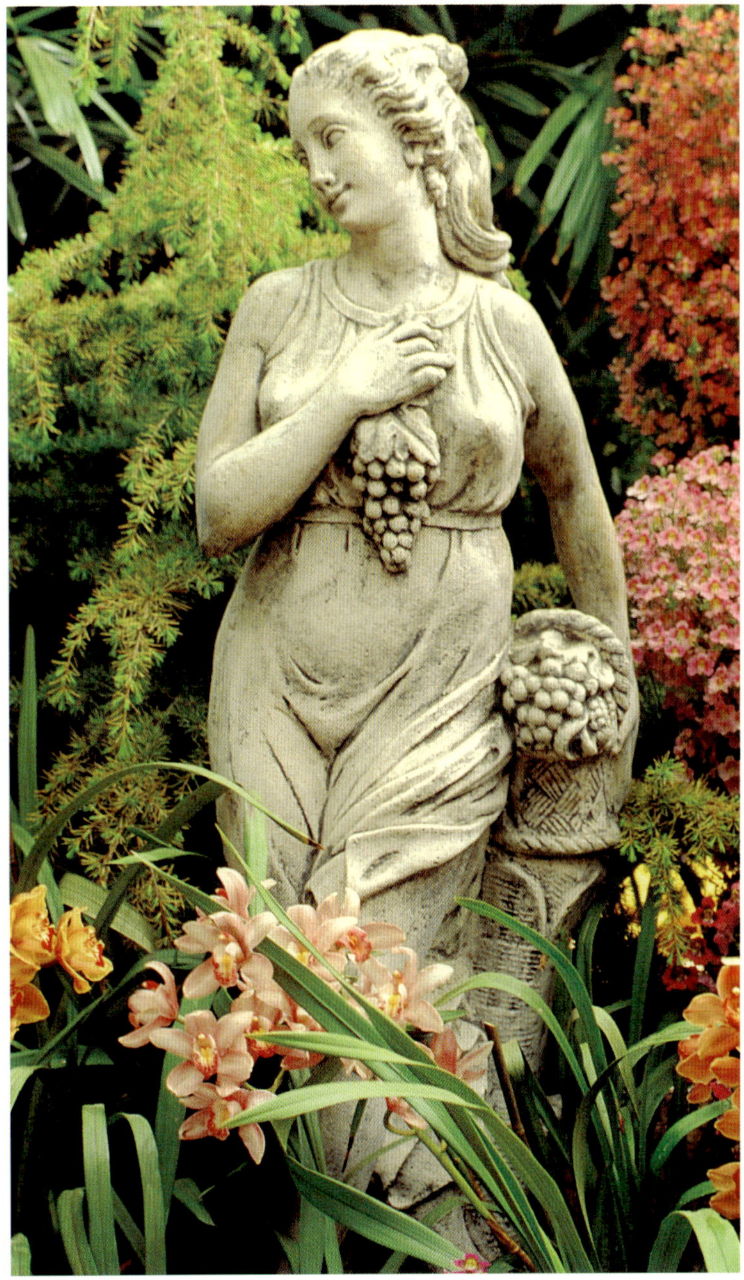

Above: A statue of a nymph in Fitzroy Gardens Conservatory.
Following pages: The Rhododendron Gardens at Olinda in the Dandenongs.

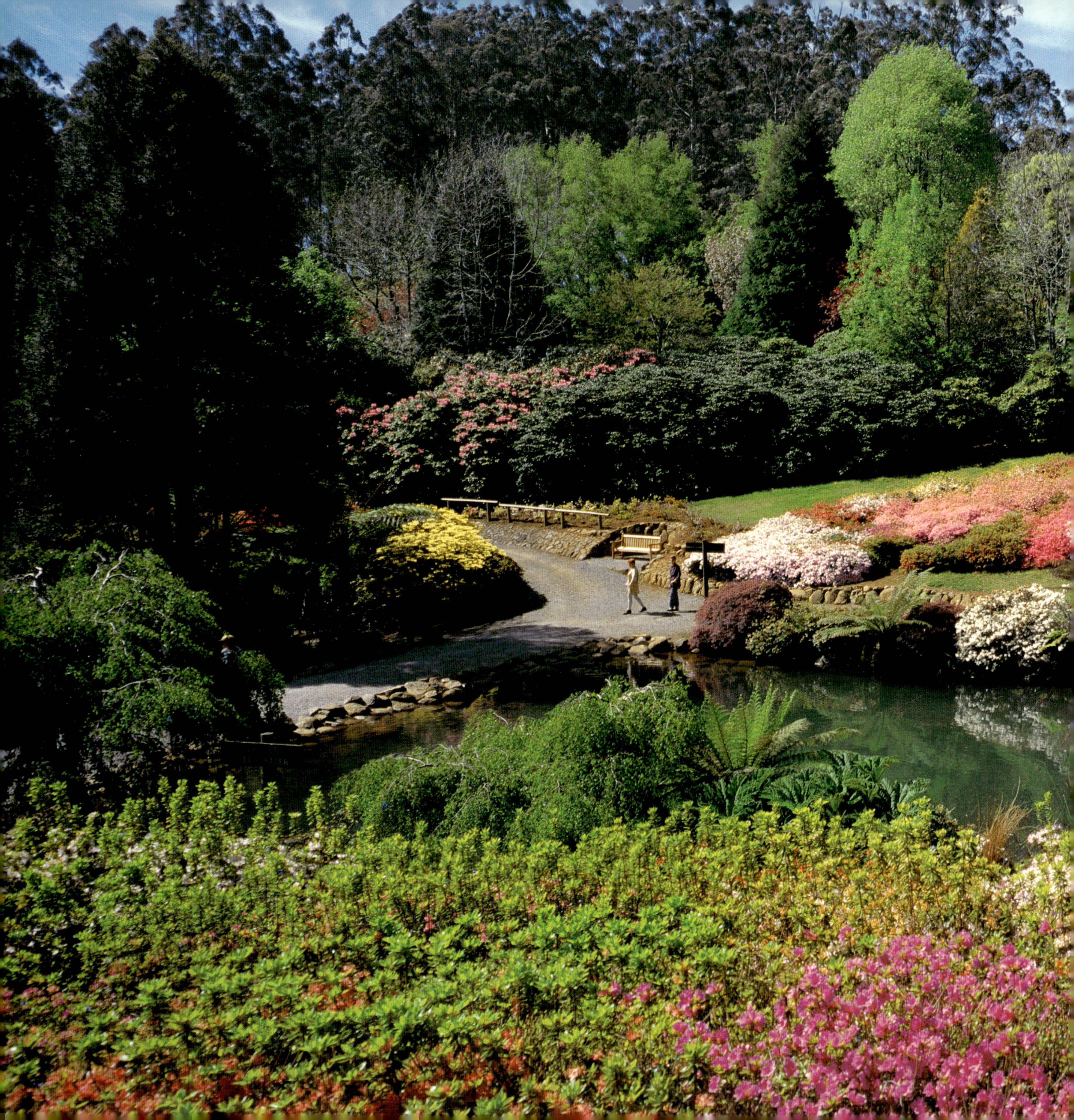

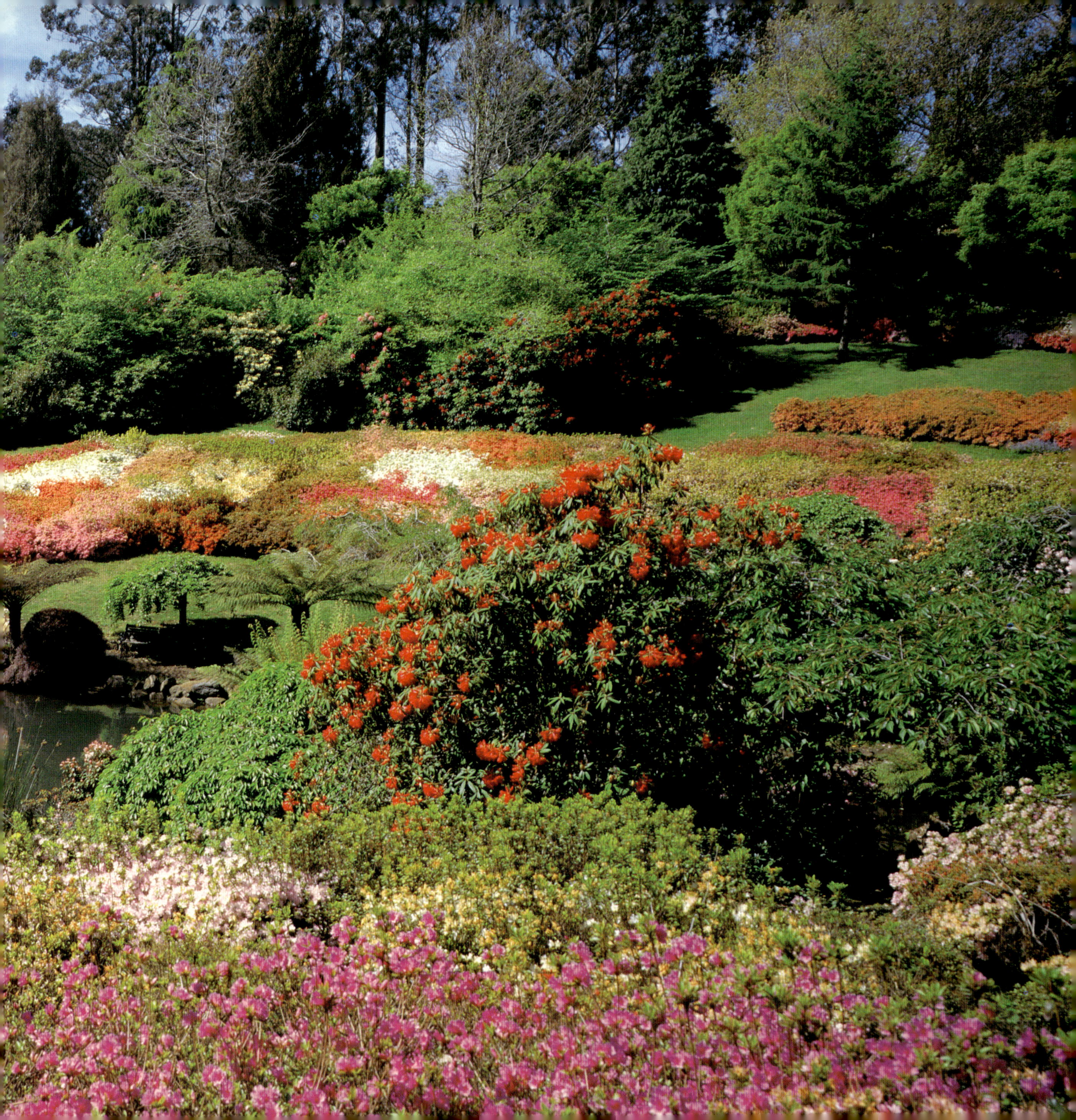

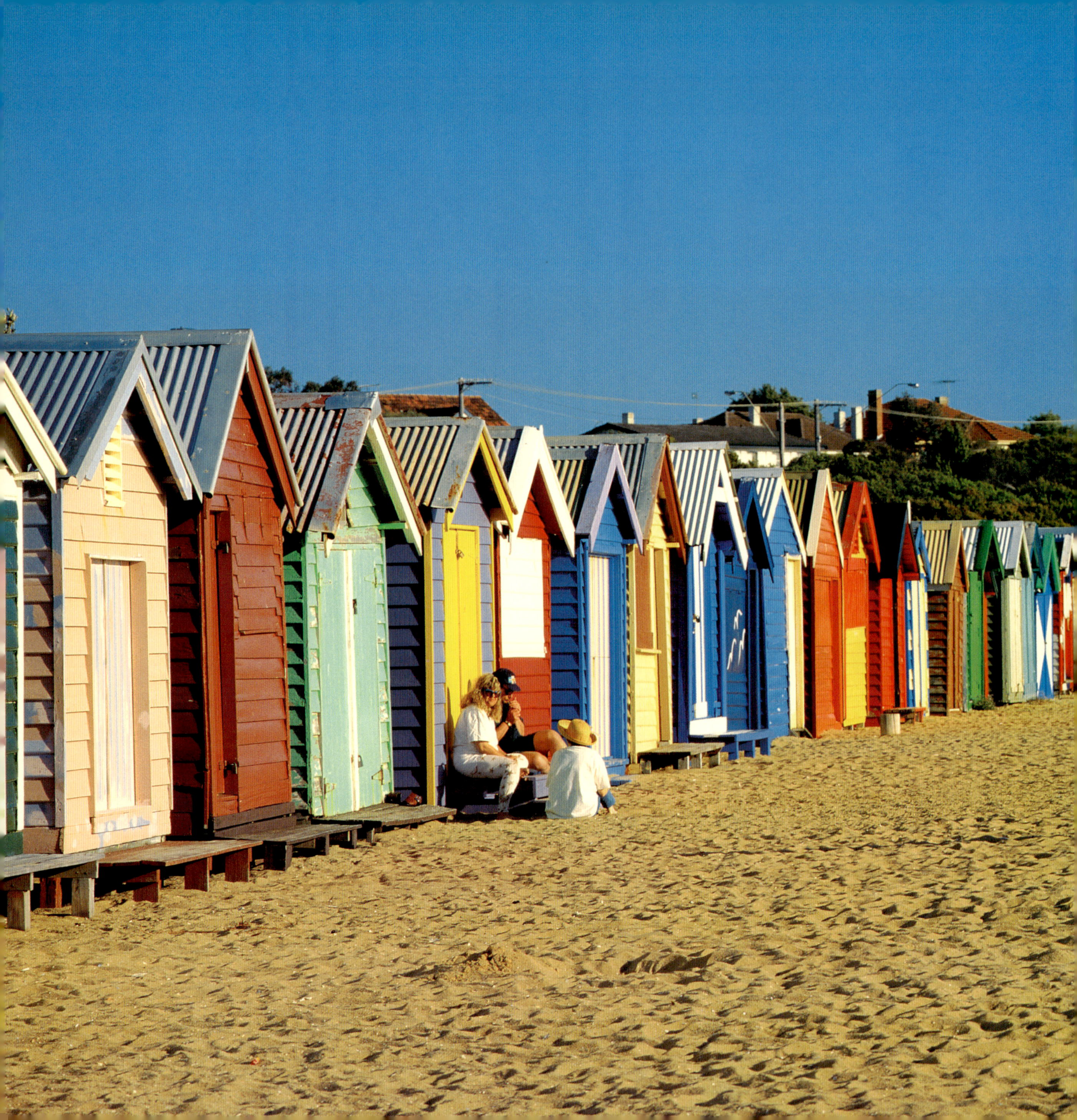

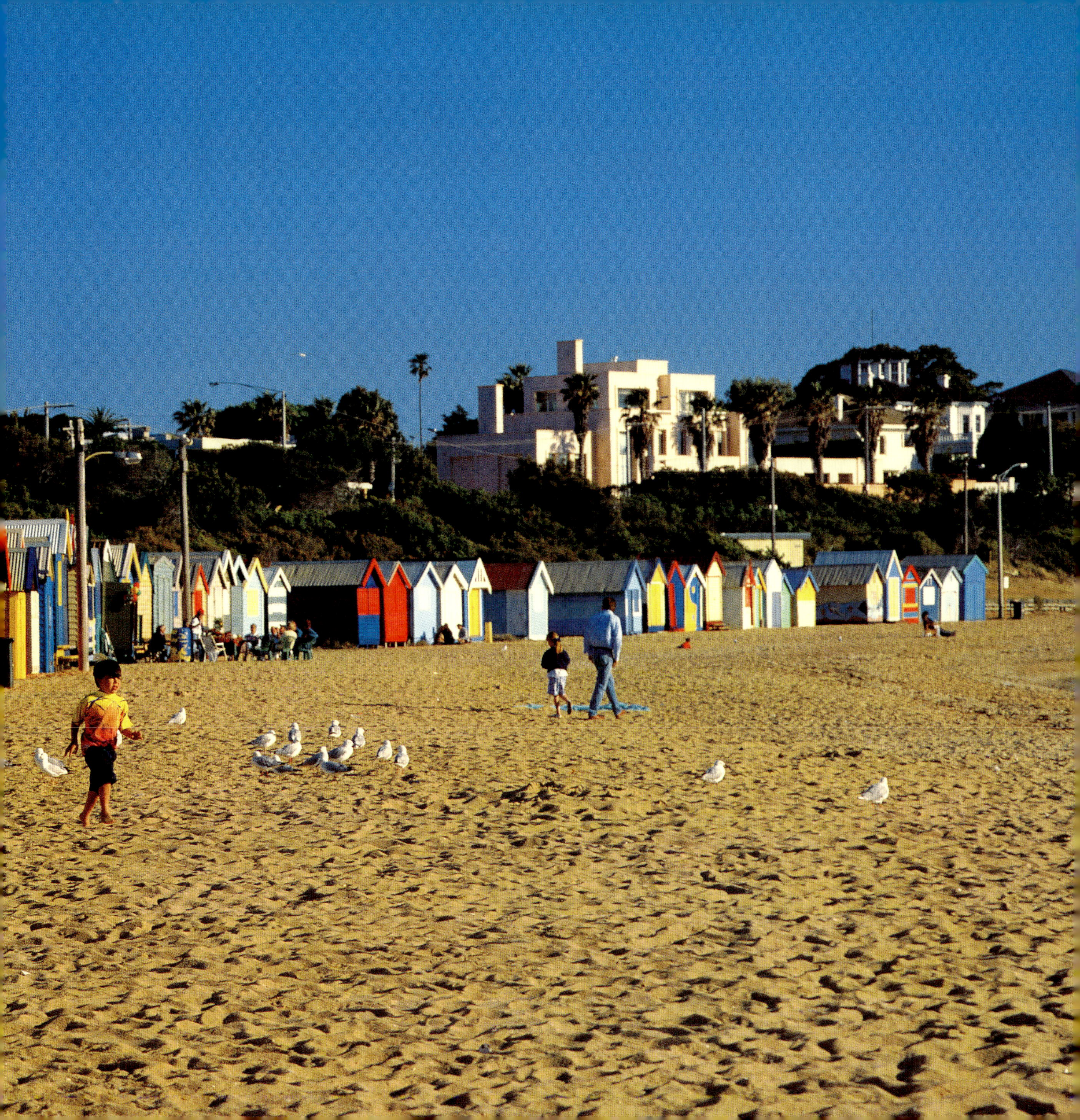

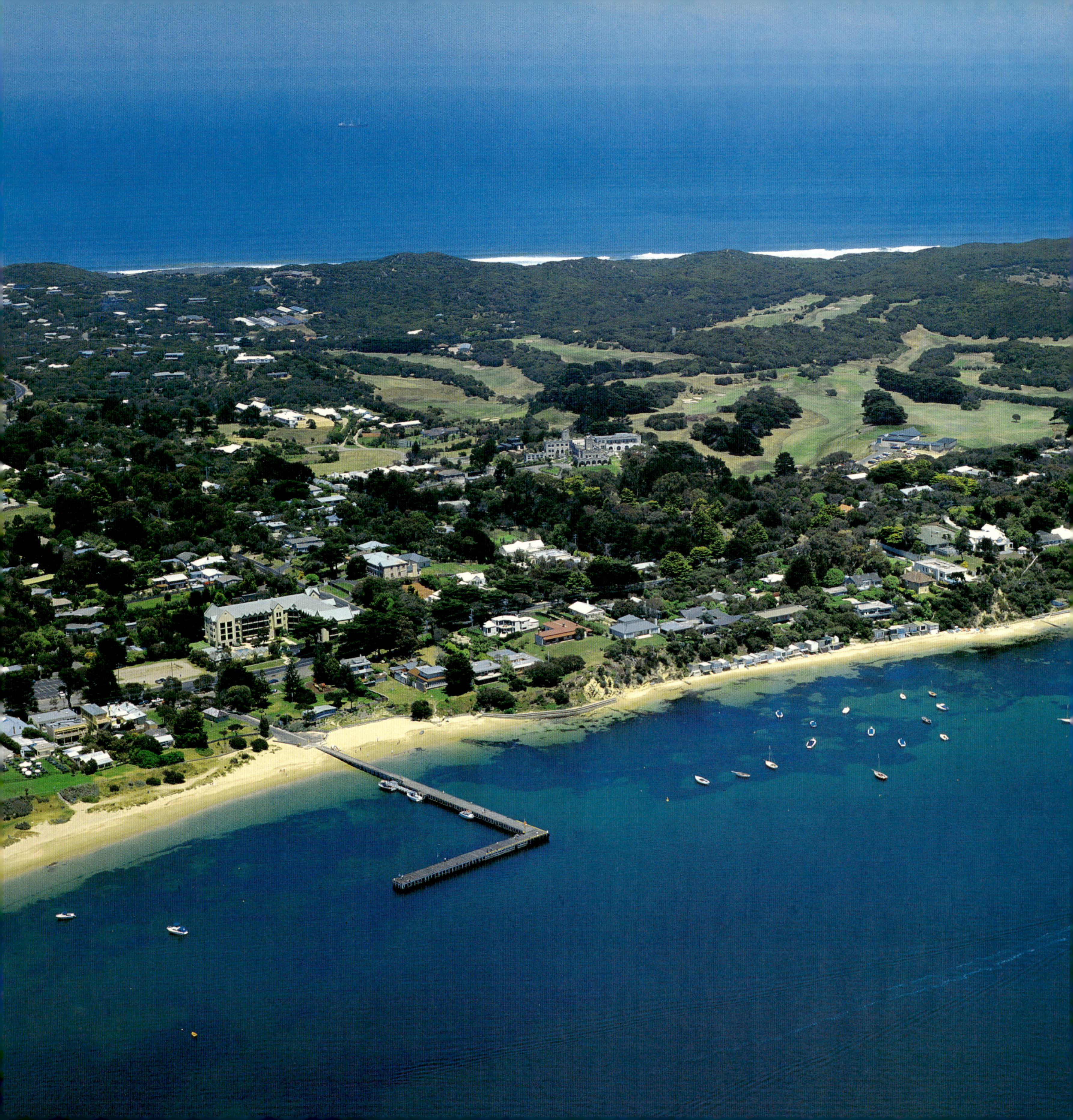

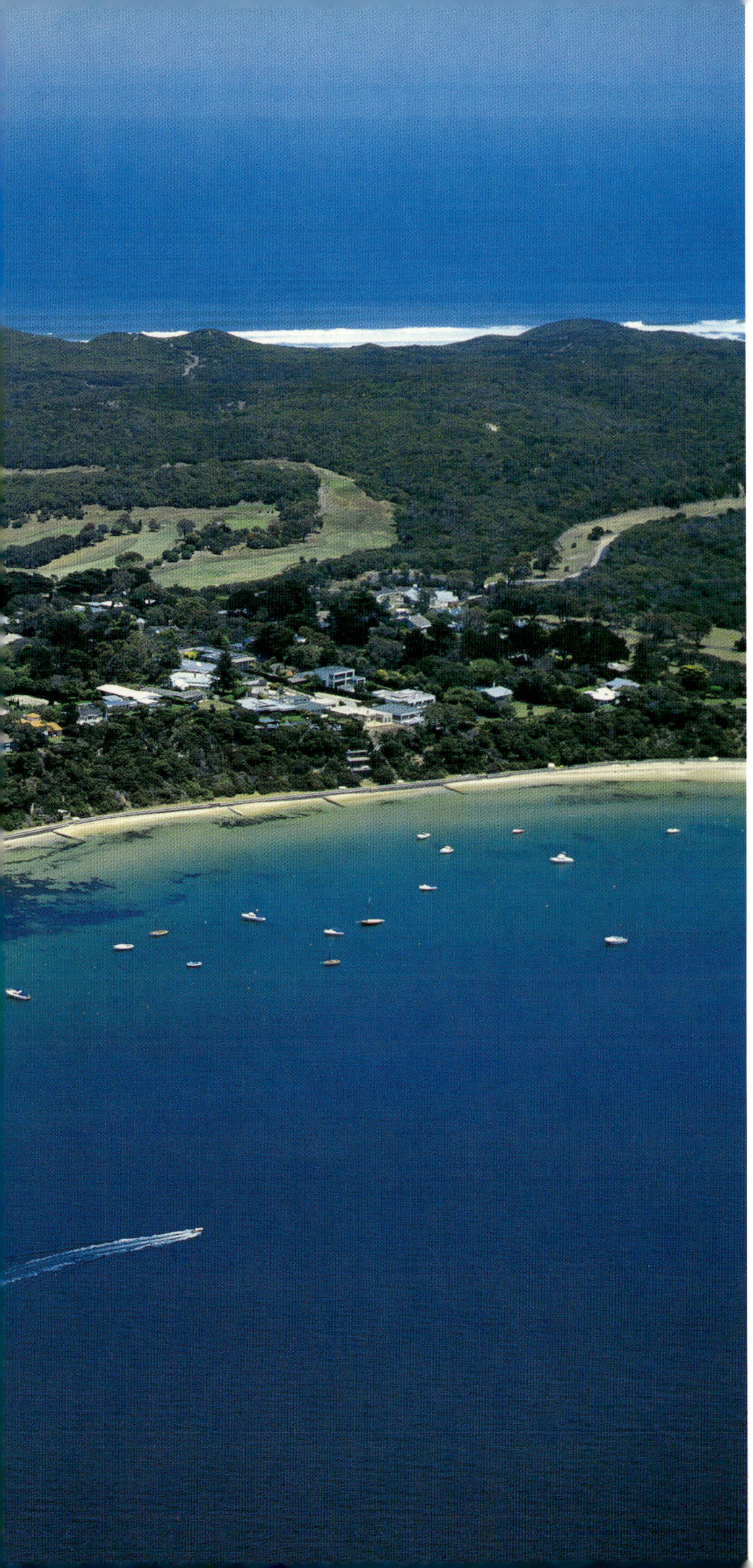

Mornington Peninsula

Few cities can equal Melbourne's marvellous location on the shores of Port Phillip Bay, with attractive beaches such as Brighton and St Kilda close to town. Mornington Peninsula forms the eastern arm of the bay, and Melburnians have been holidaying on the peninsula for many years. Today the Nepean Highway provides easy access to Point Nepean National Park, past Mt Martha, Dromana, Rosebud and other popular resorts. Along the picturesque backbone of the peninsula are farms and vineyards, and towns whose restaurants, craft shops and galleries are the objectives of many weekend expeditions from Melbourne's suburbs.

Left: The foot of the Mornington Peninsula has the calm water of Port Phillip Bay (foreground) on one side, the ocean on the other.
Preceding pages: Bathing boxes at Brighton, one of Melbourne's bayside beaches close to the city.

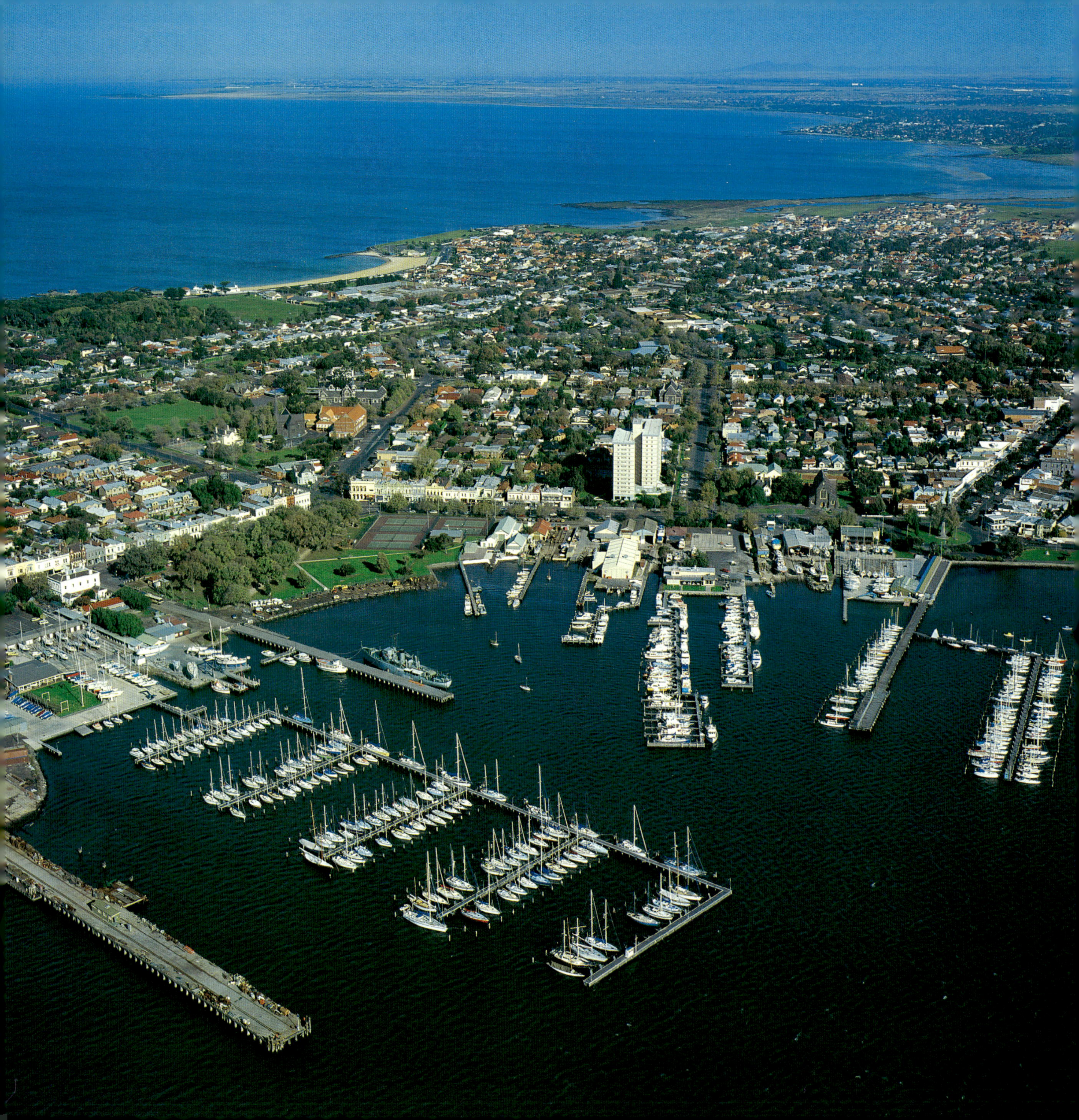

Williamstown

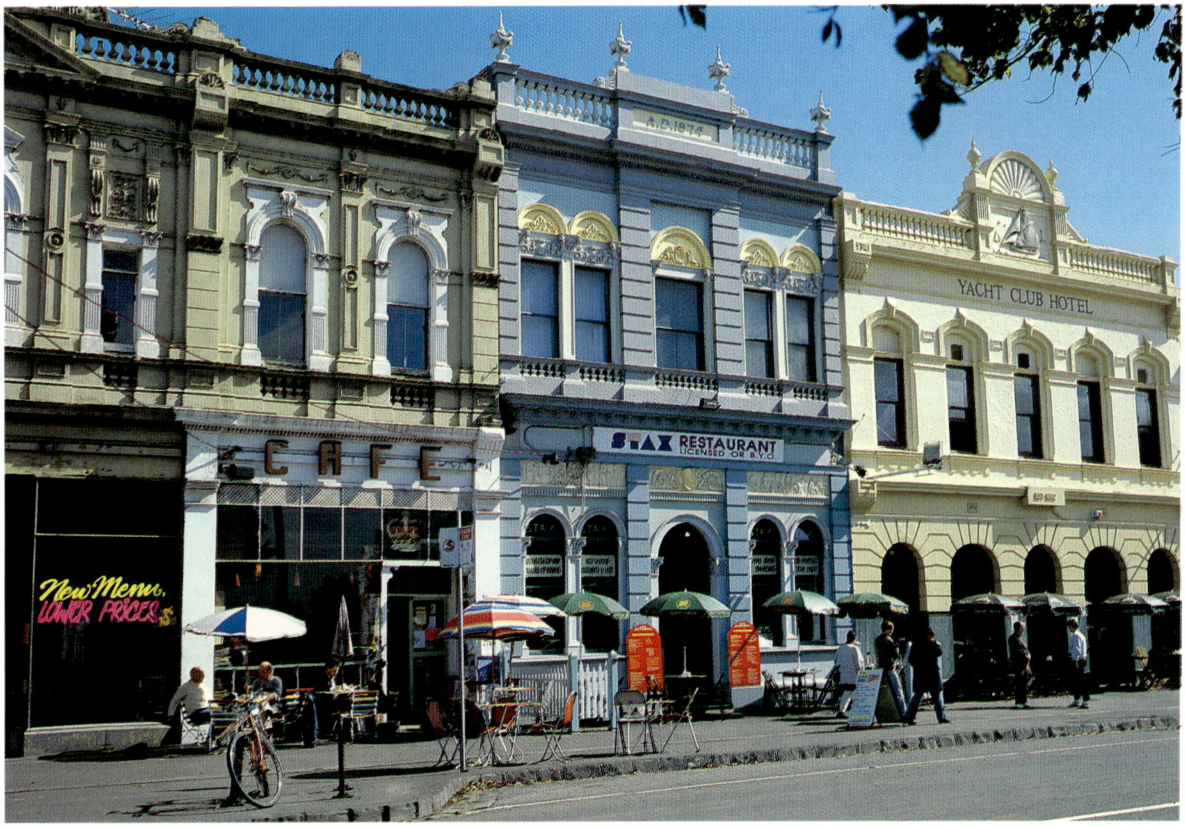

Nelson Place, Williamstown, offers a variety of places to dine, including the legendary Yacht Club Hotel at far right.

In 1837, Williamstown, on Hobsons Bay, was planned as the seaport for Melbourne and its streets were lined with solid buildings of locally quarried bluestone. When the Yarra River was deepened in the 1880s, Williamstown took a back seat to the Port of Melbourne. Today, Williamstown is a popular base for boating and an ideal place to relax by the bayside. It offers a host of excellent eating places, especially in Nelson Place which is named after the British Navy's heroic admiral. HMAS Castlemaine, moored at Gem Pier off Commonwealth Reserve, is a maritime Historical Society Museum (see photo opposite, centre left), and there is a Railway Museum. A craft market is held each month in Commonwealth Reserve.

Opposite: A marina and yacht club moorings at Williamstown.

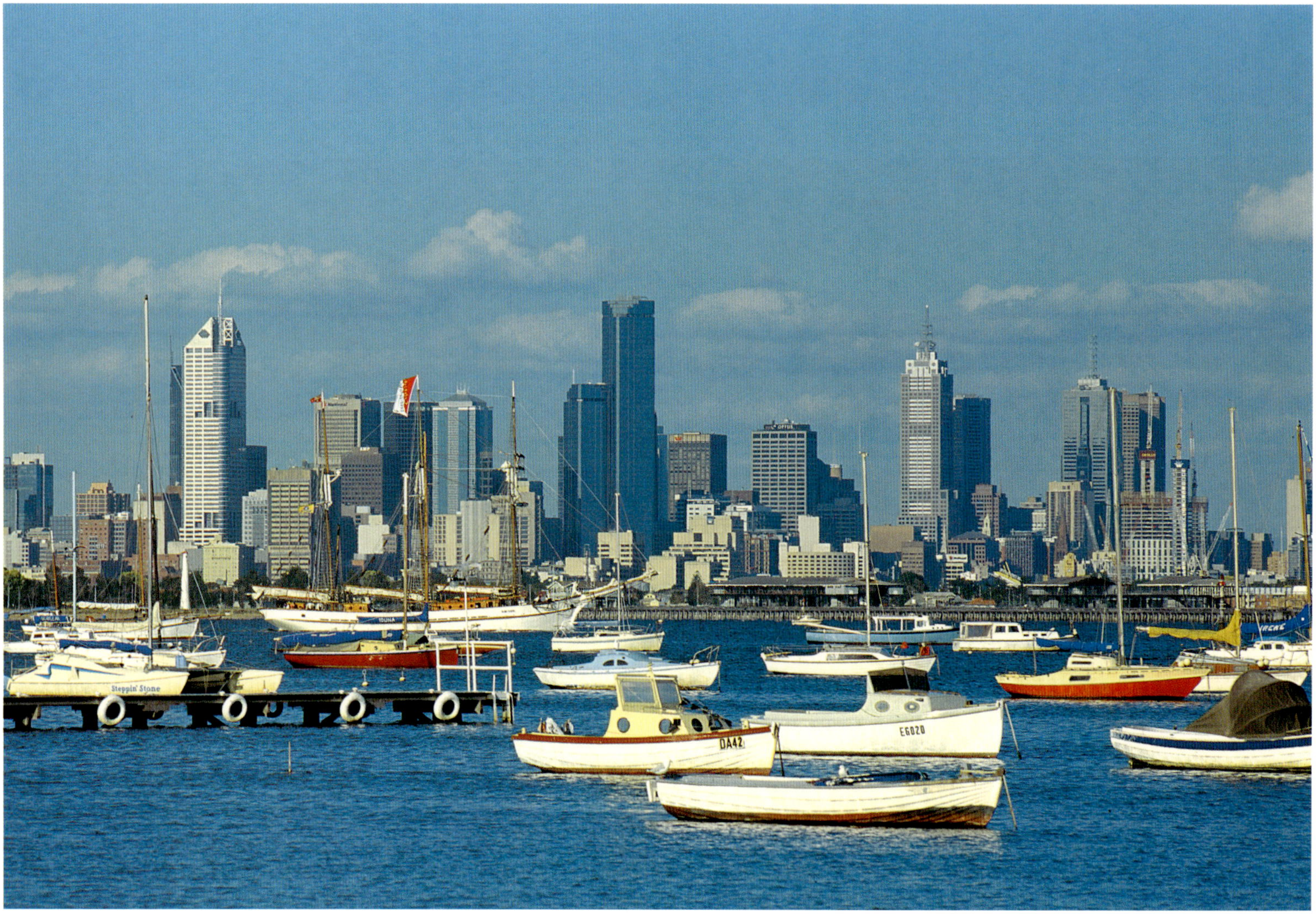

Williamstown foreshore provides mooring for a variety of pleasure craft and a fine view of Melbourne city.

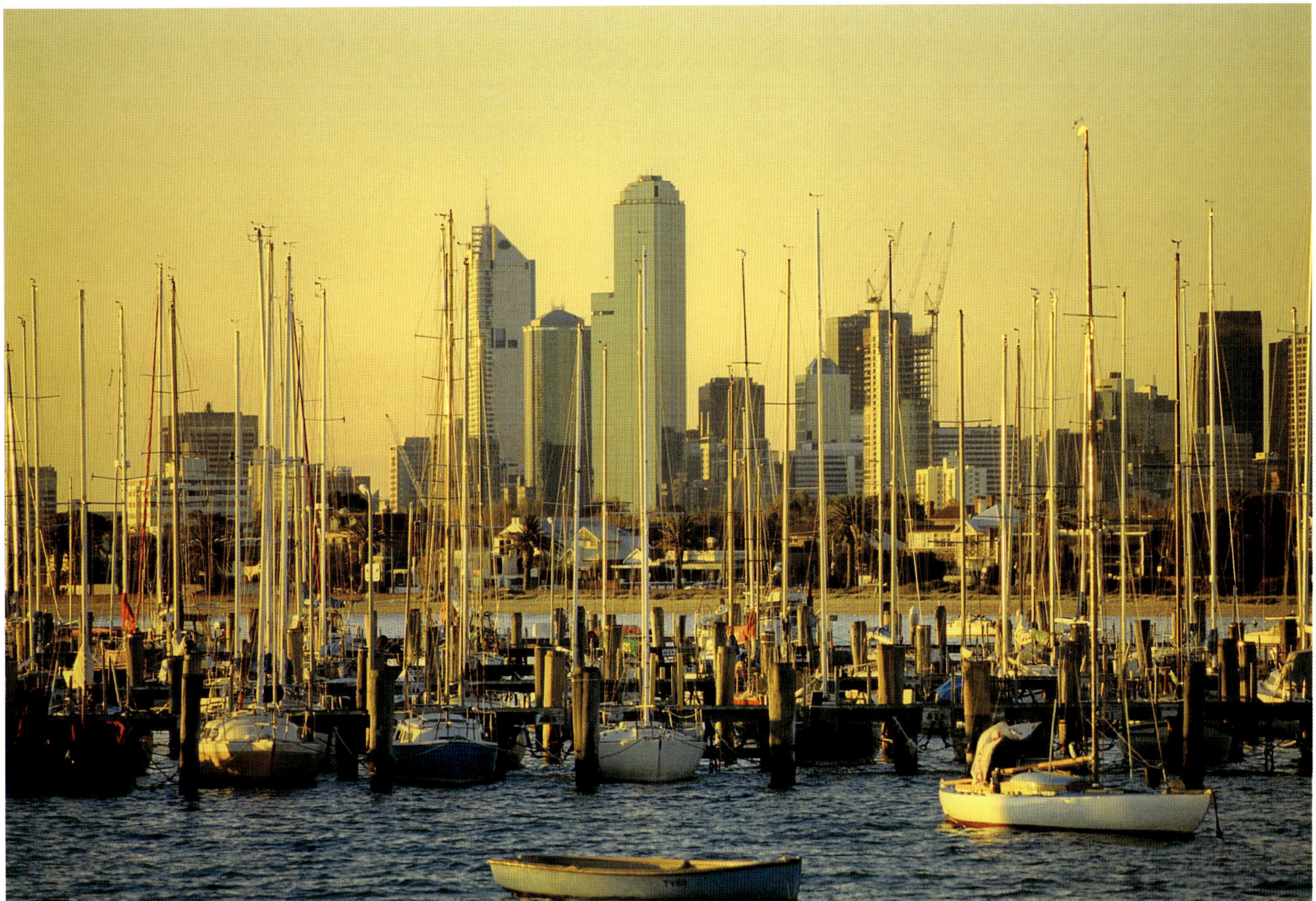

A view of the city centre from St Kilda Pier, opposite Williamstown, one of Melbourne's favourite bayside places.

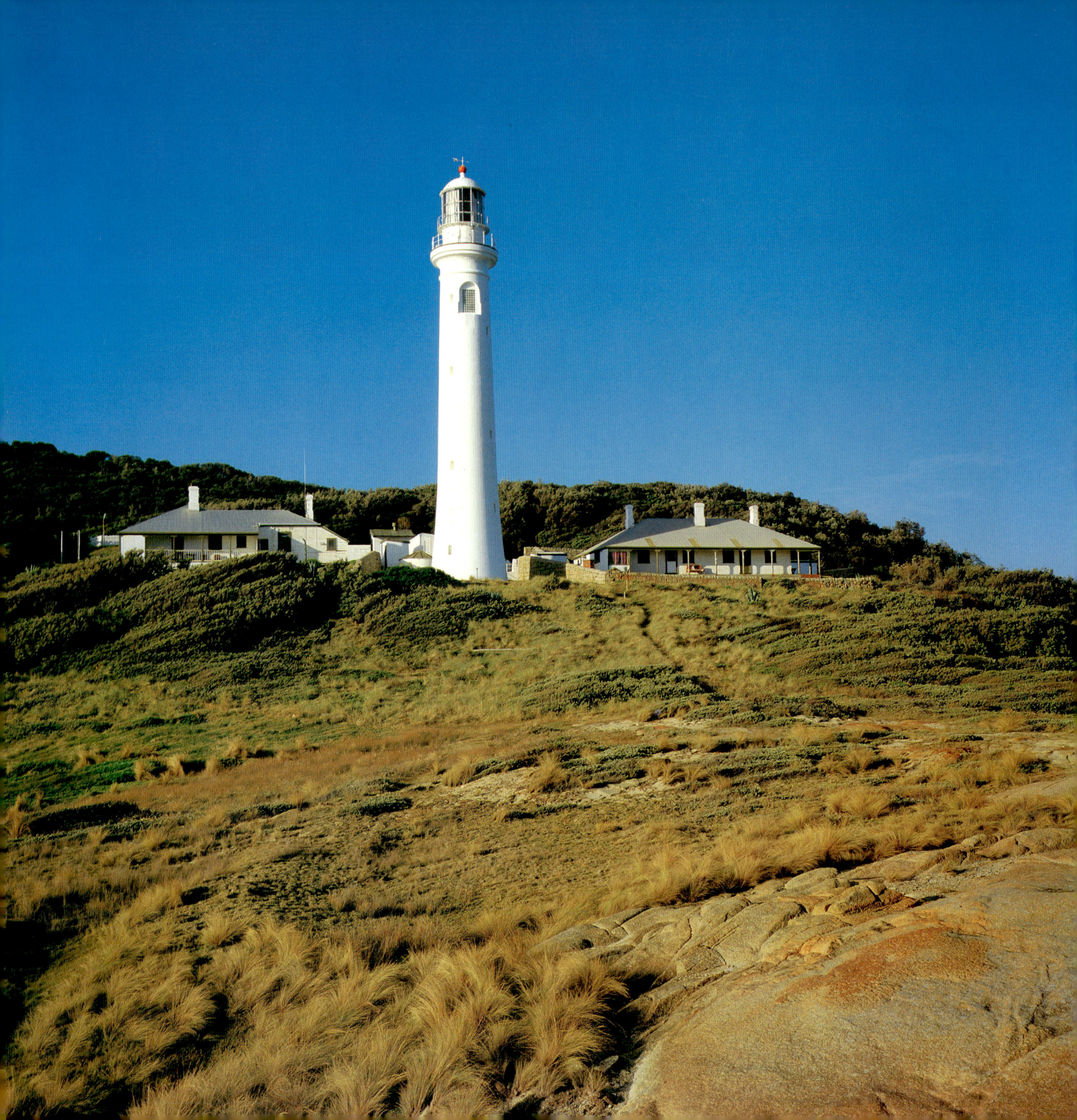

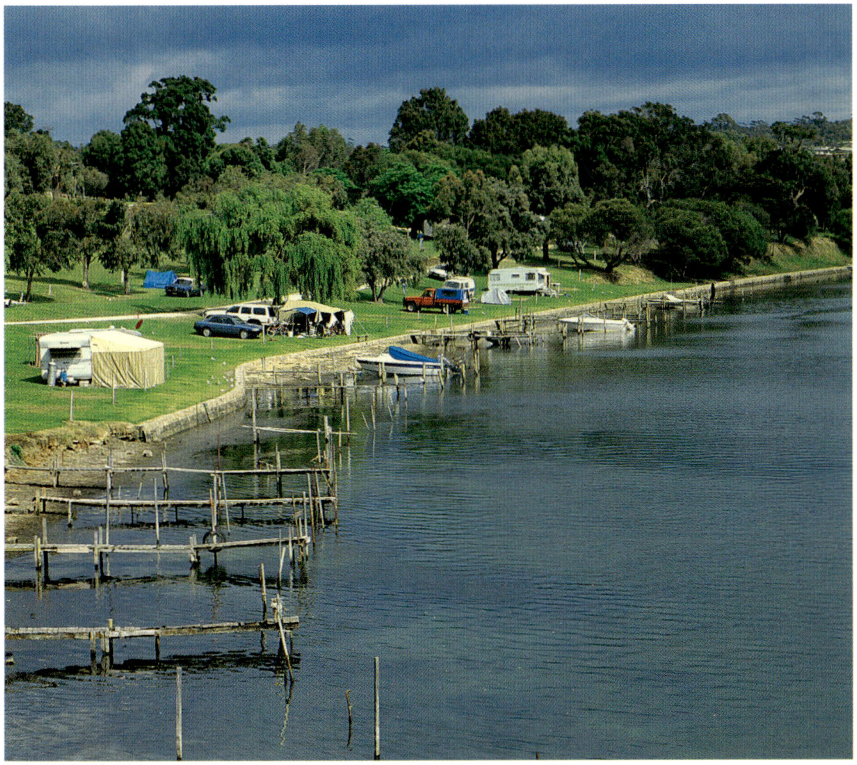

Above: An idyllic place for caravanners and campers at Mallacoota.

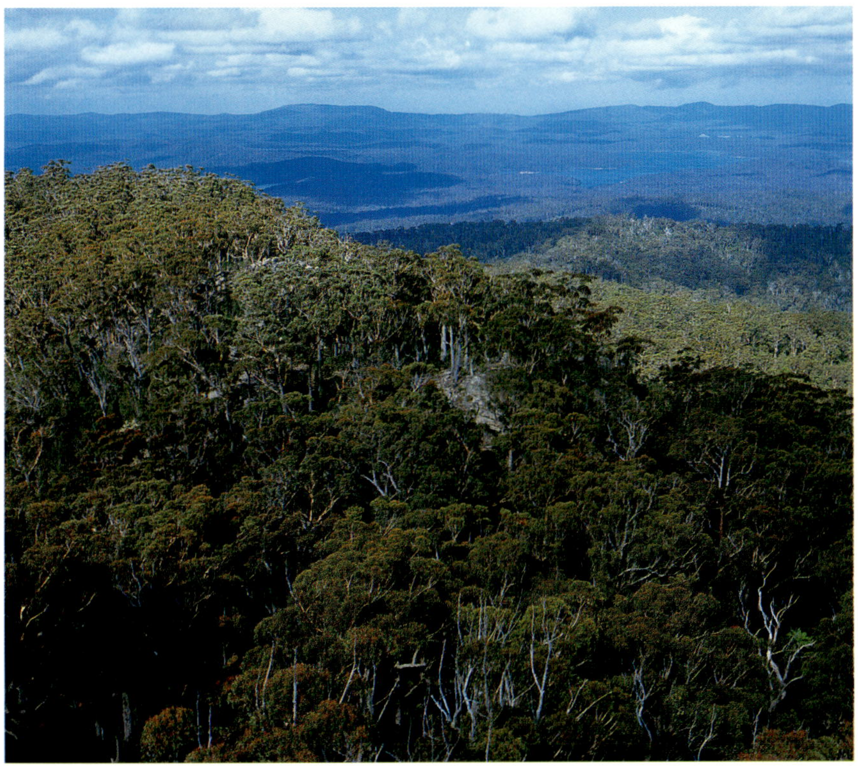

Above: The view from Genoa Peak.

Opposite: Point Hicks Lighthouse.

Croajingolong National Park

One of the most delightful ways to spend a week or so is to wander Victoria's eastern seacoast from the New South Wales border back to Melbourne. Croajingolong National Park, adjacent to the border, has 100 kilometres of unspoiled beaches sheltered by jutting headlands and it surrounds Mallacoota Inlet, which is a wonderful place to fish, sail or relax in the sun. The park has five camping areas, each on a waterway. Genoa Peak Lookout rewards those prepared for a moderately strenuous walk, with panoramic views of the coastline and surrounding forest.

Another feature of the park is Point Hicks Lighthouse, built in 1888 on a headland then called Cape Everard. The name-change commemorates the fact that this point of land was the first part of Australia sighted by any of Captain Cook's crew, the distinction going to Lieutenant Zachary Hicks.

Lakes Entrance

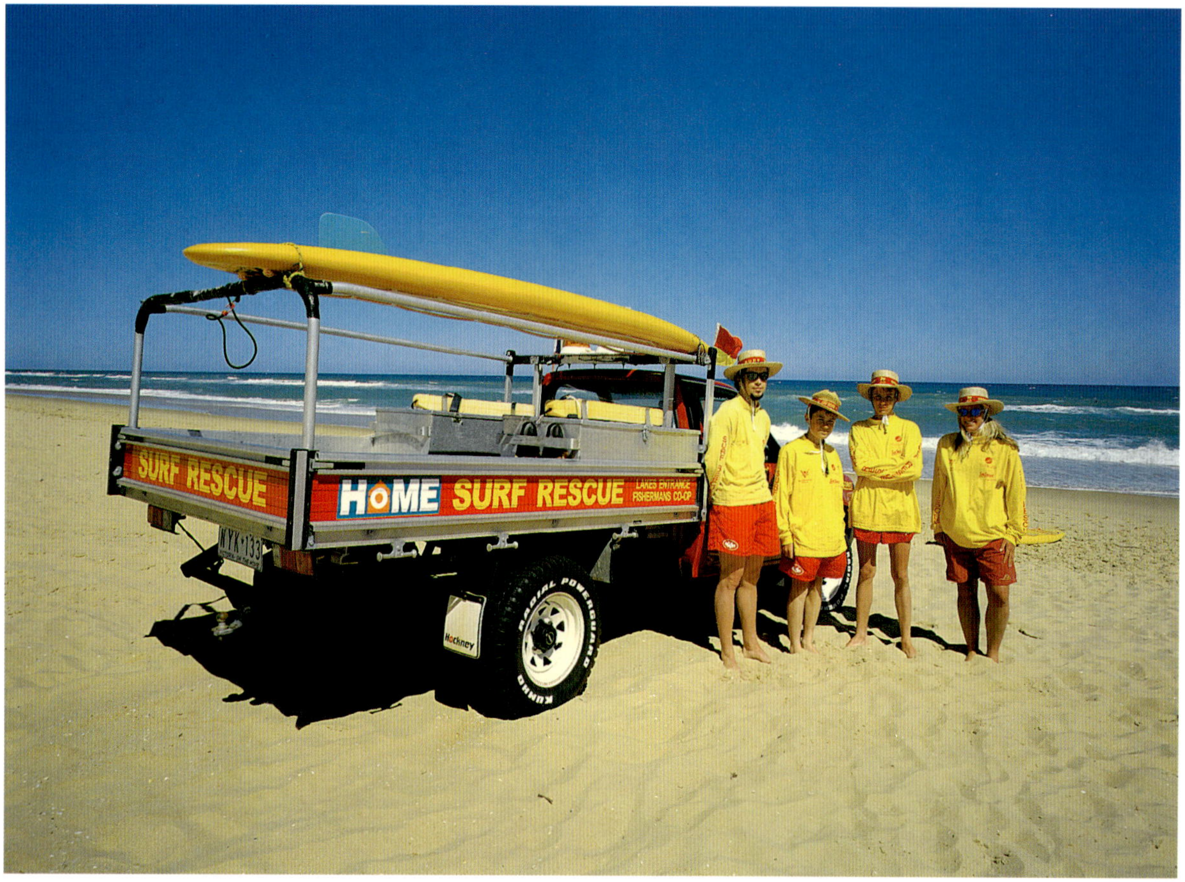

Surf lifesavers on the Ninety Mile Beach, the seaward face of the sand barrier forming the Gippsland Lakes. *Opposite and following pages:* Lakes Entrance.

The Gippsland Lakes were formed a million years ago, when the sea dumped sand to form a series of barriers behind which coastal lakes formed. The area is a paradise for people who want to catch fish: deep sea fishing craft, scallop boats, family sailcraft and powerboats of all kinds set out from Lakes Entrance, at the entrance to the 400 square kilometres of sheltered waterways.

Gippsland Lakes Coastal Park surrounds The Lakes National Park, and includes much of the Ninety Mile Beach, lakes and coastal dunes. Sperm Whale Head in the The Lakes National Park is a great place for birdwatching and for observing other wildlife, especially the resident mobs of kangaroos.

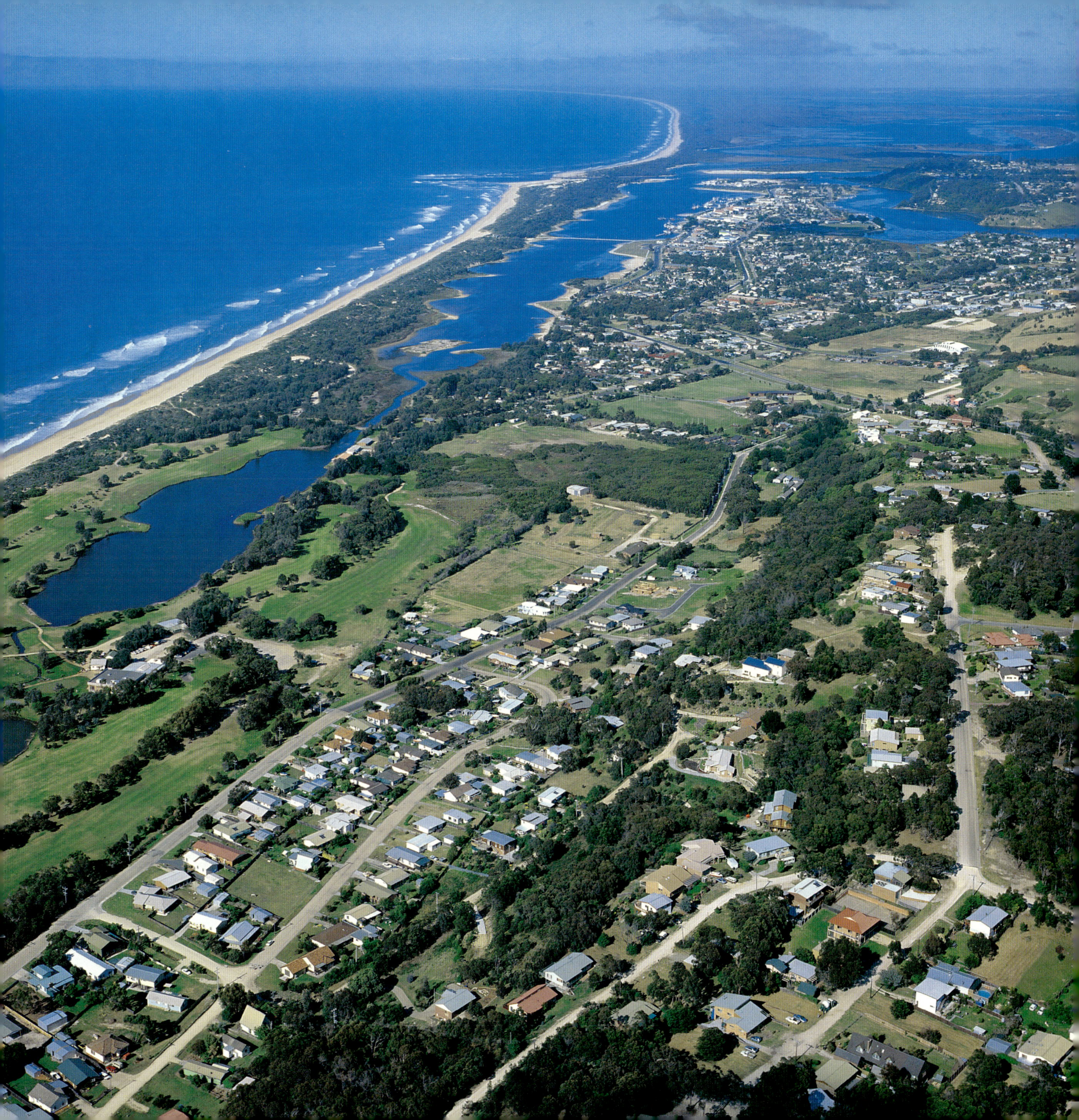

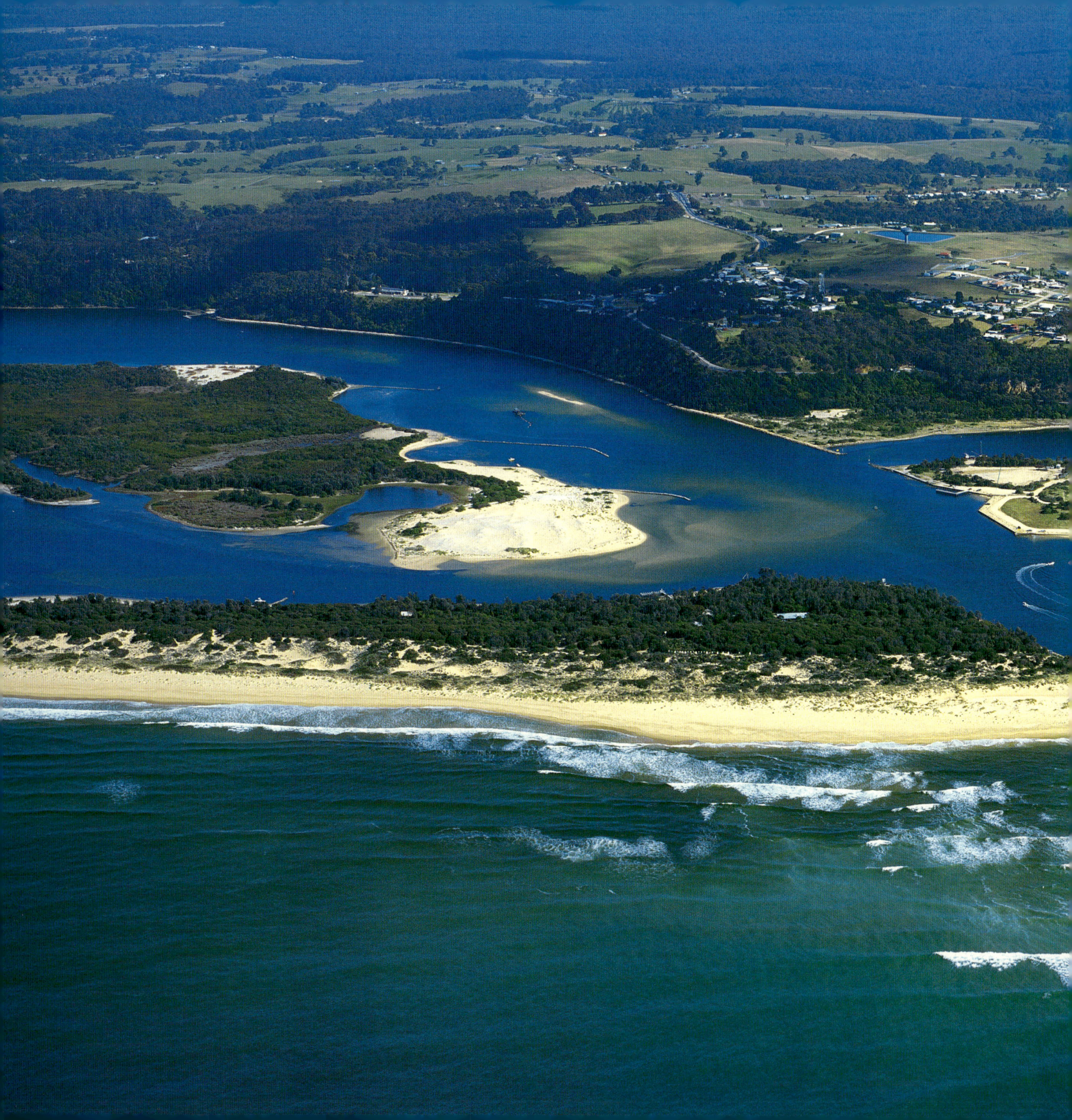

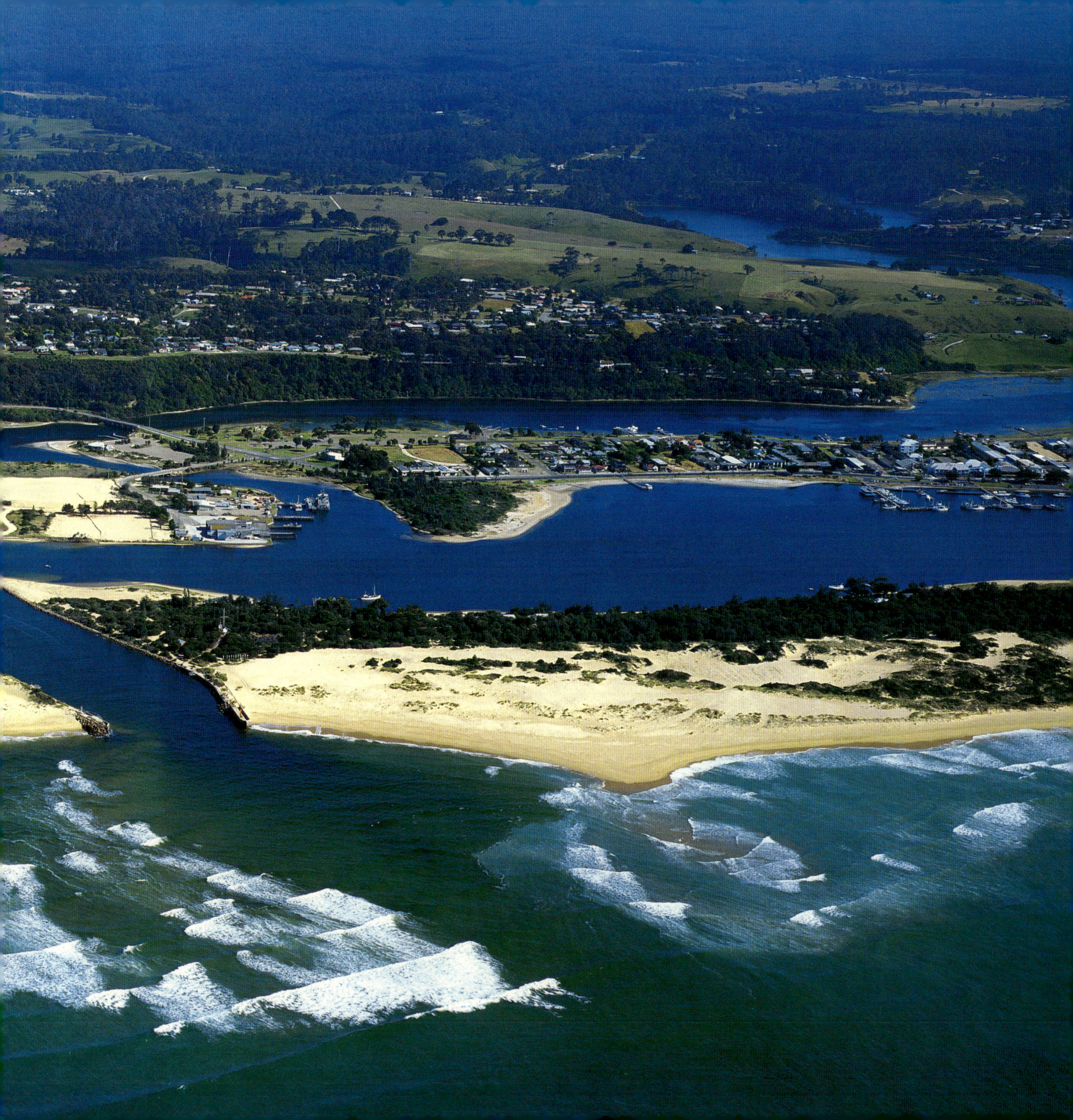

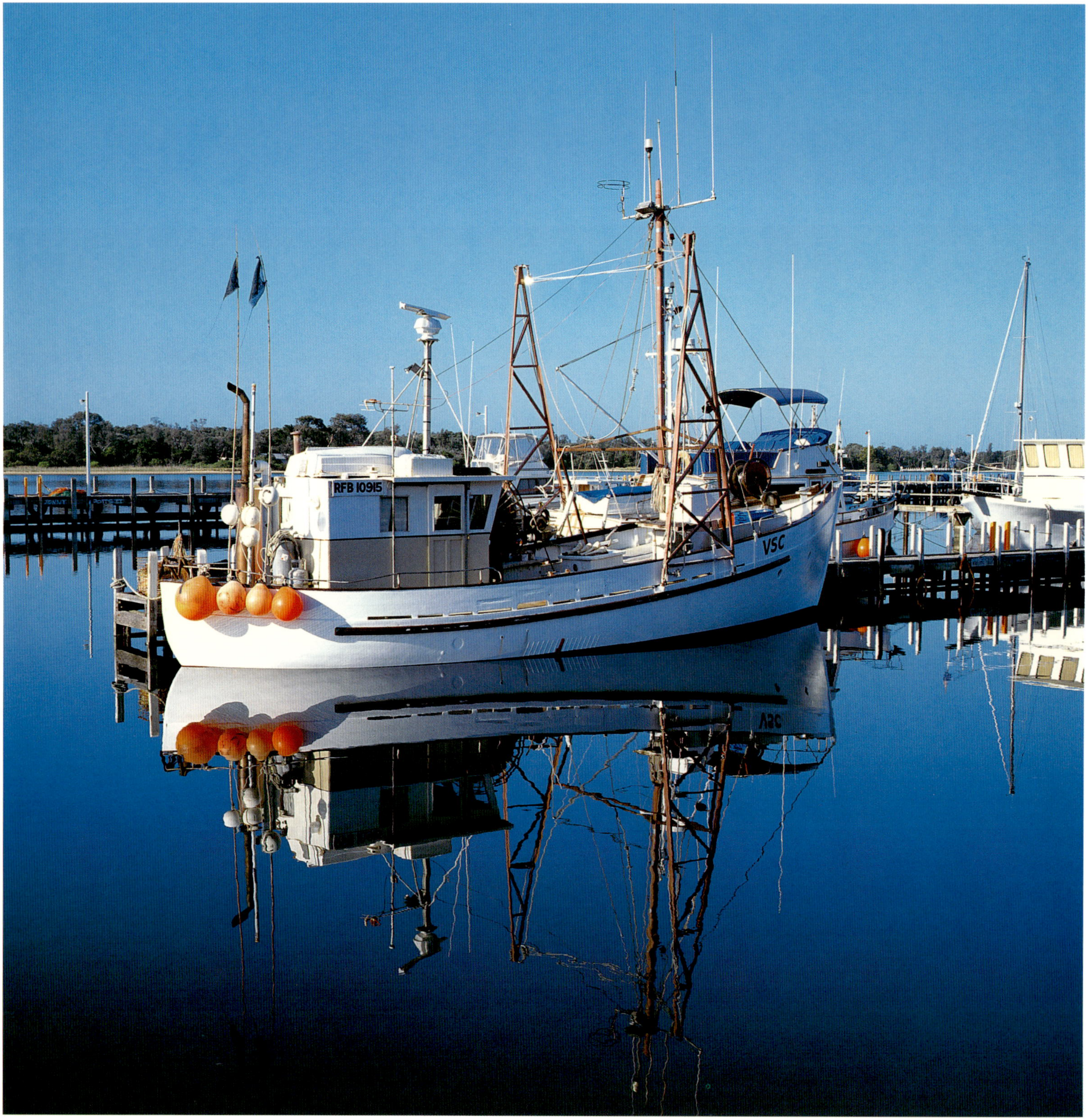

A fishing trawler mirrored in the stillness of the water at its Lakes Entrance moorings.

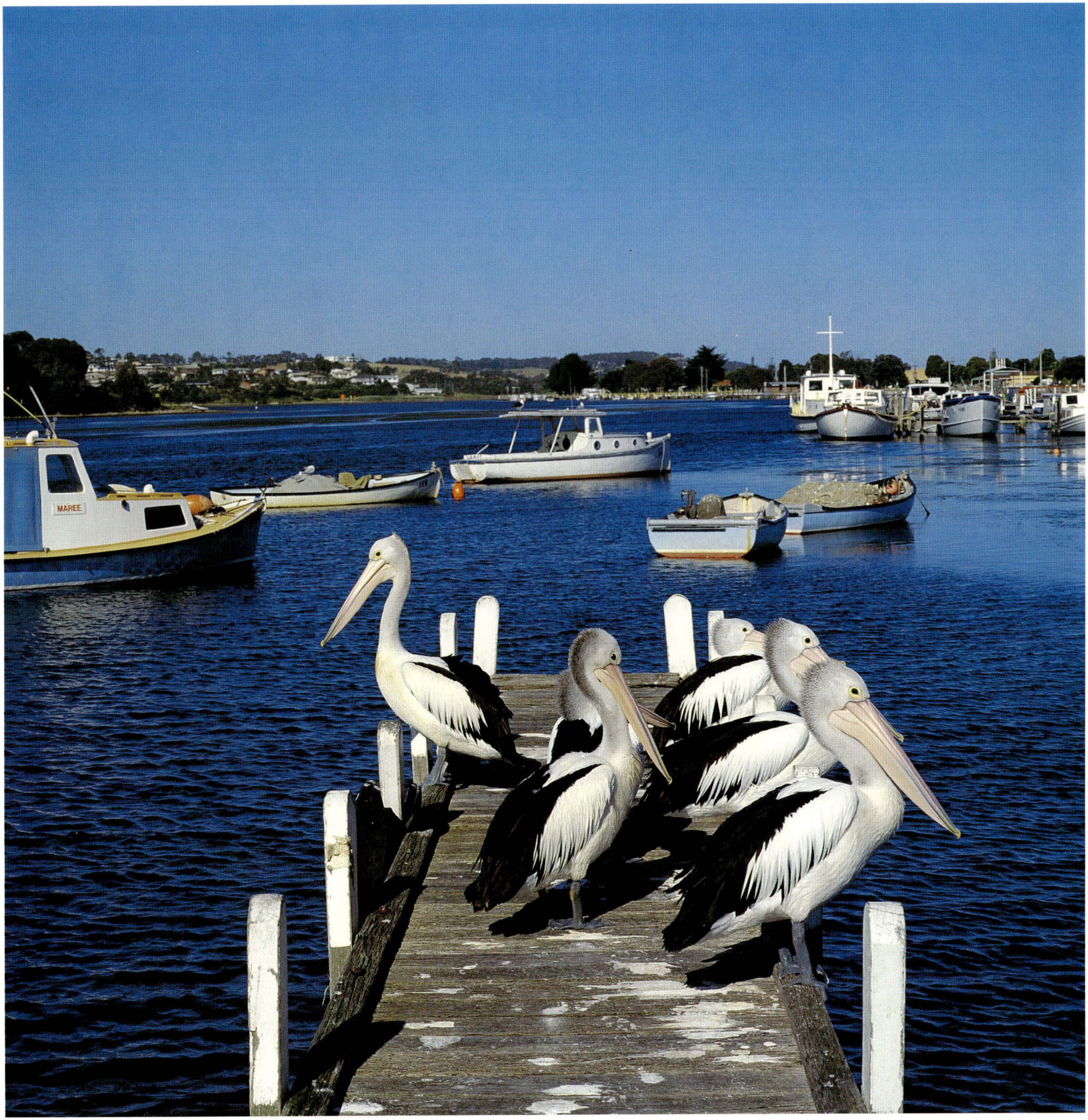

Australian Pelicans await the return of a successful fishing vessel at Lakes Entrance.

The Gippsland Lakes

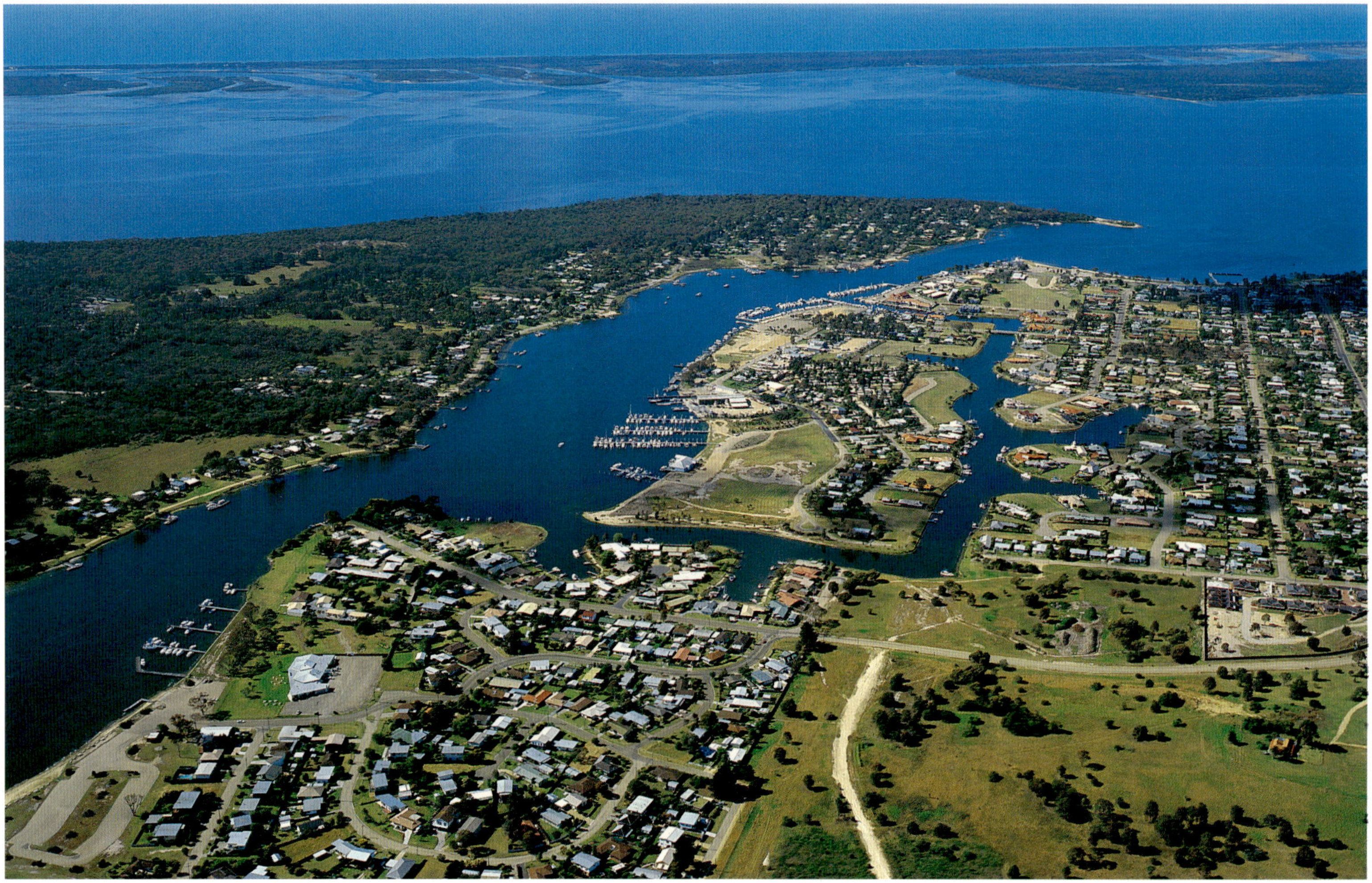

Above: Paynesville is the boating capital of the Gippsland Lakes.

Opposite: Bairnsdale has become a base for exploration of Victoria's beautiful Gippsland Lakes district.

The Gippsland Lakes area is sometimes called "Victoria's Riviera". The resort towns, such as Paynesville (above) nestle amid the natural beauties of the lakes, the Ninety Mile Beach and national and coastal parks.

Early European settlement was opposed by heroic resistance from the Aboriginal inhabitants of the area. In the 1850s the discovery of gold at Omeo made Bairnsdale into a riverboat port, linked to the Lakes by the Mitchell River. Today, the district produces sheep, cattle, timber and vegetables.

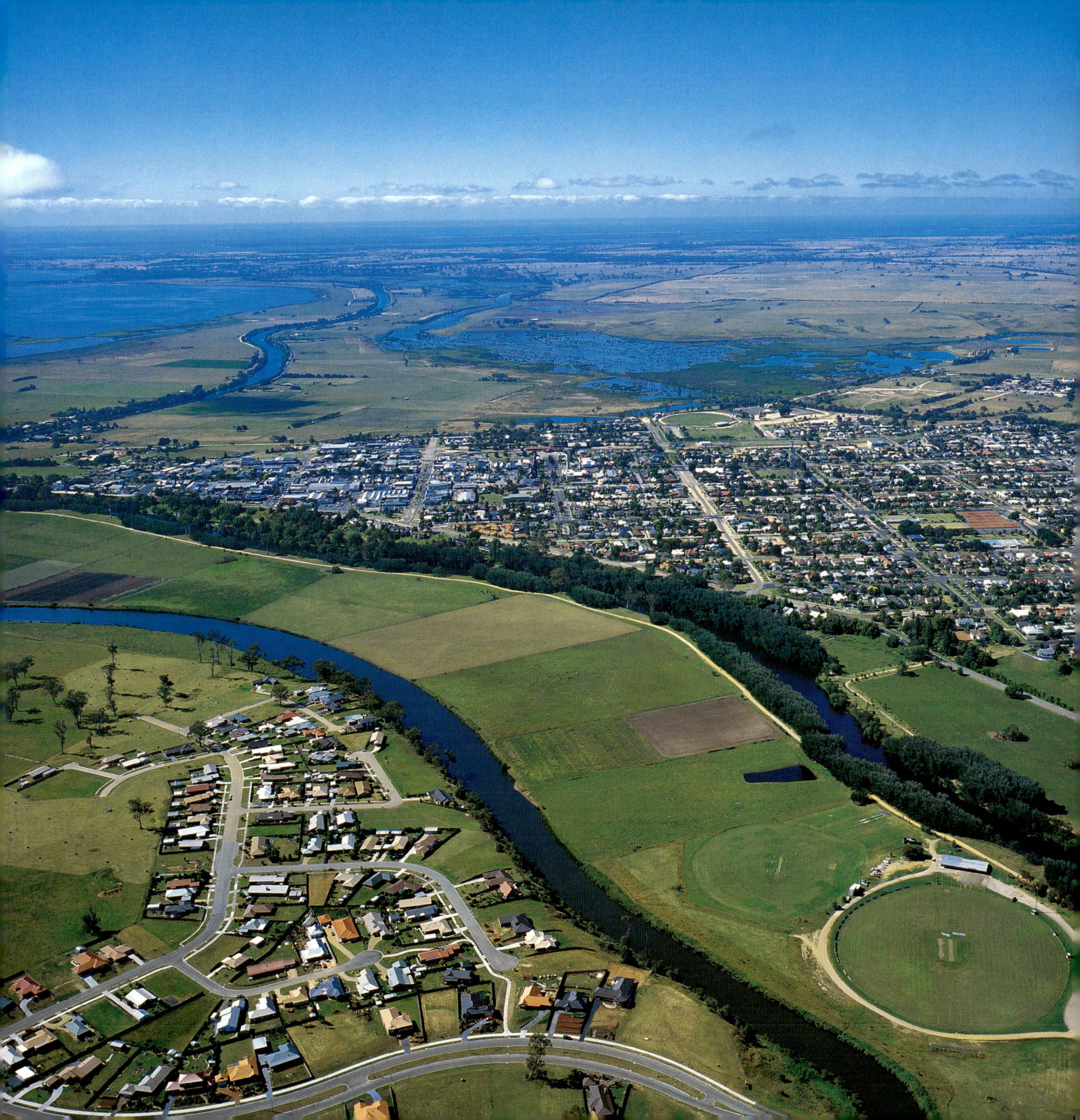

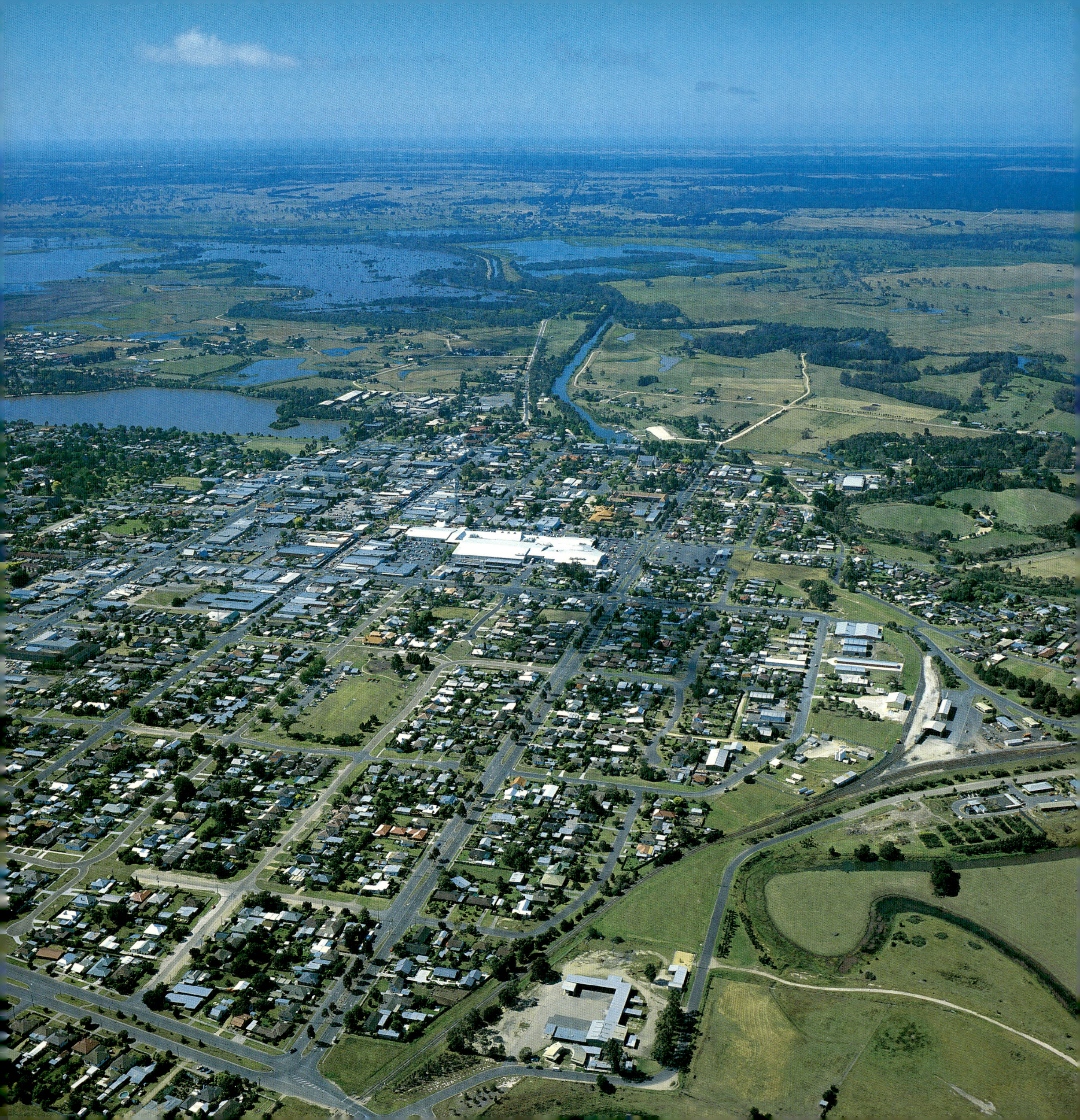

Sale

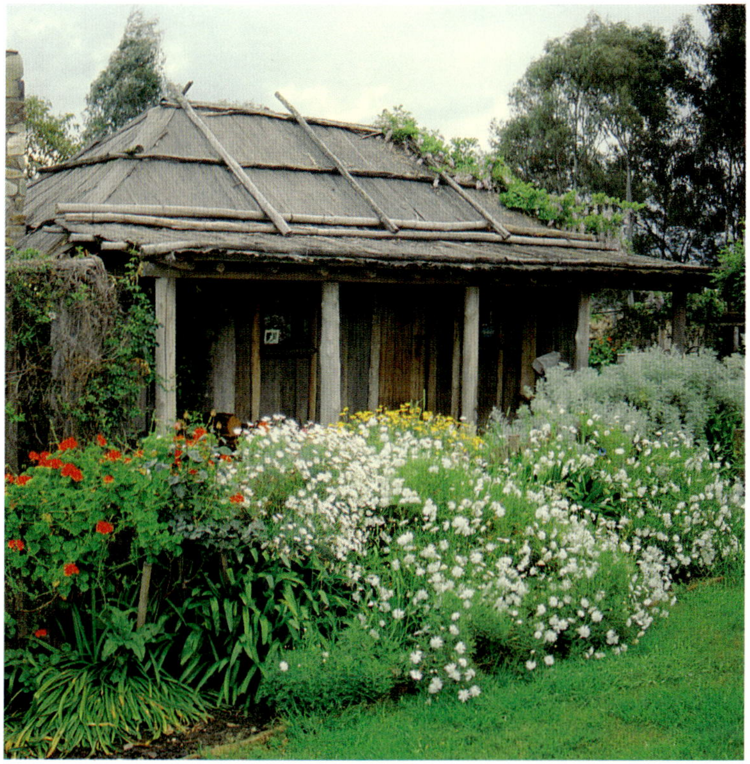

Above: Sale is a town which treasures its links with the past, such as this historic cottage.

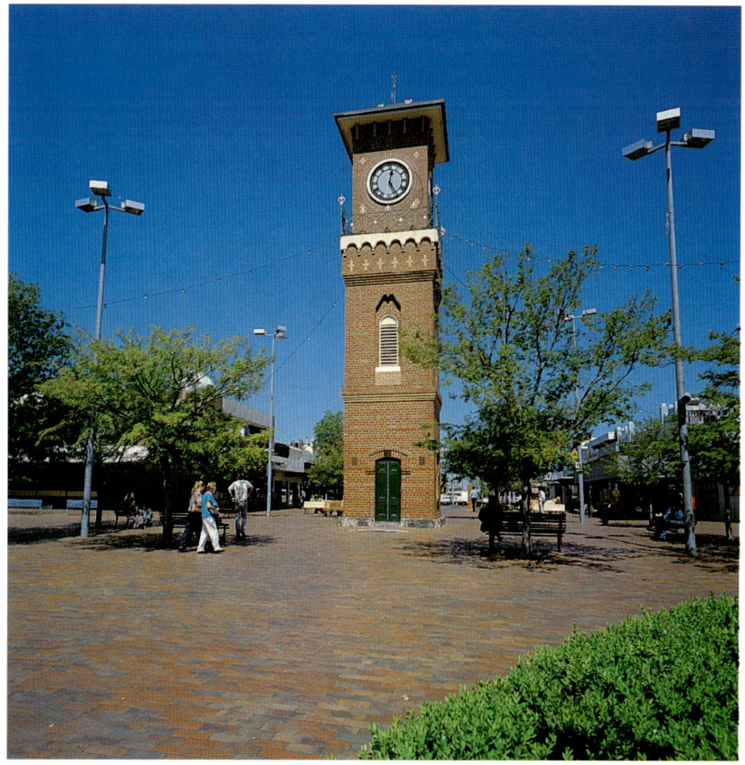

Above: The clock tower in the Mall at Sale.

Since 1965, Sale has been the centre for Bass Strait oil and natural gas interests. As well, Sale serves as a centre from which areas of natural beauty and diversity can be visited. The district is famed for its wetlands: Sale Common and Wildlife Reserve is a marvellous place to watch waterfowl.

Much of the heritage of Sale has been preserved. The town was named in 1840 and it served as a centre for settlers in the Gippsland area and supplied would-be miners heading to the Omeo and Walhalla Goldfields. From 1880, steamers and barges provided the links between the town and the sea, and a canal to the La Trobe River carried vessels and their cargoes to Lake Wellington.

Opposite: Sale from the air.

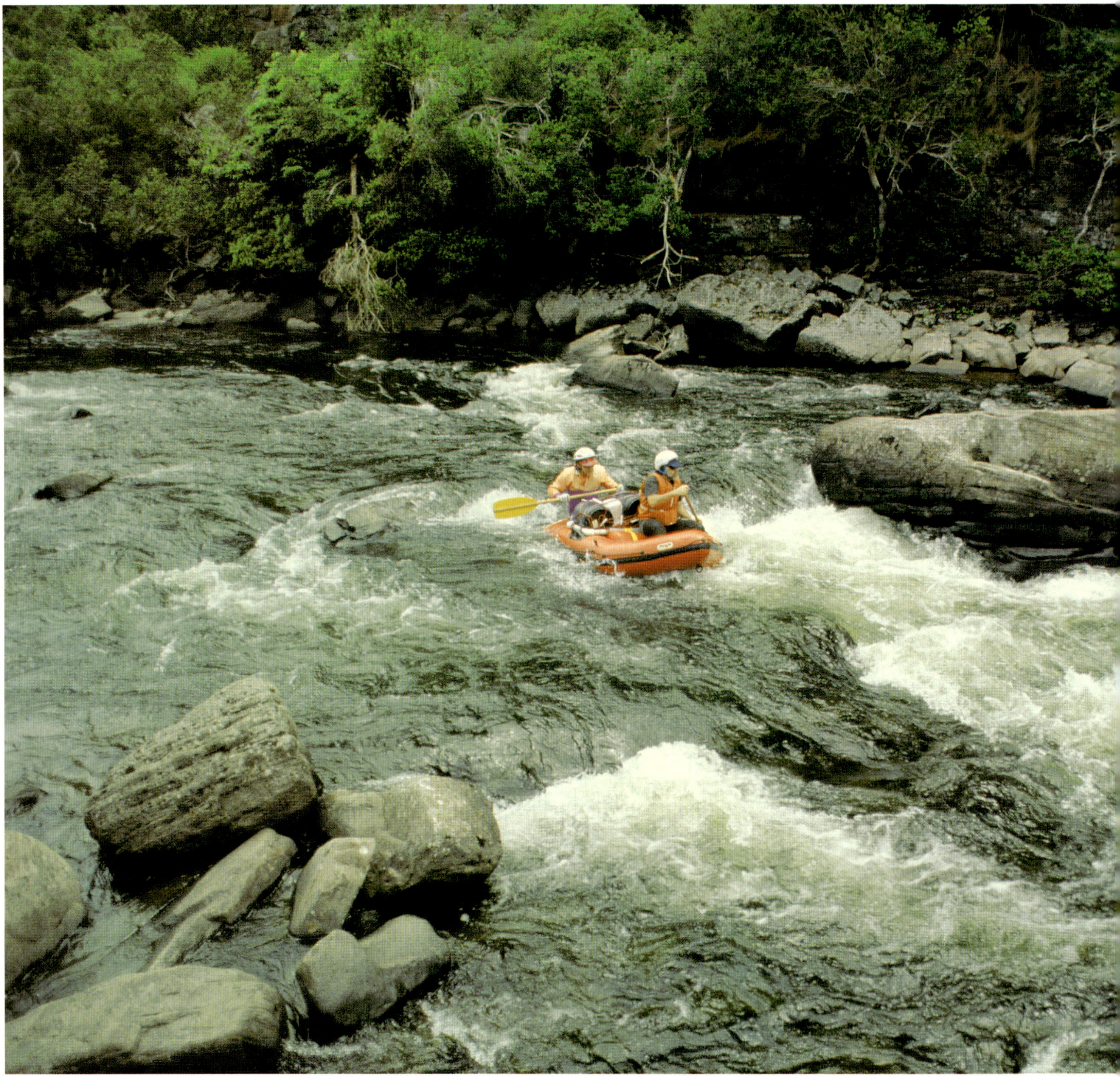

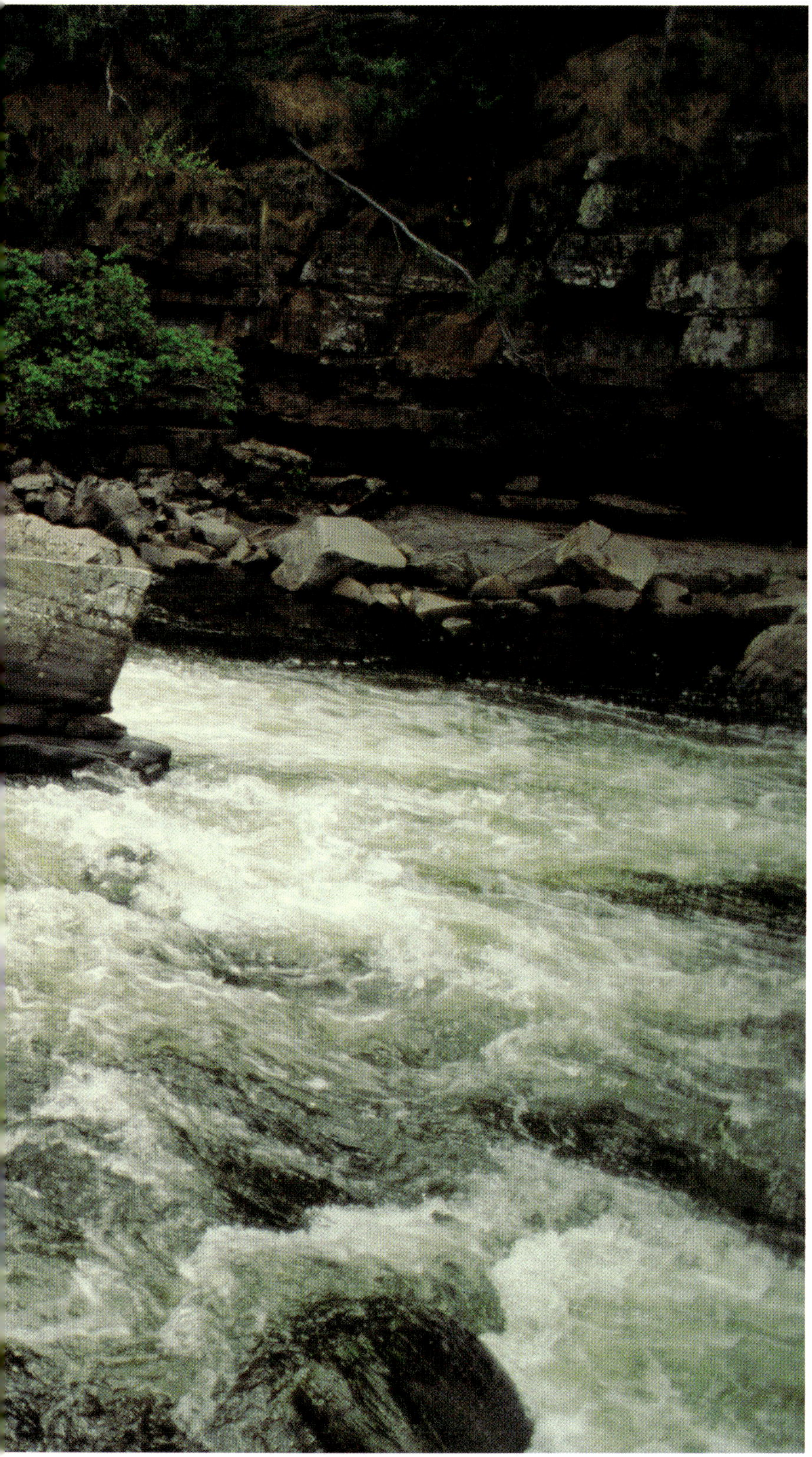

Mitchell River National Park

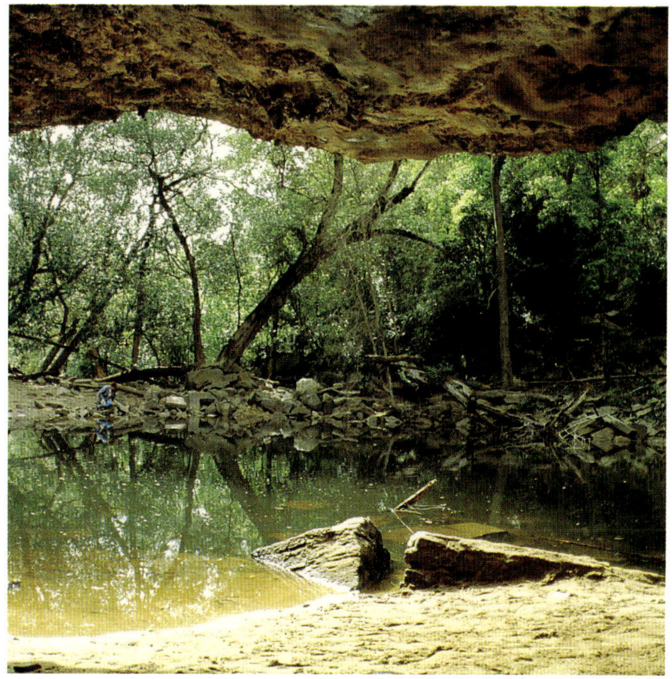

Above: The Den of Nargun, a creature of Aboriginal legend.

Some of Gippsland's most beautiful forested country is enclosed in Mitchell River National Park, north-west of Bairnsdale. The river rushes through gorges it has carved through the rocks of the southern extremity of the Great Dividing Range, past remnant pockets of warm temperate rainforest. Satin Bowerbirds and Gippsland Water Dragons are amongst the wildlife which add to the park's attractions.

A legendary wild creature of the area is the Nargun, whose den may be seen along Woolshed Creek. A fearsome creature of the Dreaming, the Nargun is said to be part animal but mostly stone, a predator on unwary passers-by.

Left: White water rafting on the Mitchell River.

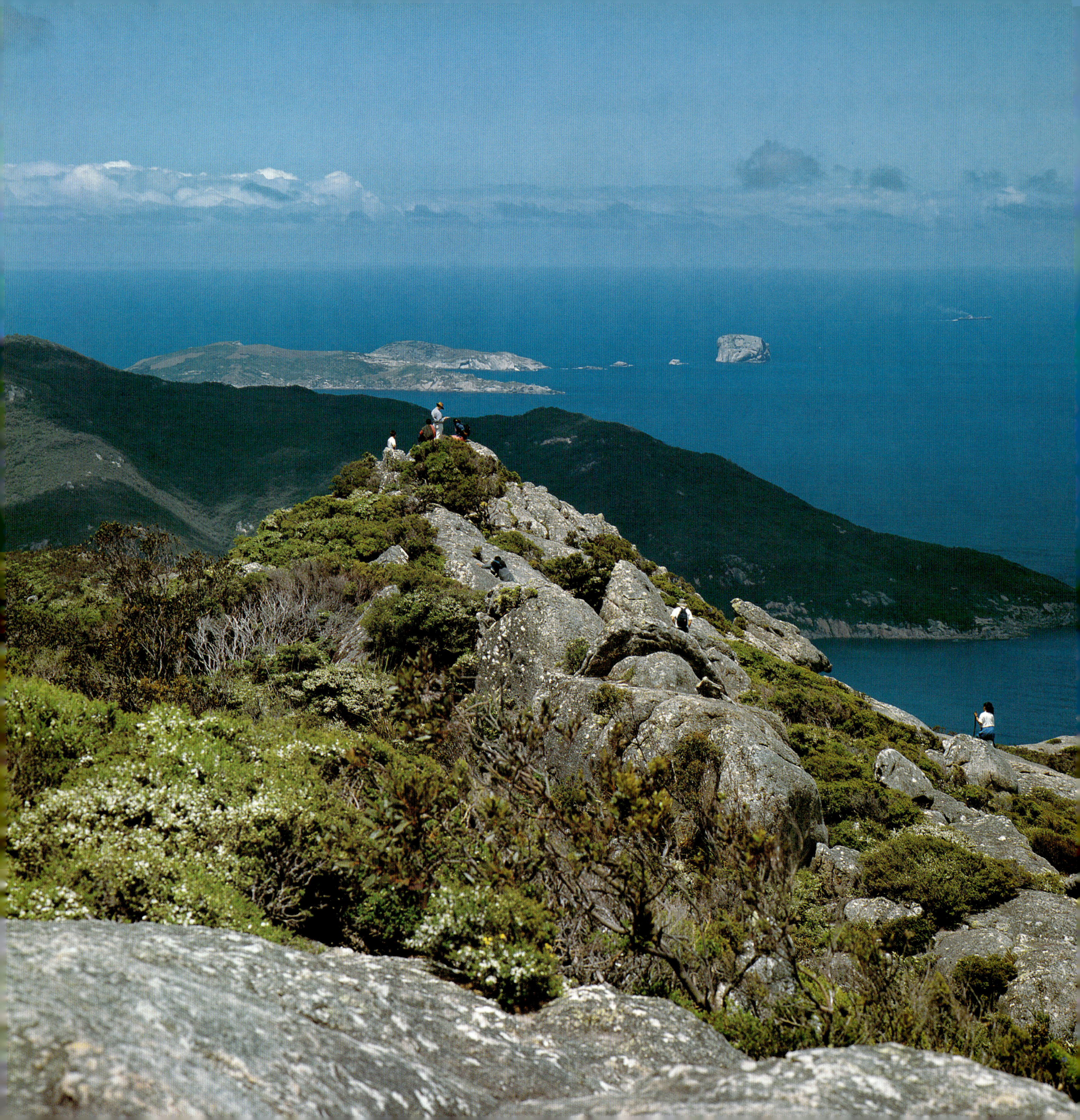

Wilsons Promontory

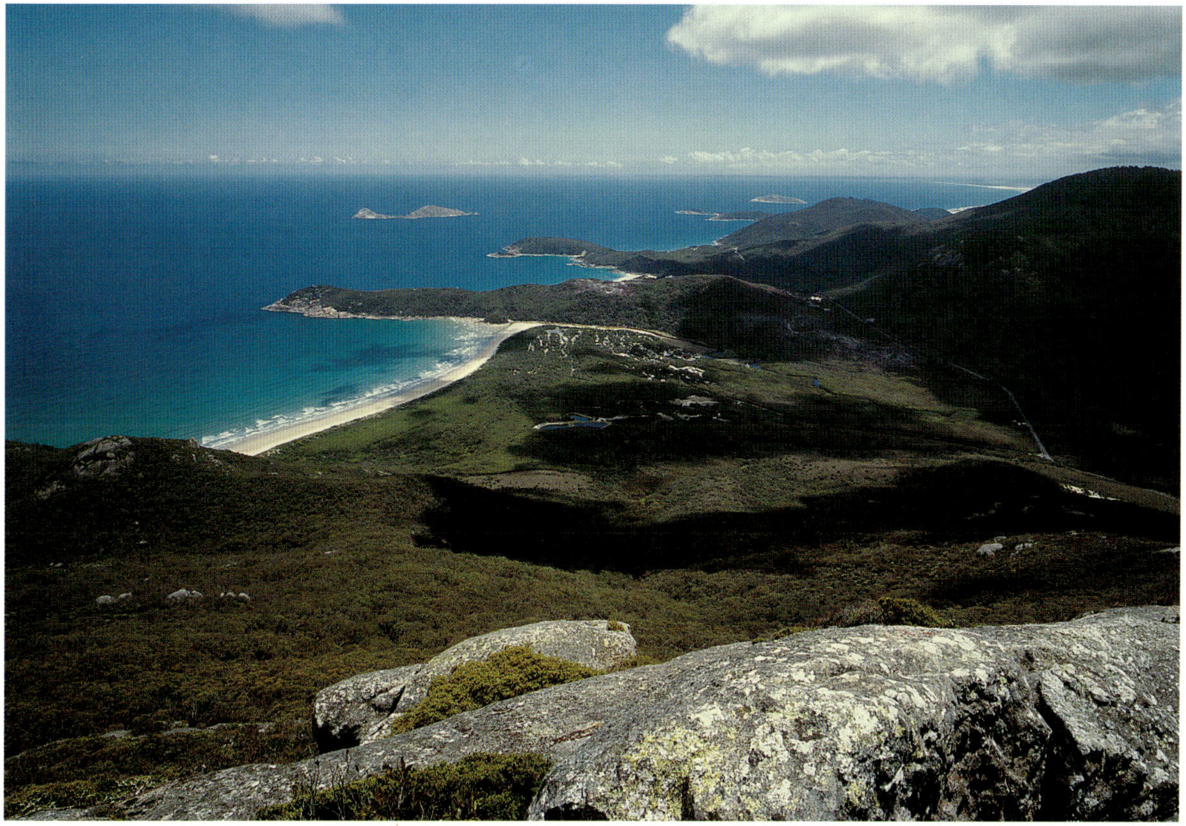

Above: A view from Mt Oberon which overlooks Tidal River.

Wilsons Promontory is a giant outcropping of granite connected to the mainland by the Yanakie Isthmus. During the early 1800s, sealers and fur-trappers exploited its wildlife, but the promontory has been a National Park since 1905. There is only one road giving vehicle access to Tidal River village, so walking is the preferred way of seeing most of the area's magnificent scenery and abundant animal and plant life. Some of the most popular features of the Prom, such as Squeaky Beach, Picnic Bay, Mt Oberon and Lilly Pilly Gully are within a short distance of Tidal River.

Opposite: "The Prom", as those who love its wild places call it, is mecca for bushwalkers, photographers and wildlife enthusiasts.
Following pages: Squeaky Beach is noted for the sounds made by its sand.

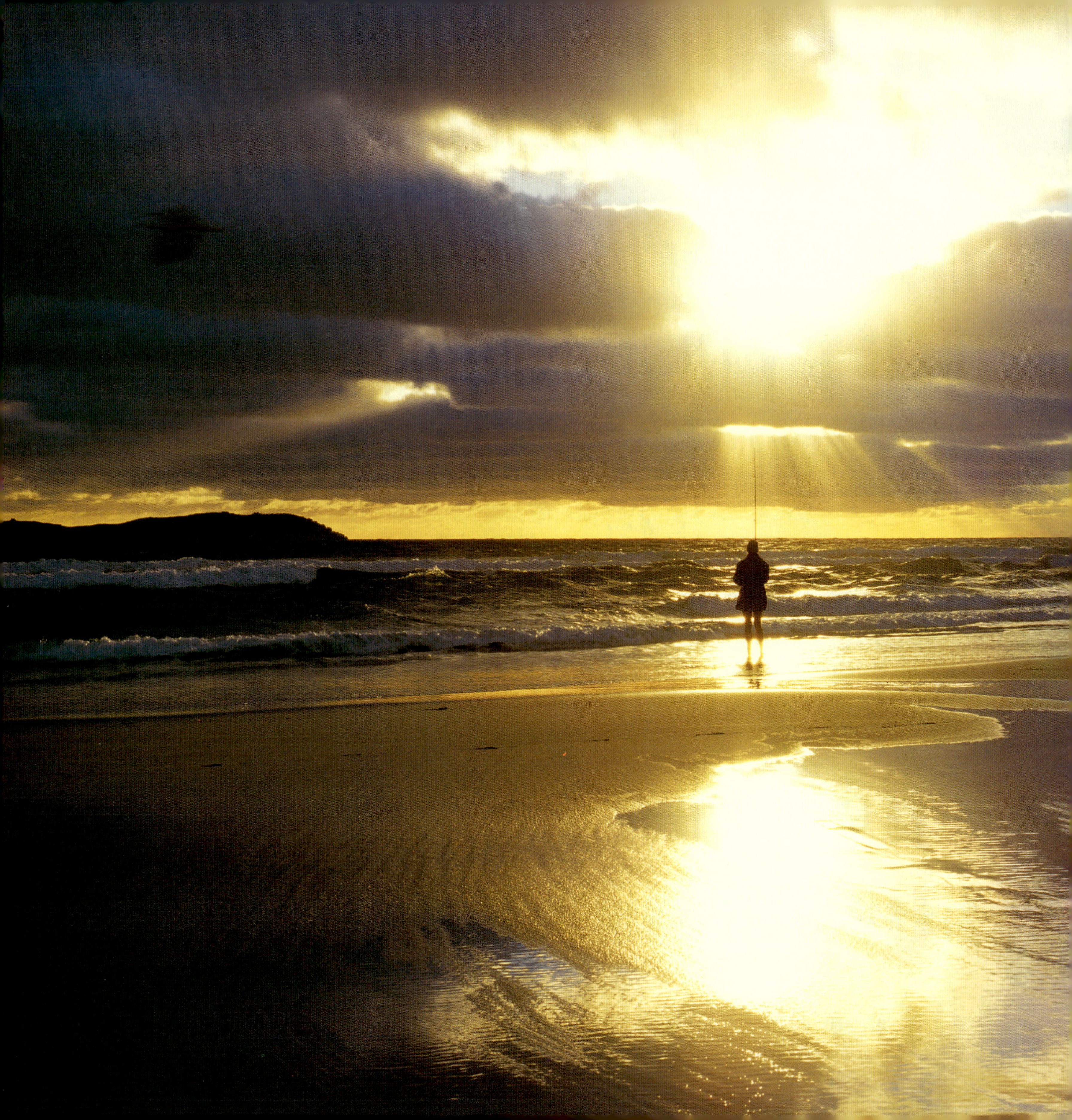

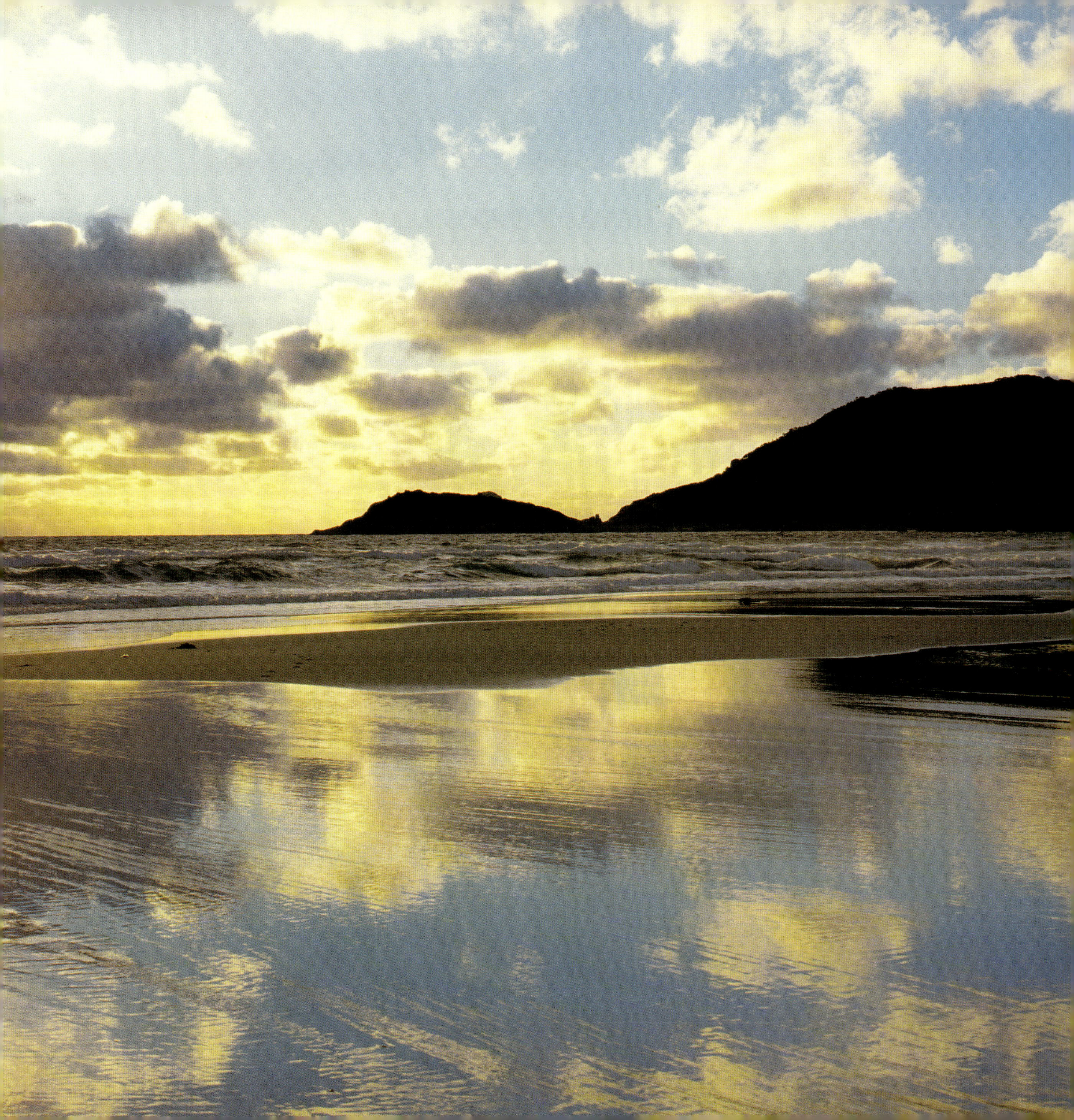

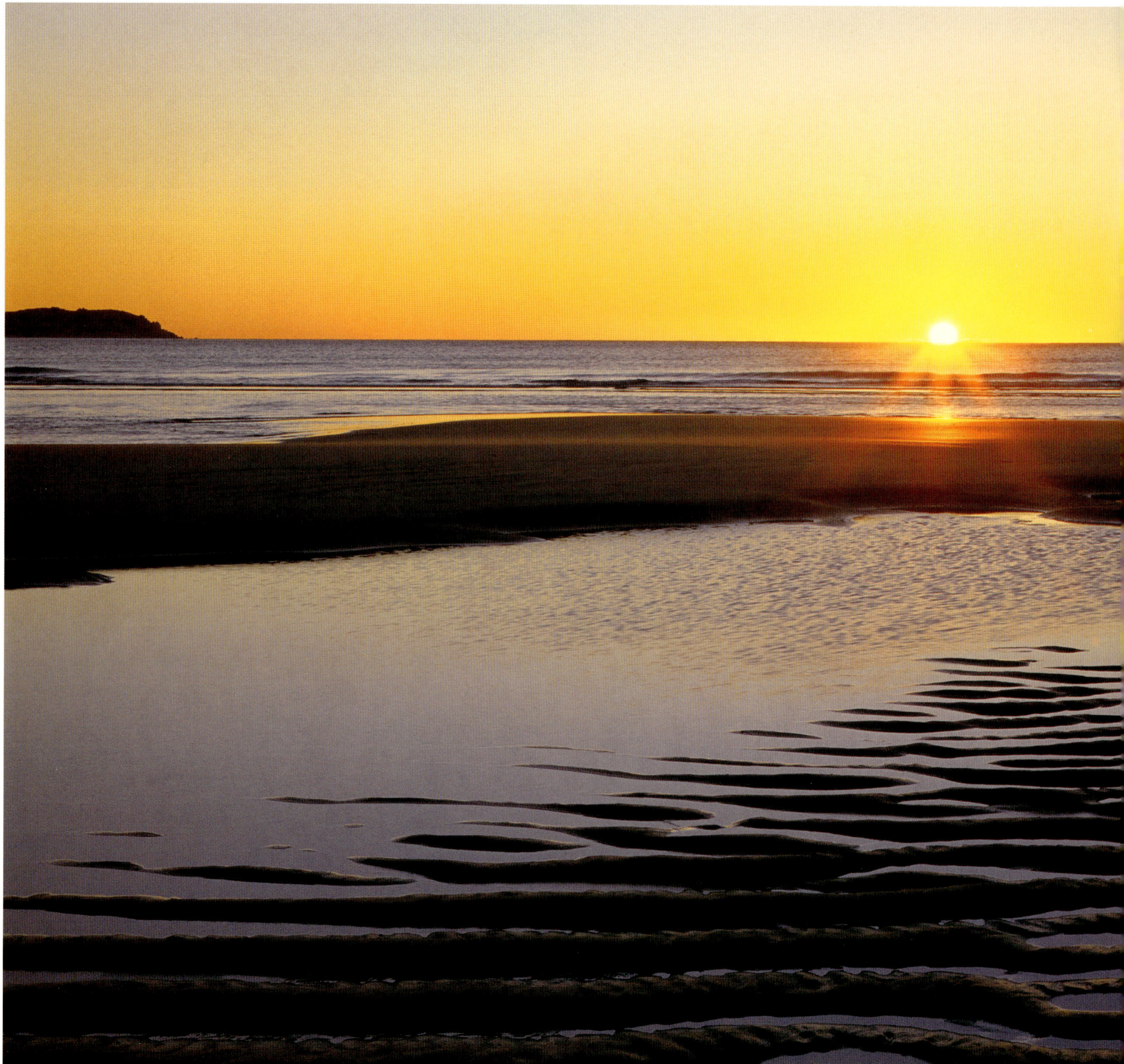
In the glow of an exquisite sunset, the sands of Whisky Bay await the returning tide.

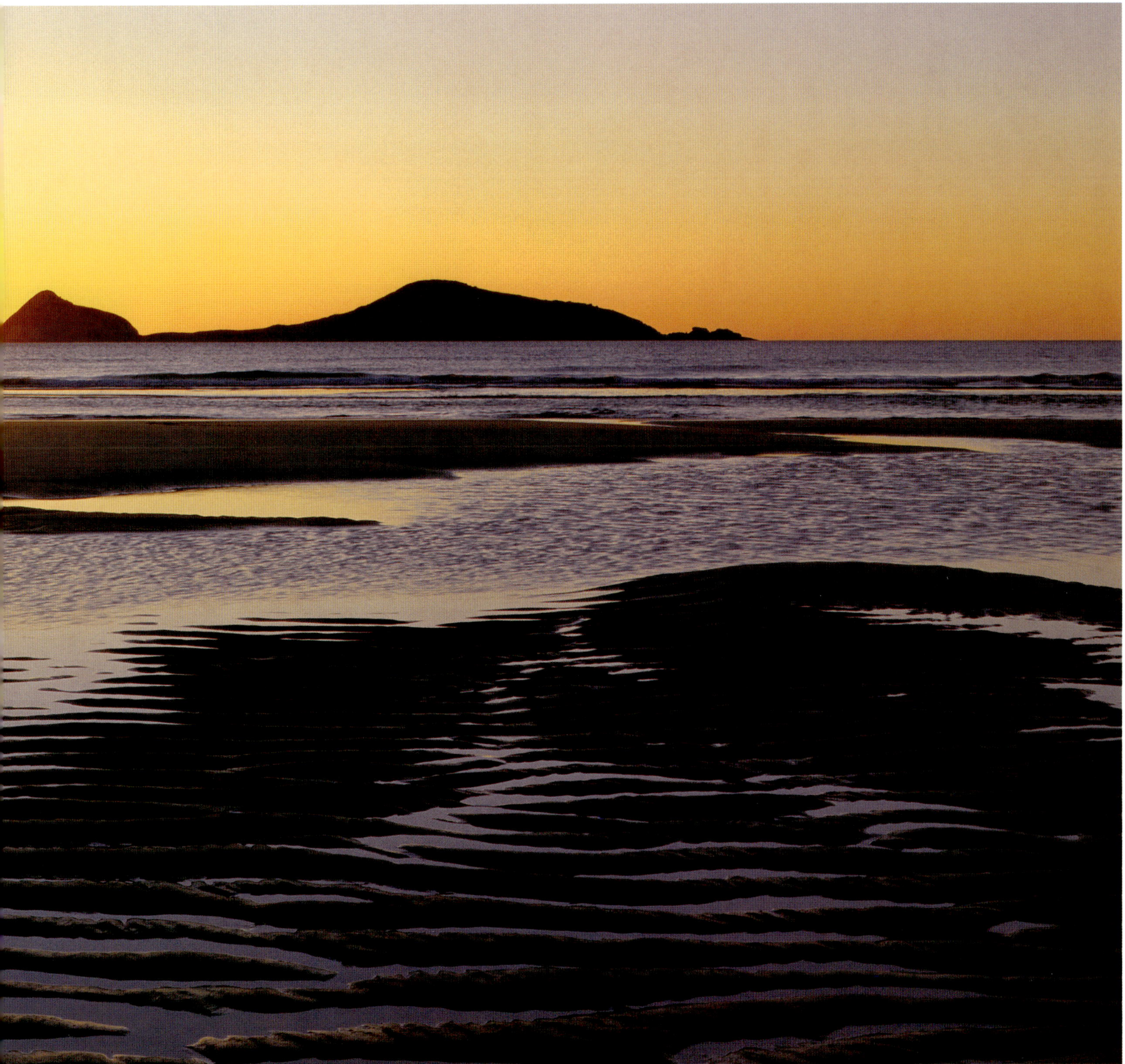

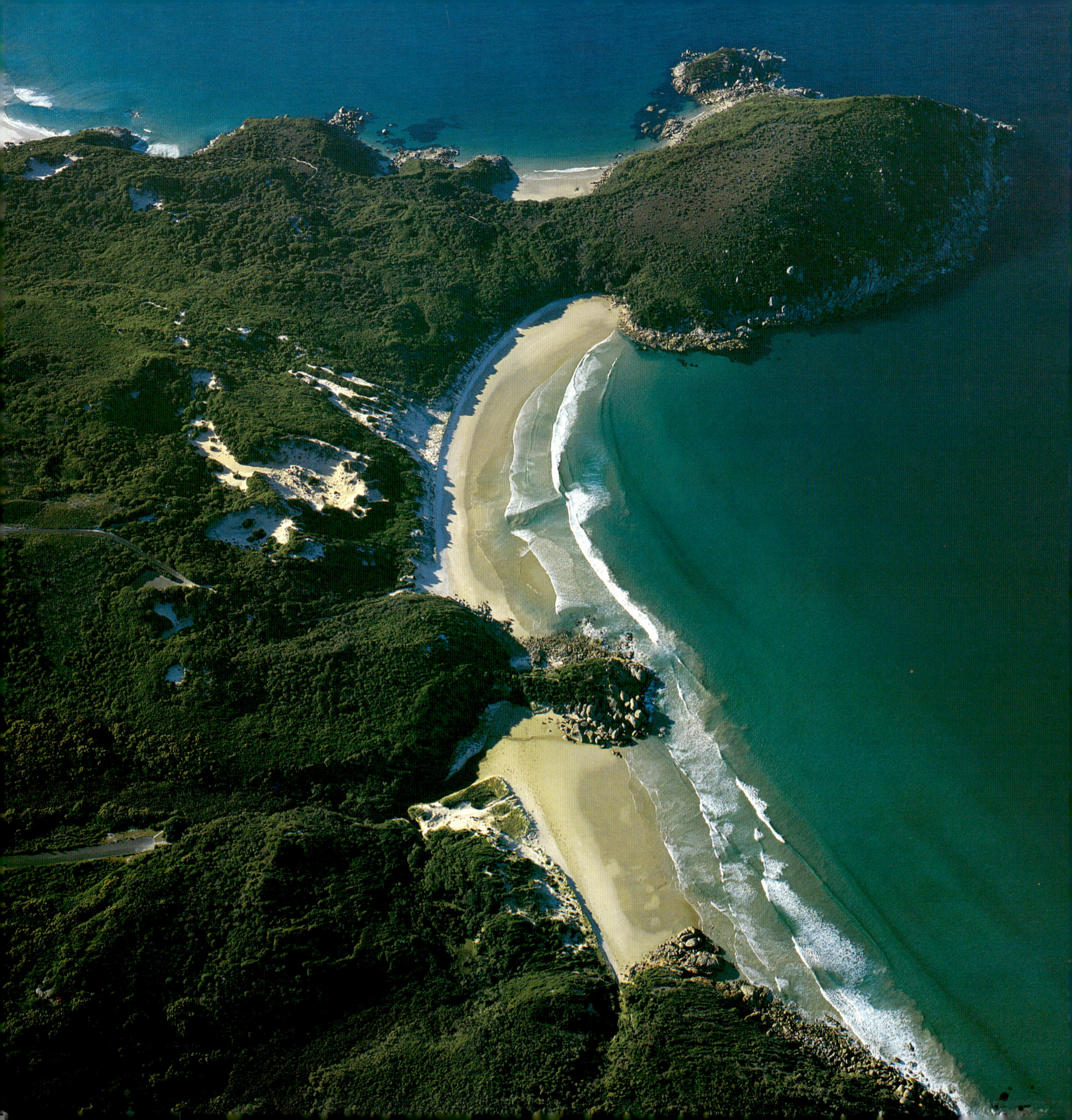

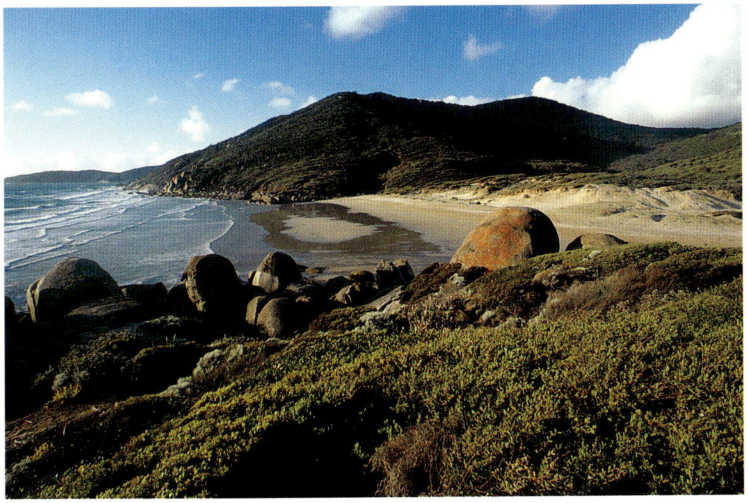

Above: Secluded bays are surrounded by vegetation pruned by salt winds.

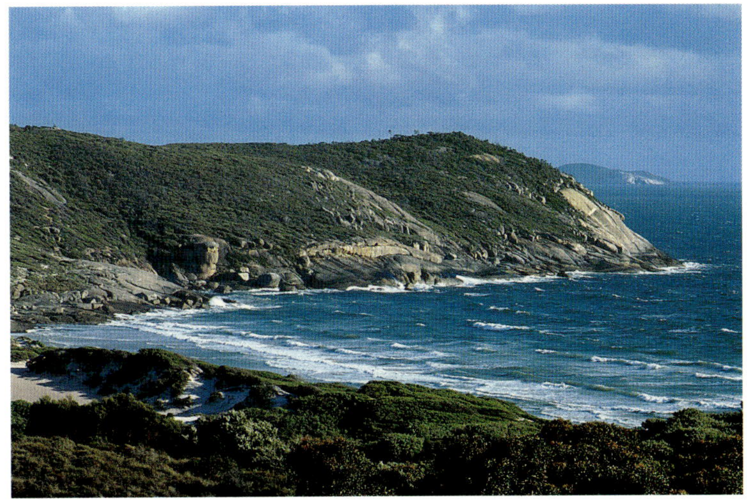

Above: Massive granite headlands are typical of Wilsons Promontory.

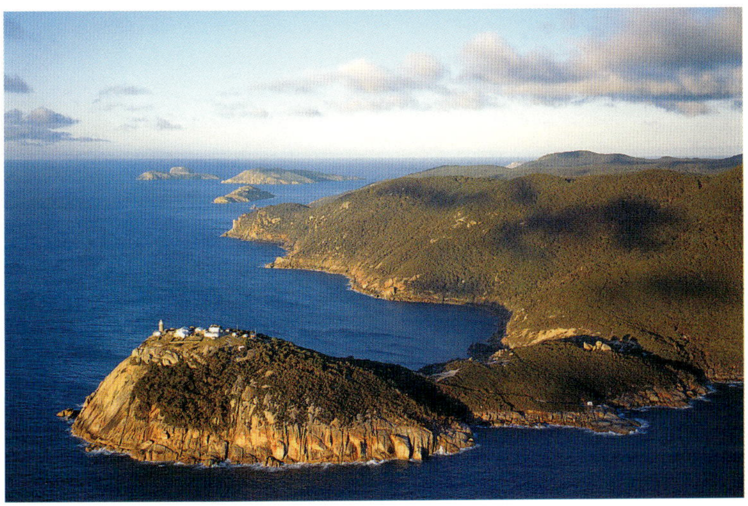

Above: An operational lighthouse stands on South East Point on Wilsons Promontory.

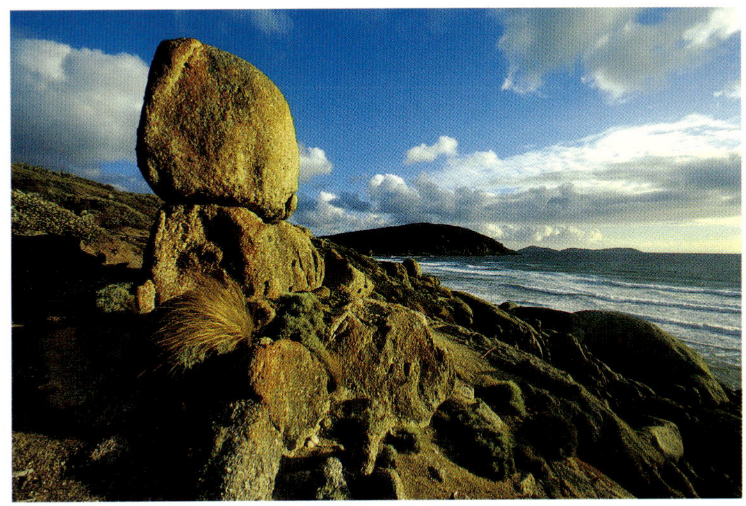

Above: The granite rocks of the promontory have been eroded into picturesque forms.

Leonard Bay, Whisky Bay and Picnic Bay are just north of Tidal River. Leonard Bay, which is reached by a short Nature Walk, contains Squeaky Beach, so named because of the noise the fine silver sands make when walked upon. Whisky and Picnic Bays are divided by a granite headland whose boulders are fretted into fanciful shapes by salt-carrying sea winds. The Prom's granites are often stained with colourful lichens, and may have crystals of semi-precious stones embedded in them.

Opposite: The rolling surf and pristine beaches of Whisky Bay and Picnic Bay.

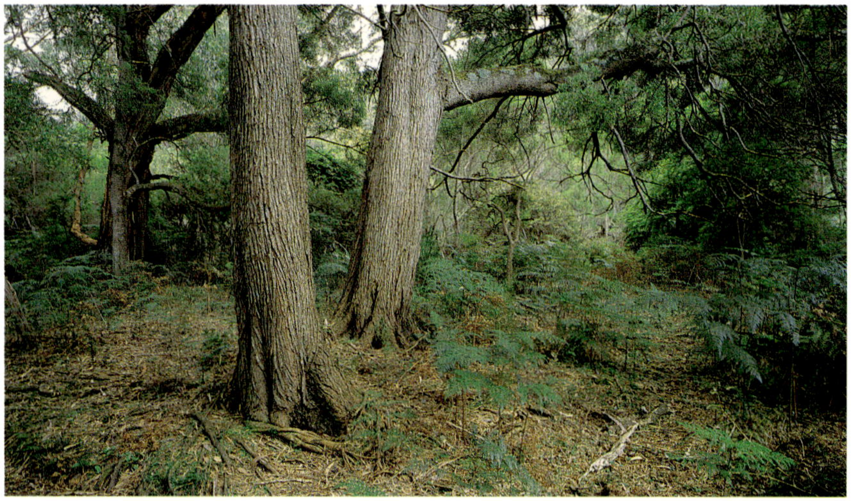

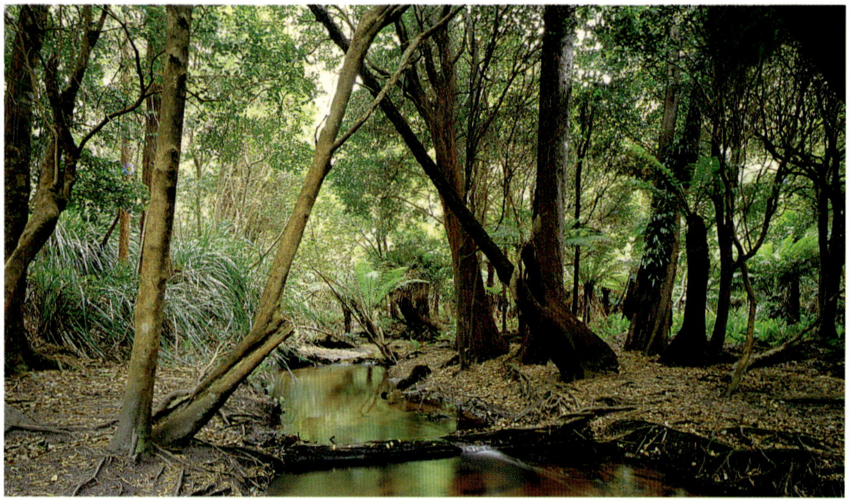

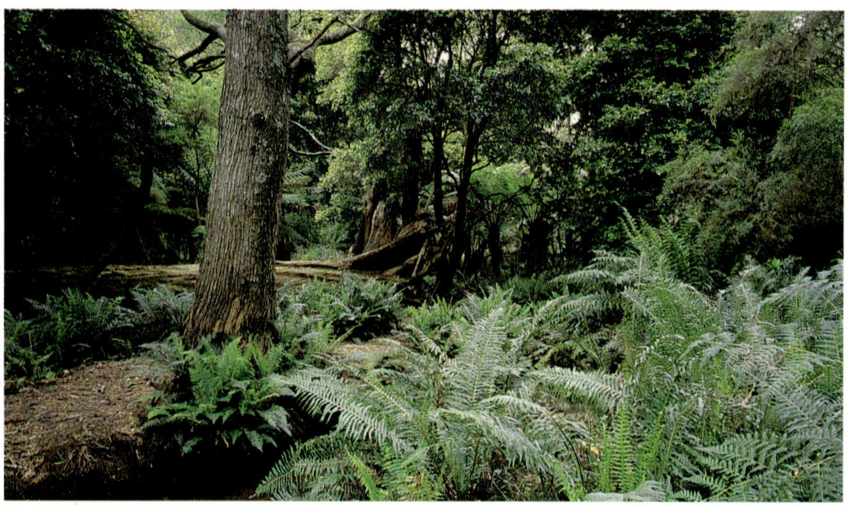

Lilly Pilly Gully

About 750 species of native plants have been recorded from Wilsons Promontory National Park. Many species are also common in Tasmania, part of the mainland before it was separated by the rising waters of Bass Strait. In spring, the heathlands are splendid with wildflowers, including native orchids. The Lilly Pilly Gully Nature Walk introduces bushwalkers to a variety of environments in its 5 kilometre length, through the heathland and eucalypt forests to warm temperate rainforest. A stream coloured topaz by tannins from Swamp Paperbarks runs through the shade cast by tall tree-ferns, Swamp Gums, Blackwoods and Lilly Pilly trees.

Left: Three scenes from a walk along the Lilly Pilly Gully Nature Walk.
Opposite: Prickly Tea-tree, Wilsons Promontory National Park.

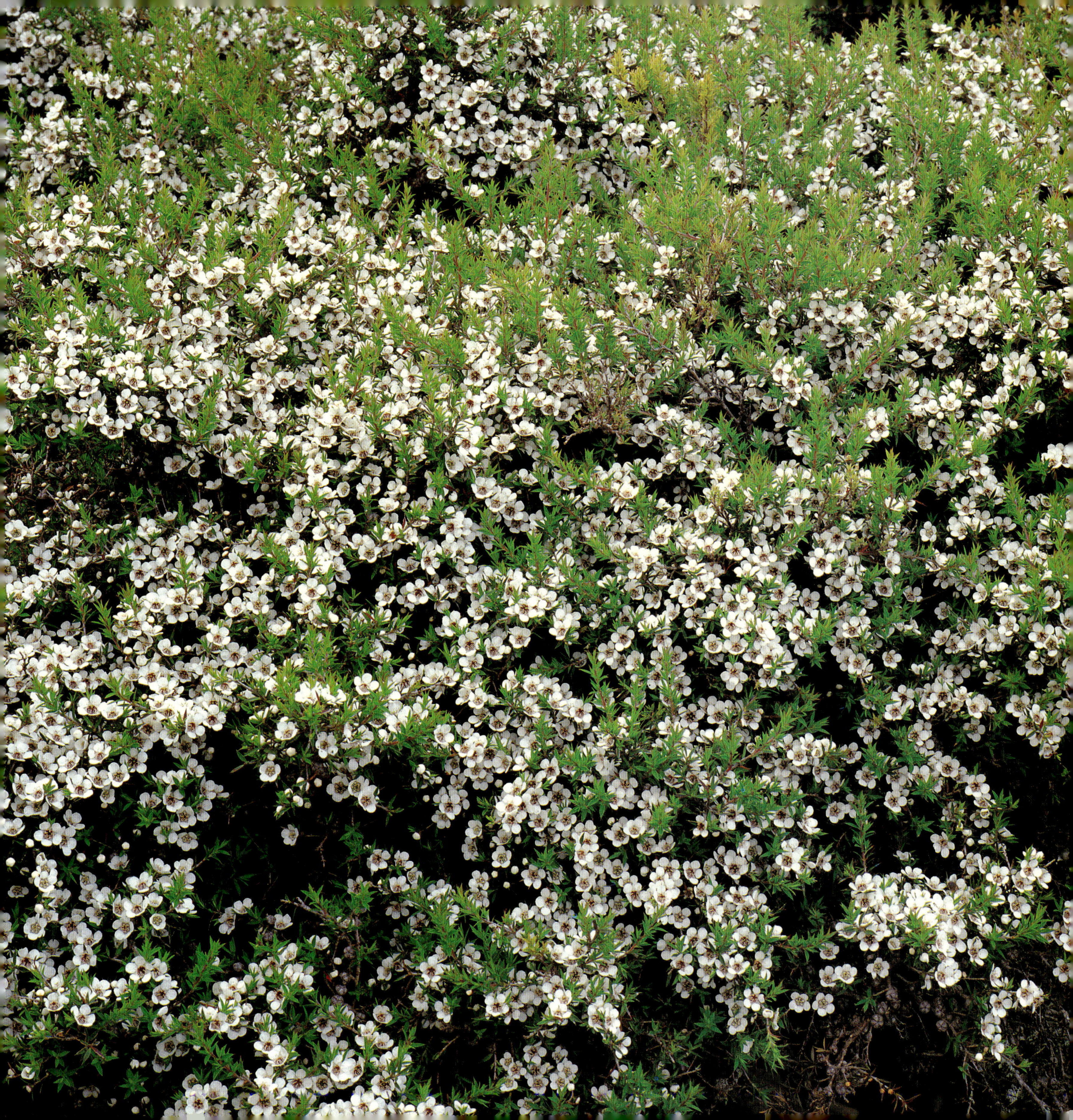

Tarra-Bulga National Park

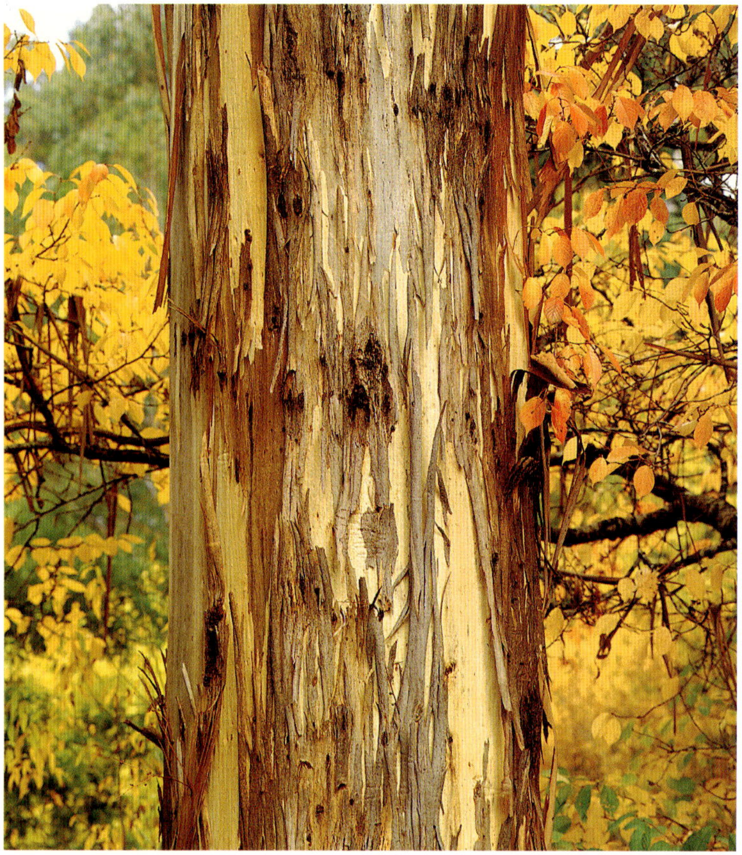

Above: The Mountain Ash is one of the world's tallest and most magnificent trees.

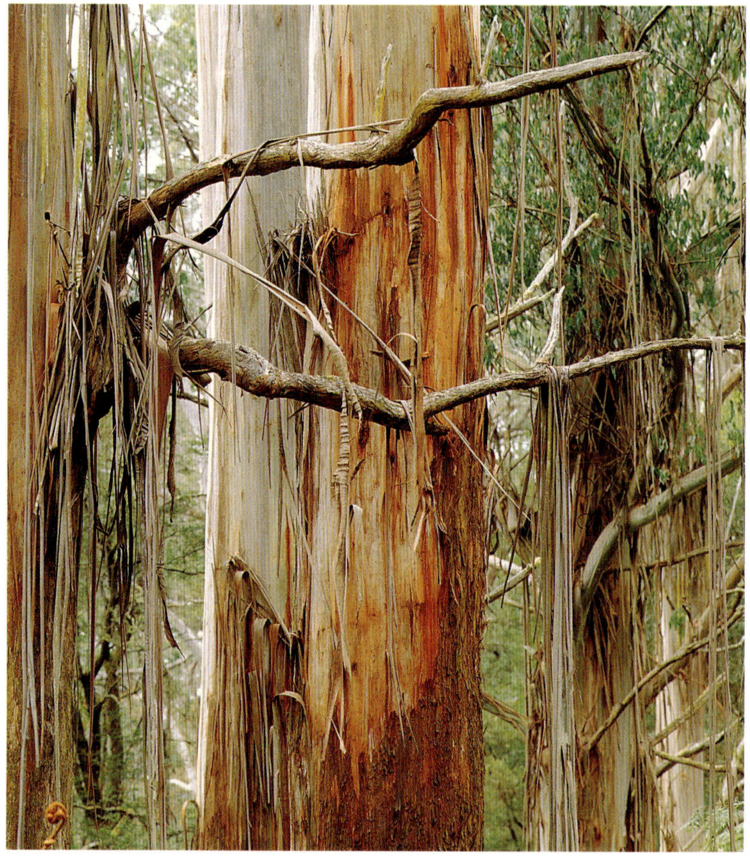

Above: Early European settlers were astounded to see these trees shed bark, not leaves.

The Strzelecki Ranges, in South Gippsland, were named after the Polish nobleman who was the first European to venture into their forested depths. In spite of many years of deforestation, some of Australia's tallest trees still remain in the area which includes Tarra-Bulga National Park, named for Charlie Tarra, Strzelecki's Aboriginal guide, and *bulga*, an Aboriginal word meaning mountain. This rainforest depends on regular, high rainfall to maintain its luxuriant growth. It harbours fascinating, and sometimes unique, native plants and animals and the protection of remaining areas is vital.

Opposite: Tree-ferns, ancient Myrtle Beech and Mountain Ash grow in Tarra-Bulga's cool temperate rainforest.

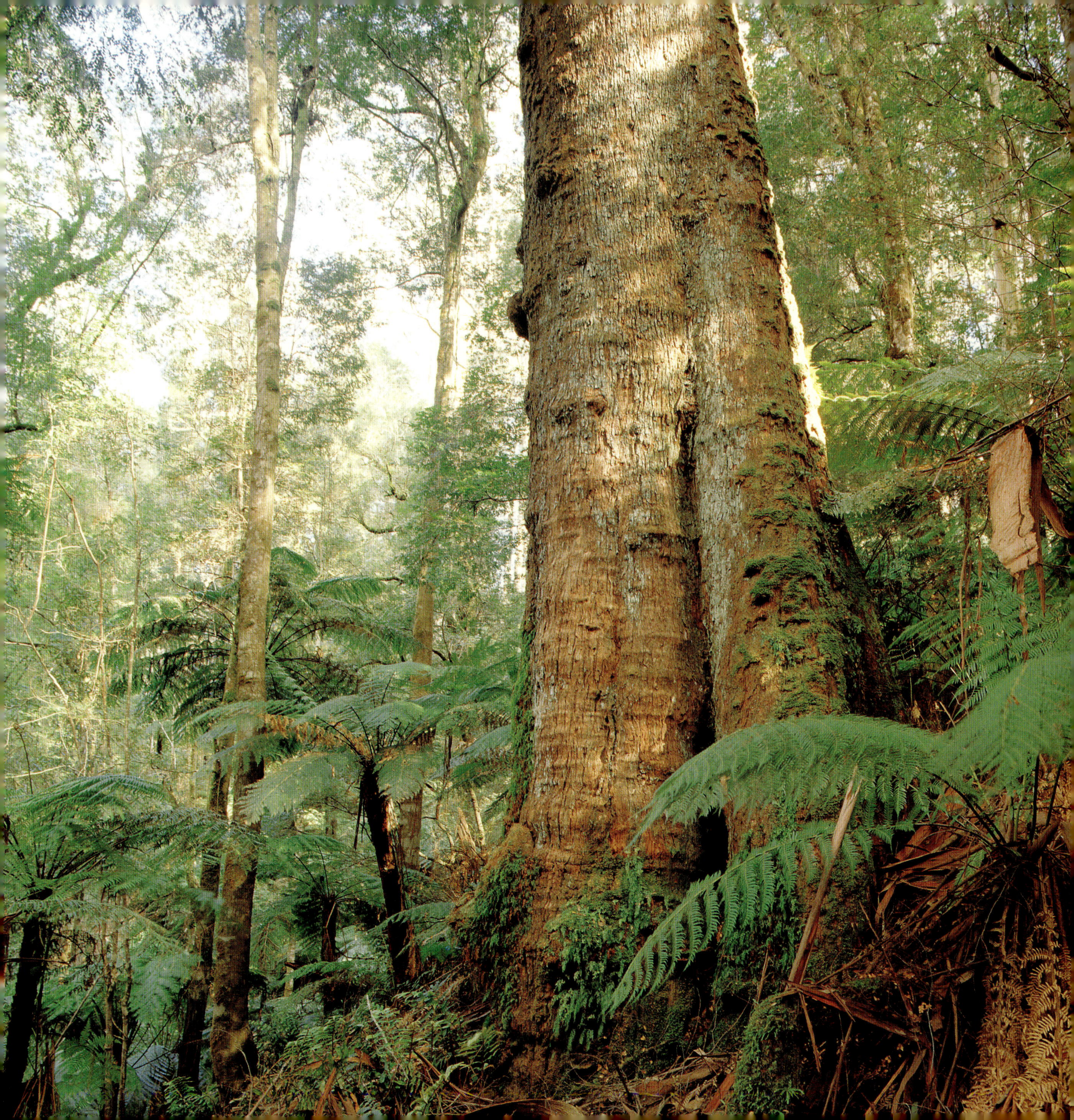

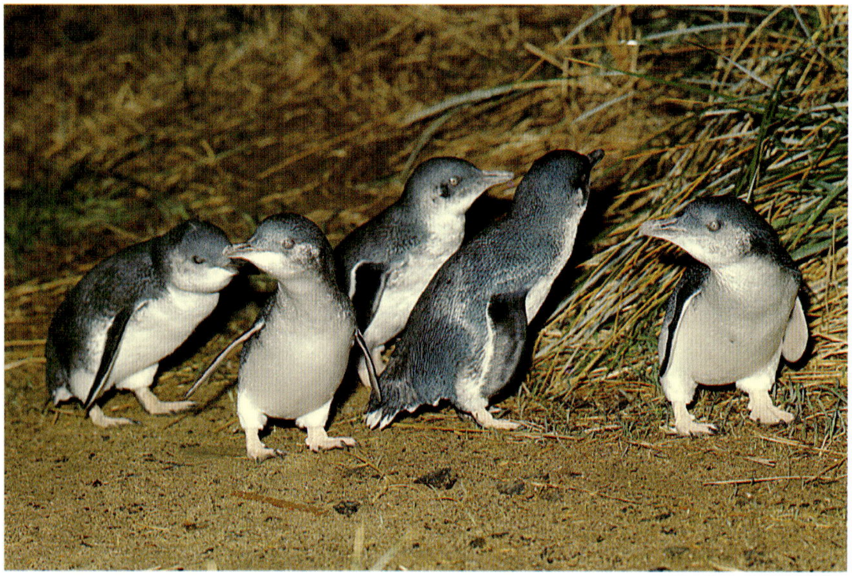

Above: The "parade" of Little Penguins returning to their nest burrows is a popular Phillip Island event.

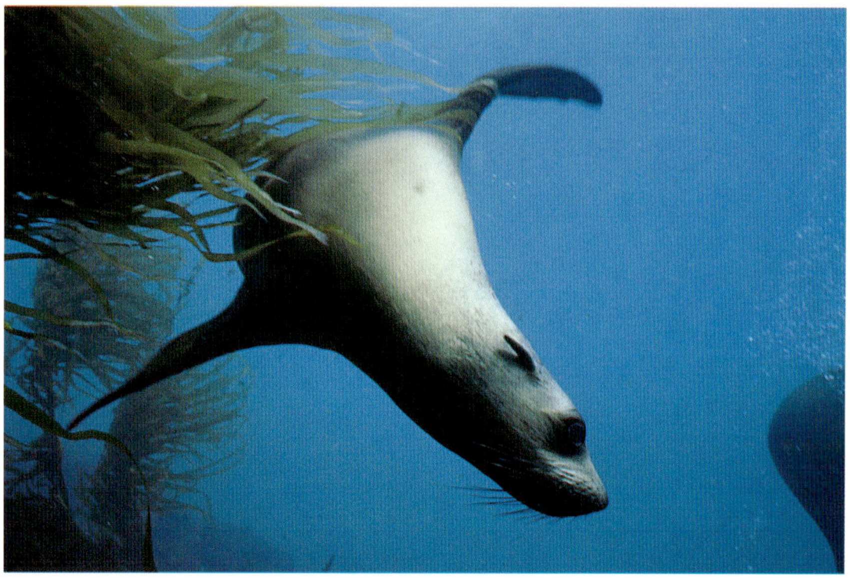

Above: Australian Fur-seals may be seen at close quarters at Phillip Island.

Phillip Island

Phillip Island lies across the entrance to Western Port Bay, just across the Mornington Peninsula from Port Phillip Bay. More than three million people visit the island each year to fish, surf, go boating, see the famous Penguin Parades, the Koalas at the Koala Conservation Centre, or to watch the Australian Fur-seals frolicking at Seal Rocks. A spectacular blowhole is only one of many coastal scenic attractions.

Opposite: The rugged and scenic coast of Phillip Island.

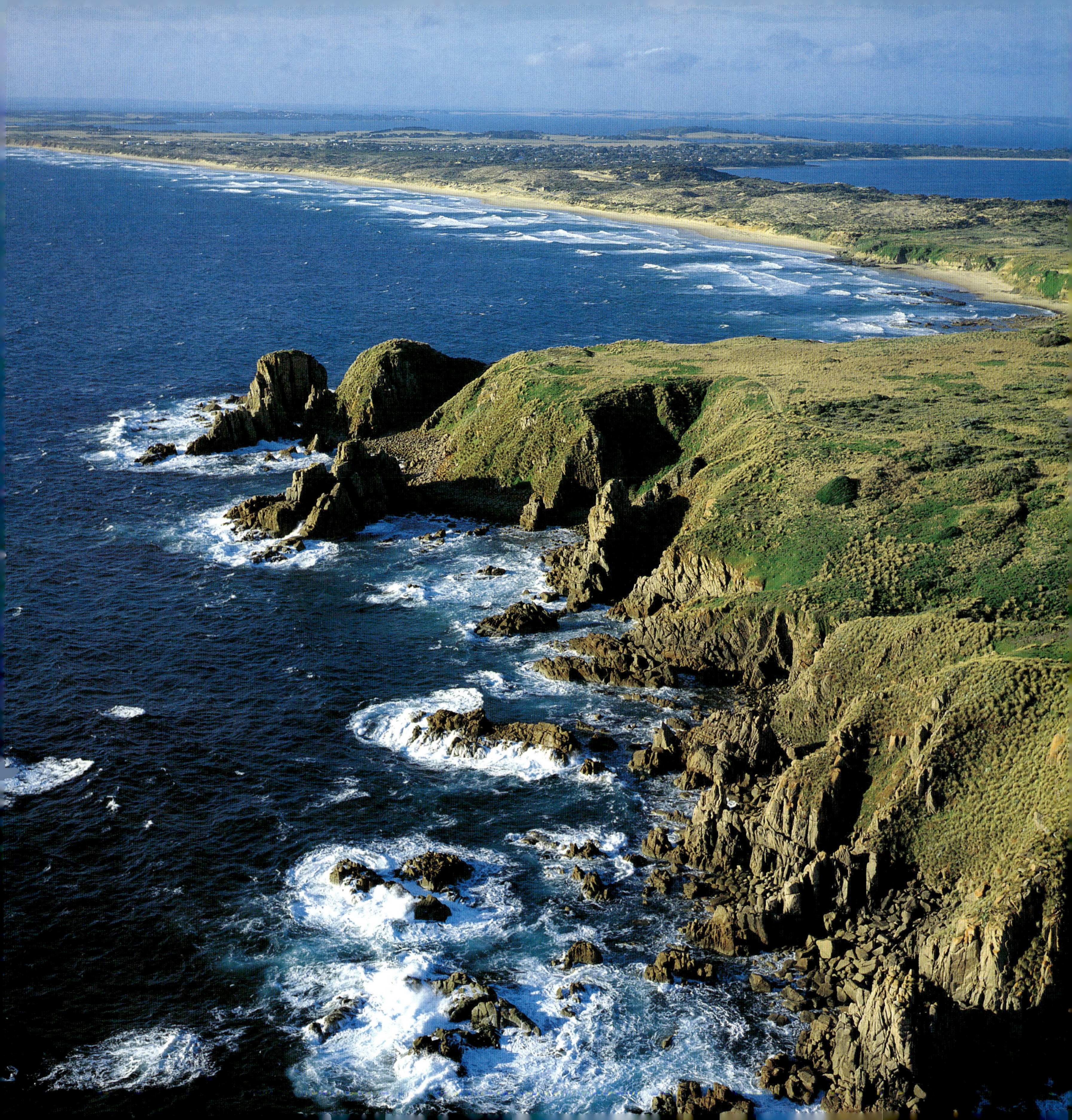

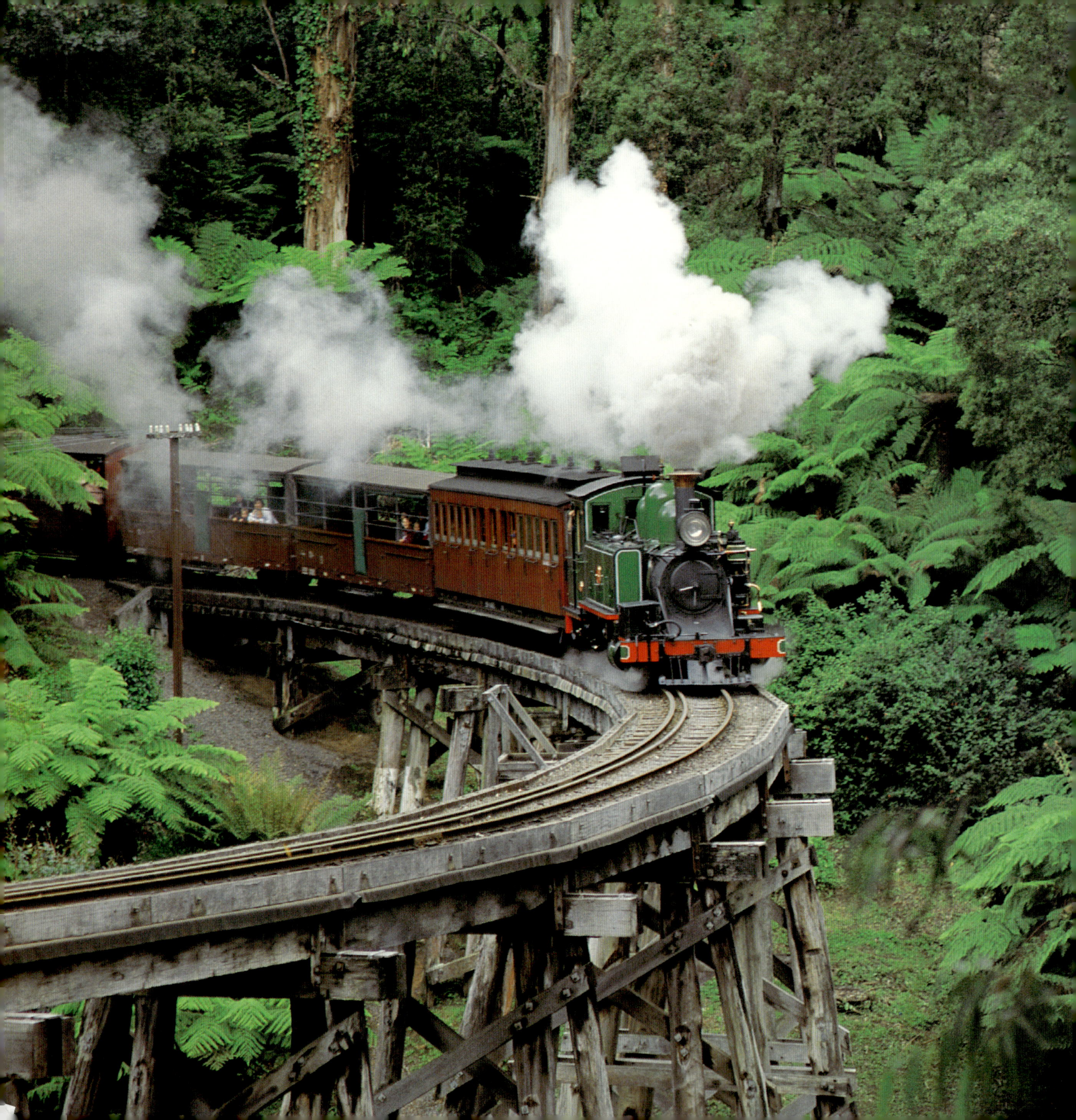

The Dandenong Ranges

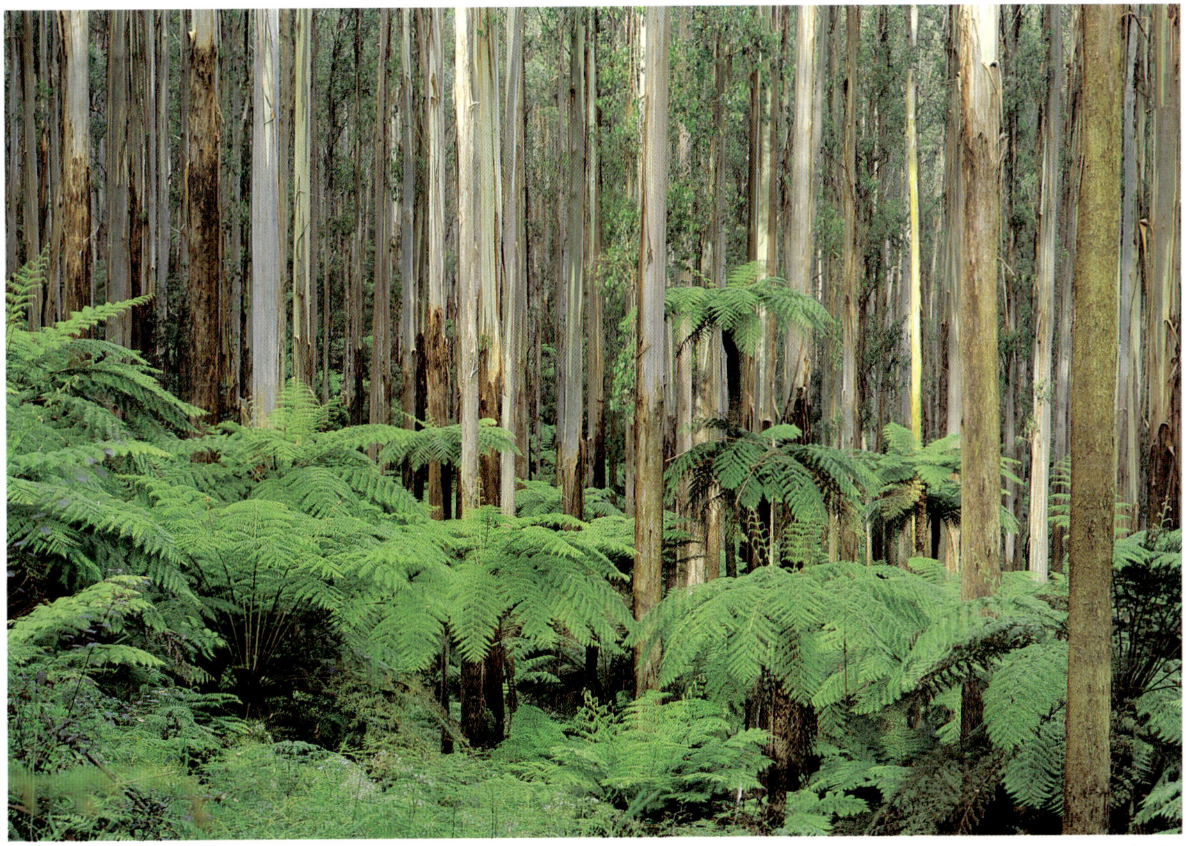

Opposite: Puffing Billy chugs 13 km between Belgrave and Emerald Lake. *Above:* Mountain Ash and tree-ferns in the Dandenong Ranges National Park.

Only 32 kilometres from Melbourne, the Dandenong Ranges have long provided Melburnians with a cool, relaxing getaway from the city. These forested hills, centred on 633-metre-high Mt Dandenong, an ancient volcanic peak, have been popular places for picnics and sight-seeing since the nineteenth century. In the small towns nestling in the ranges are plant nurseries, tea rooms, restaurants and galleries. Puffing Billy, a steam train which runs over a track laid for it in the early 1890s, is a drawcard for visitors. The creation of the Dandenong Ranges National Park, which covers just under 2000 hectares, is a step towards saving the natural life of this wonderful area for posterity.

Healesville Sanctuary

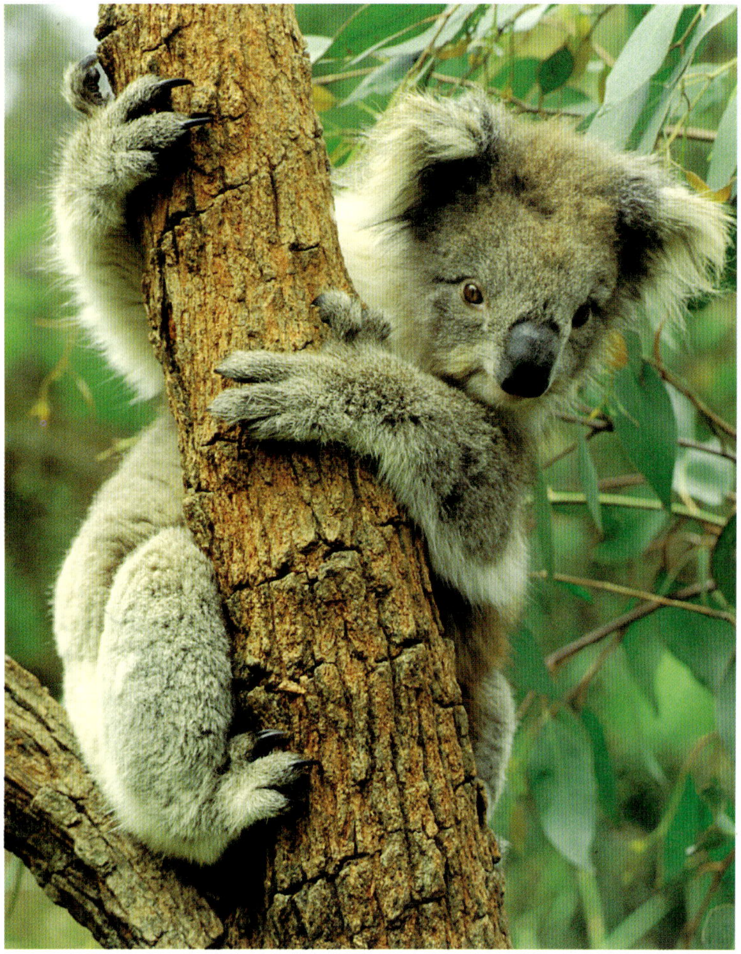

Healesville is home to a breeding colony of Koalas.

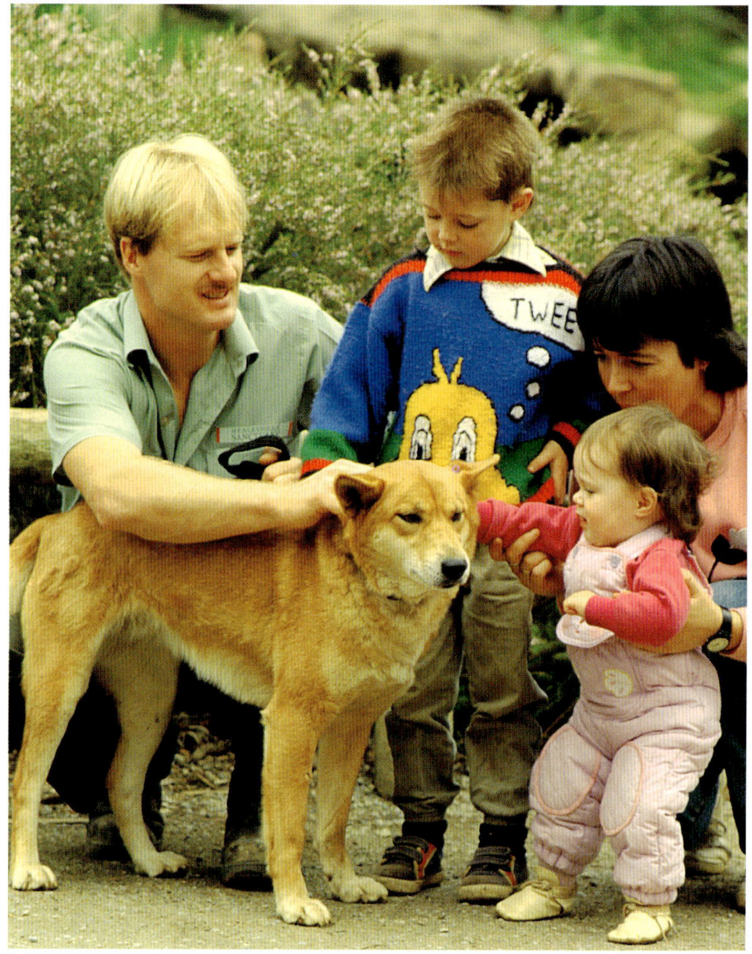

This Dingo is used to being admired. Healesville educates visitors about wildlife.

Since 1934, Healesville Fauna Park has been a magnet for those interested in Australian animals. Today, more than 350 000 people visit this sanctuary 65 kilometres from Melbourne each year. They join kangaroos and wallabies in spacious walk-through habitats, marvel at the power and beauty of birds of prey, are entertained by a Koala colony and meet many other sorts of animals. Healesville is noted for breeding and research programs which help native species.

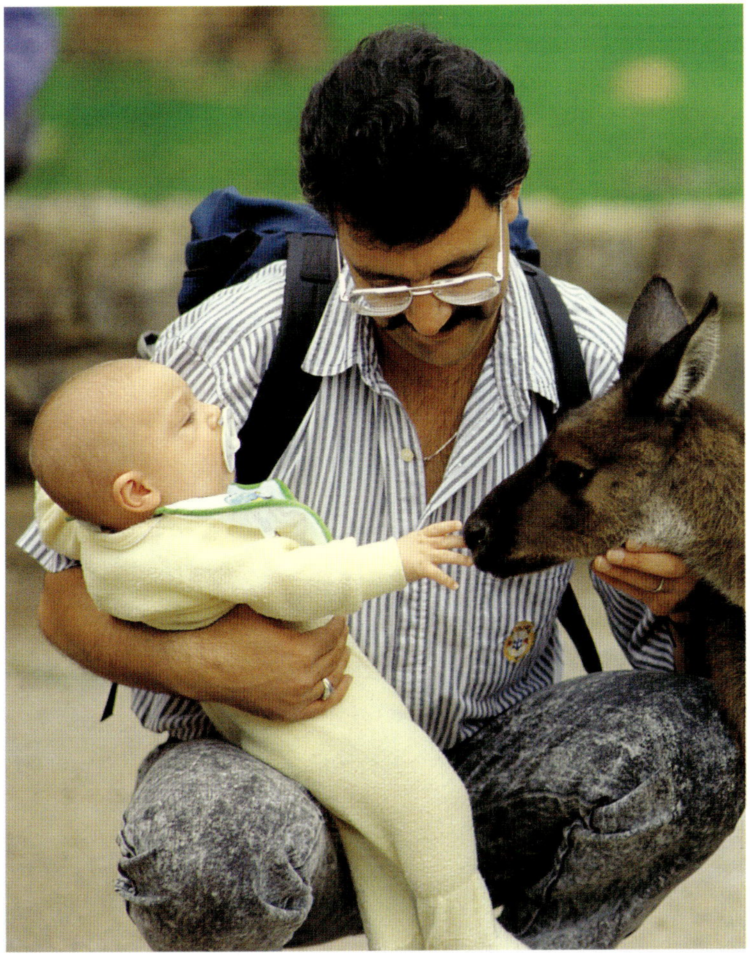

You're never too young to be introduced to a friendly kangaroo.

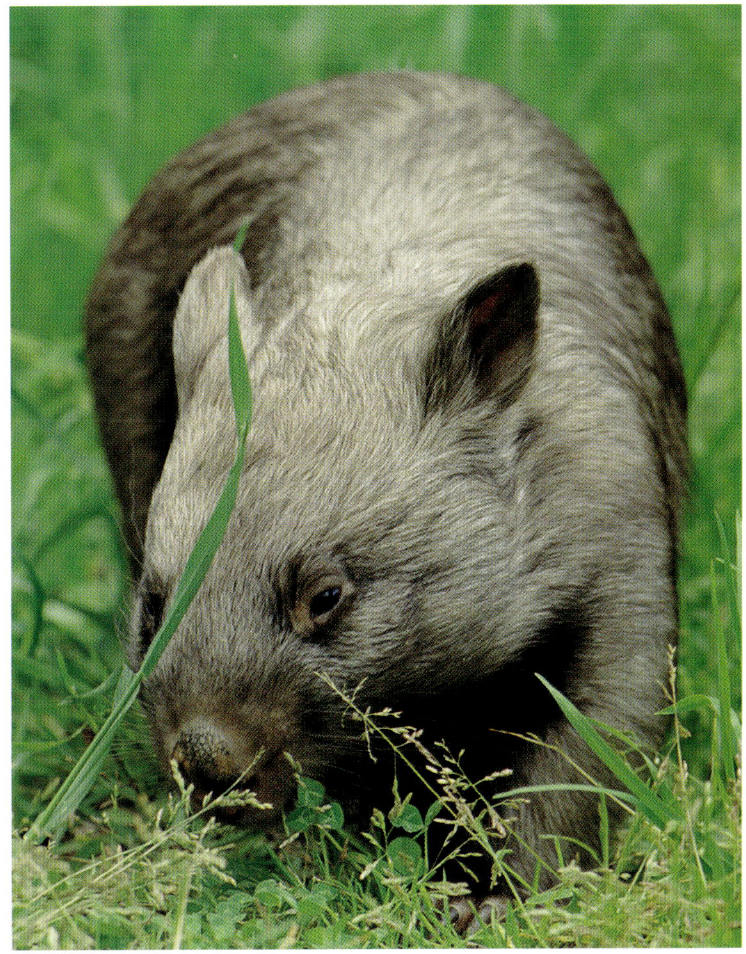

The Common Wombat is one of Healesville's most popular residents.

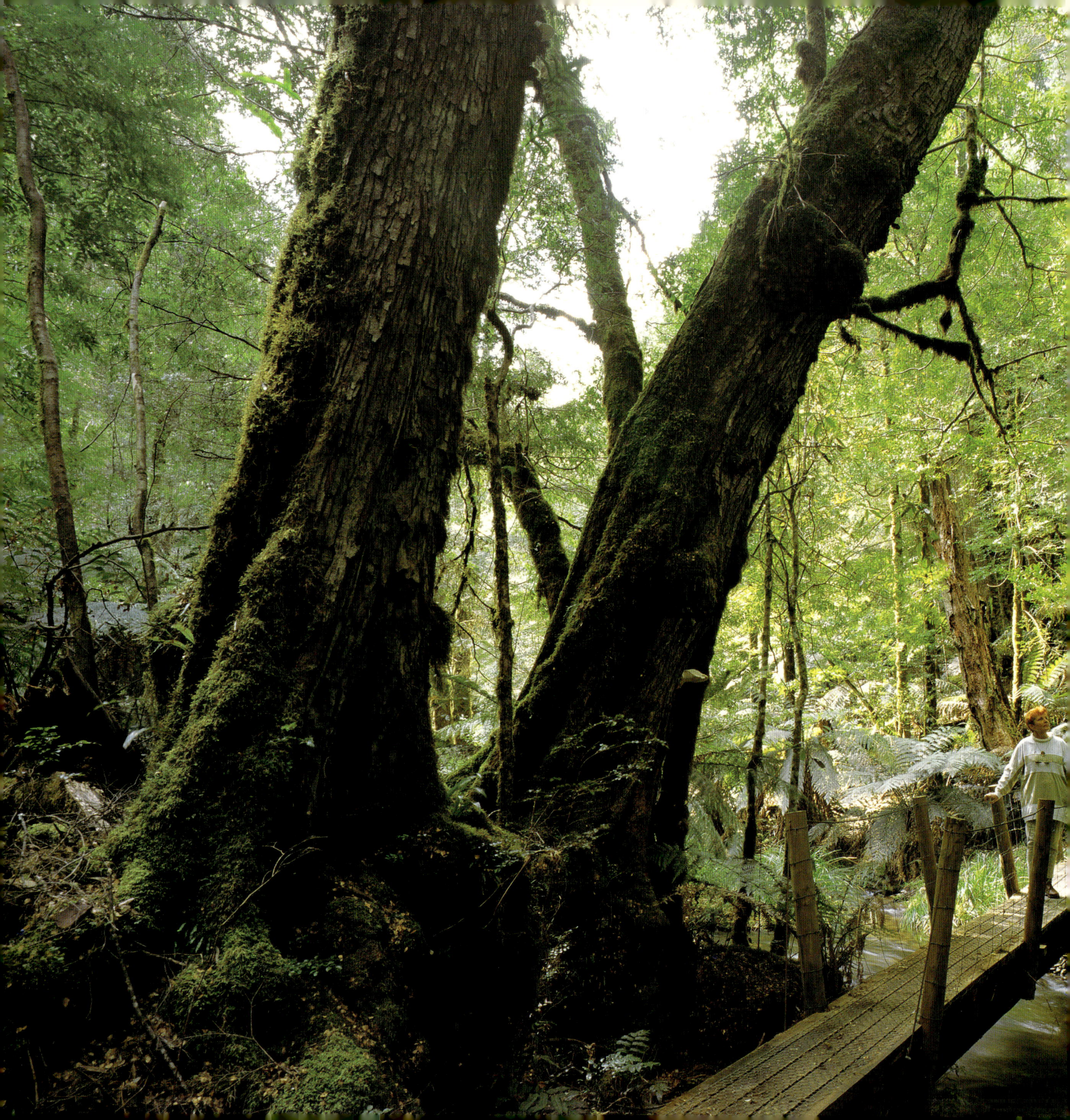

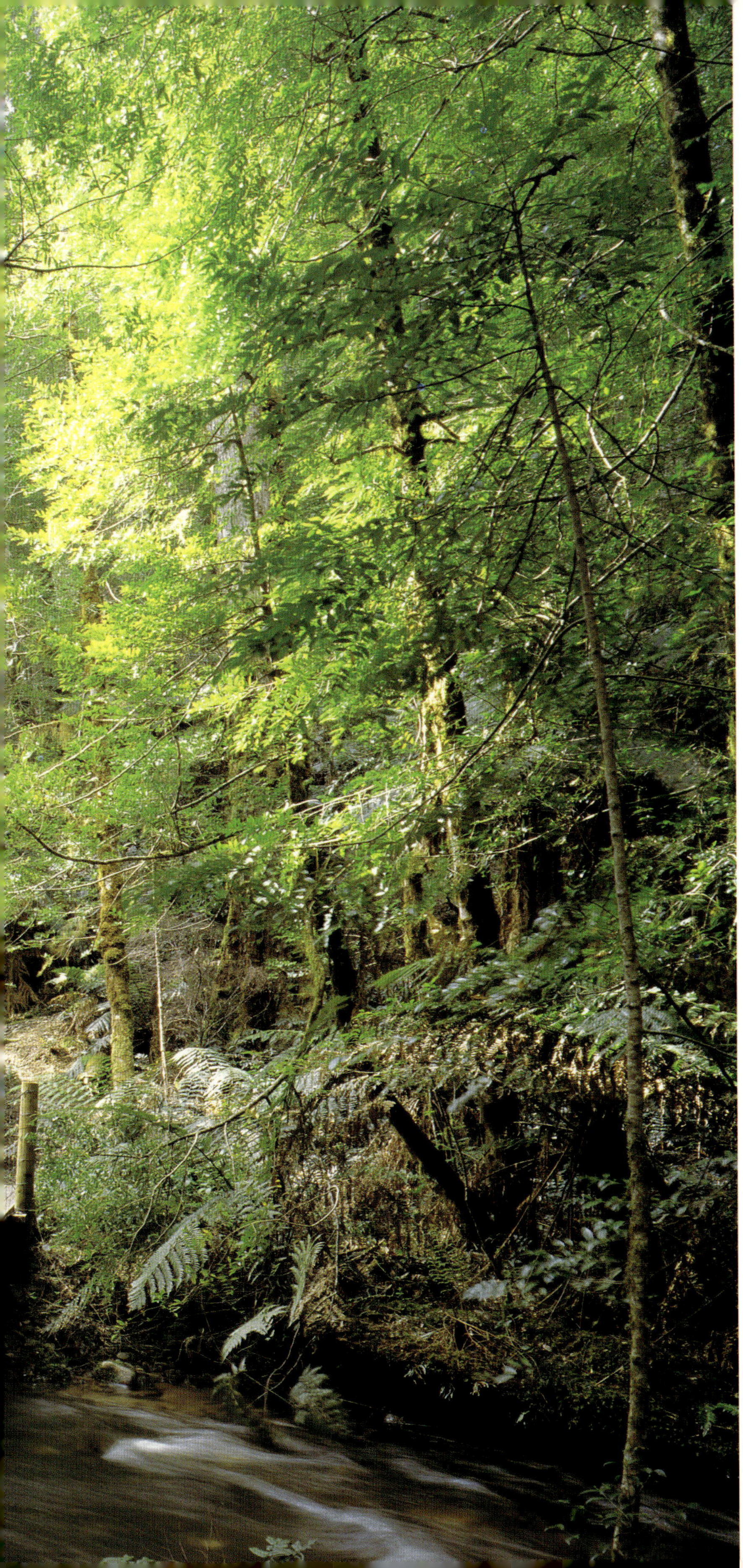

The Central Highlands

A drive along the Maroondah Highway north-east of Melbourne via Healesville for about 100 kilometres ends in Victoria's Central Highlands. The lovely town of Marysville is a wonderful base from which to explore the foothills of the Great Dividing Range, snow-covered in winter, bright with wildflowers in early summer. In the Cumberland Scenic Reserve are Mountain Ash and Myrtle Beech forests.

The lifespan of a Myrtle Beech tree may be 3000 years. Around 60 million years ago, when Australia was still part of the ancient supercontinent Gondwana, beech forests were widespread across the land. Today, these majestic trees survive only in a few temperate parts of Australia, where the rainfall is heavy and regular.

Victoria's southern forests are often carpeted with bracken-like ferns and ornamented with tall-trunked tree-ferns. These ferns are even more ancient than the beech trees and have changed little with time. A cross-section through the trunk of the tree-fern shown on page 67 would be almost identical with a section made across the stony trunk of a fossilised tree-fern which grew in a similar habitat 250 million years ago.

Left: Creepers, moss and lichen cover the mighty tree trunks in the Myrtle Beech forest, Marysville. *Following pages:* Phantom Falls tumbles over rocks in the rainforest near Marysville. *Page 66:* A Myrtle Beech stretches up through ferns to life-giving sunlight. *Page 67:* The crown of a fern with new shoots, or croziers, unfurling.

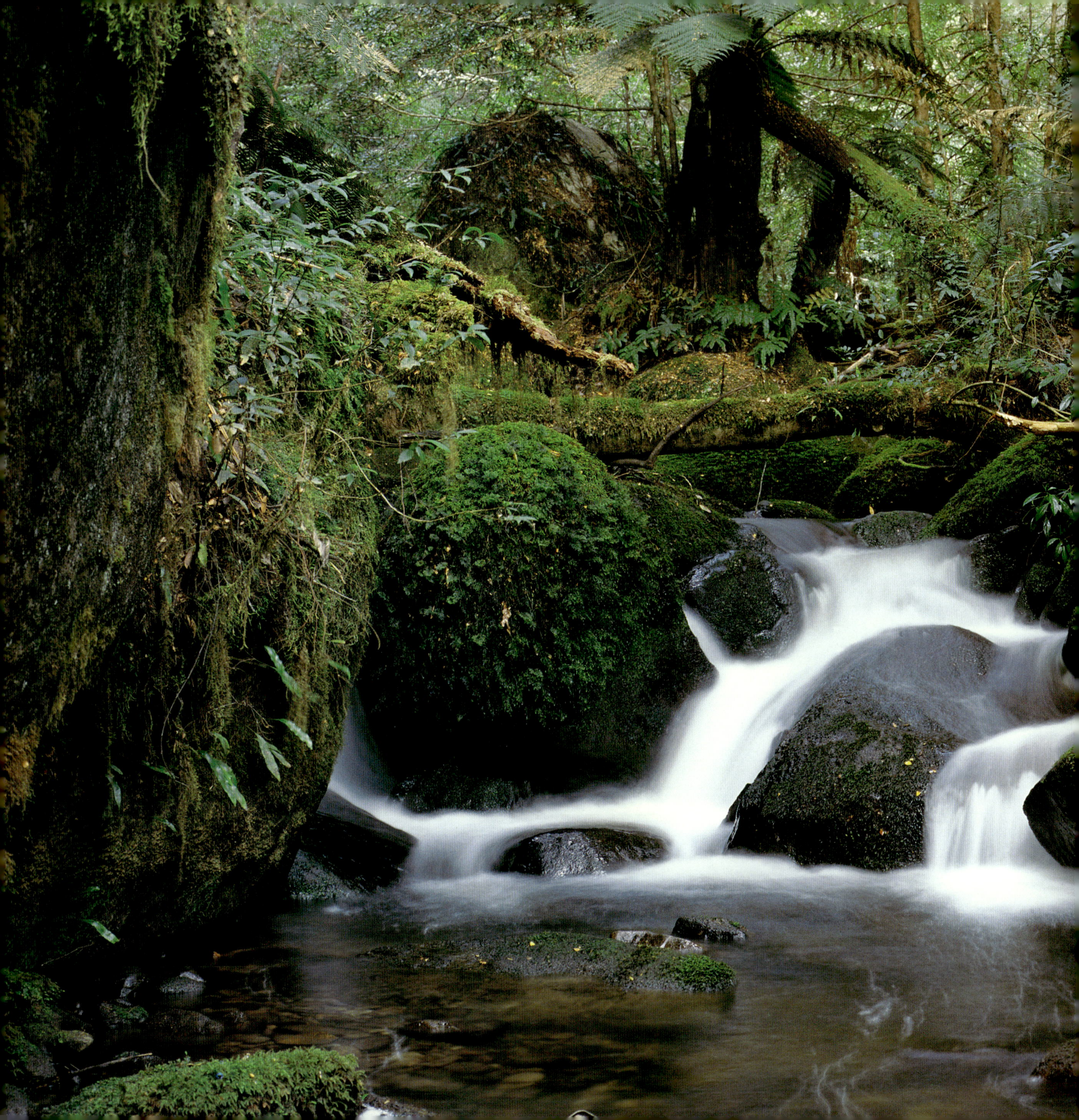

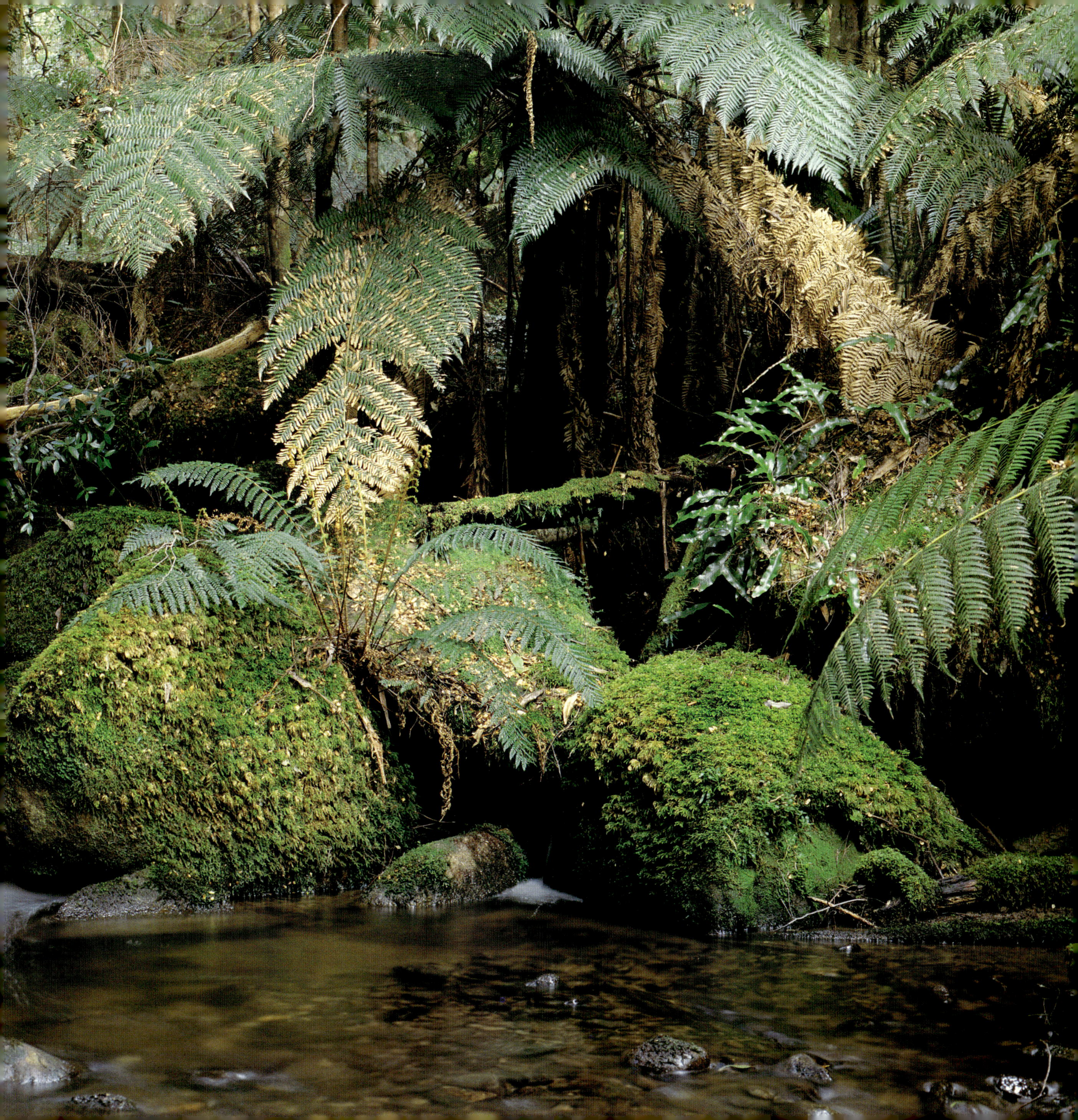

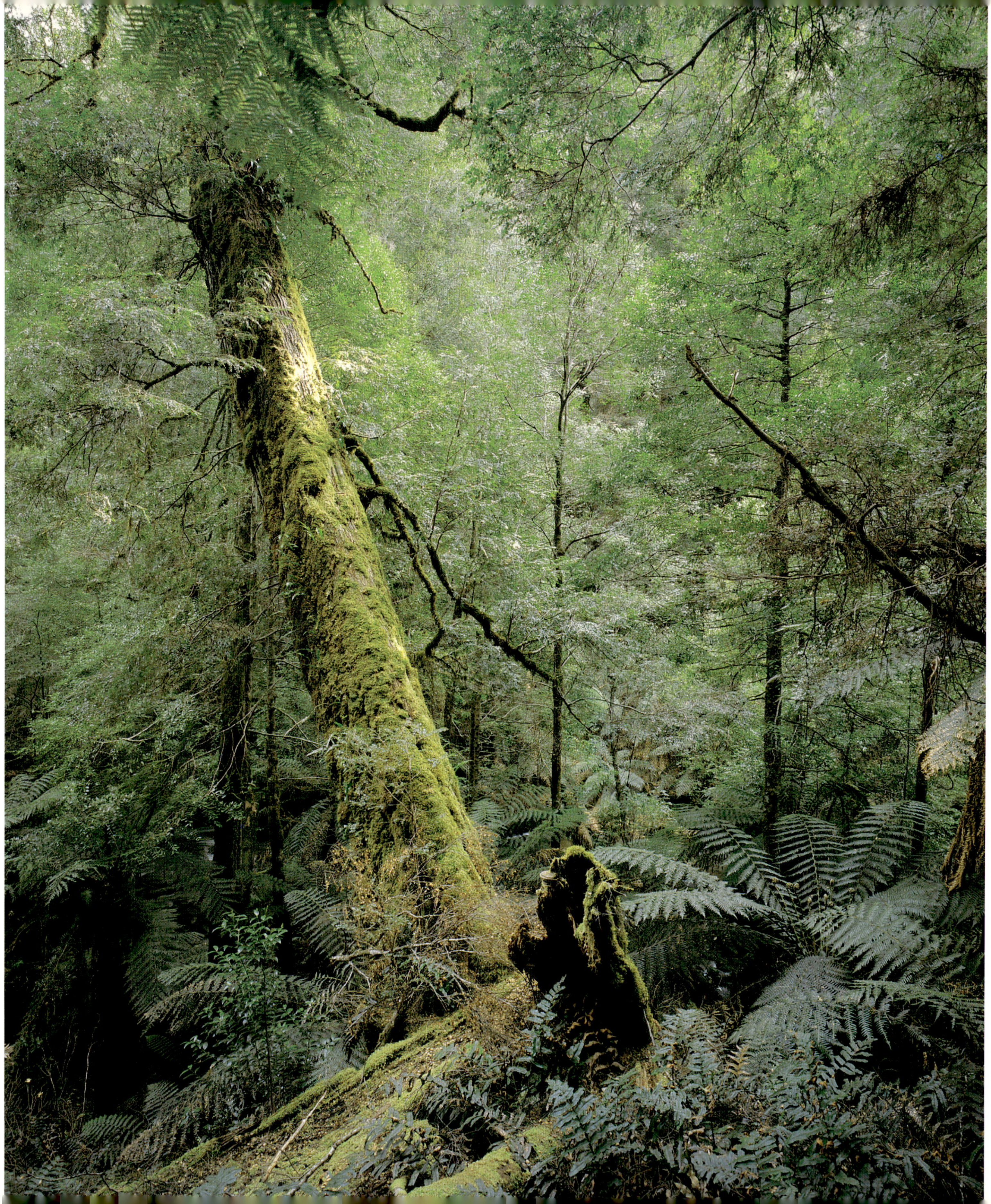

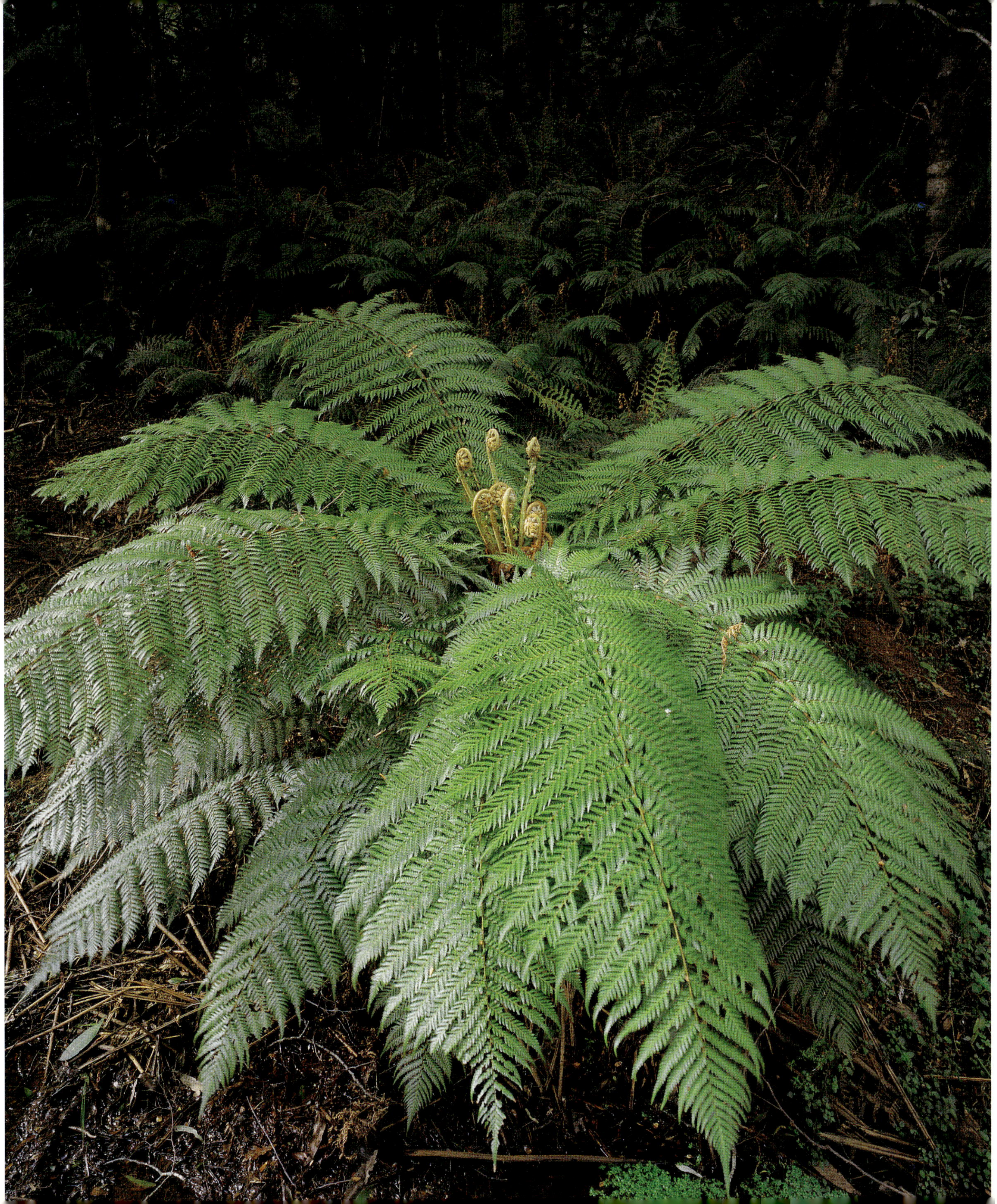

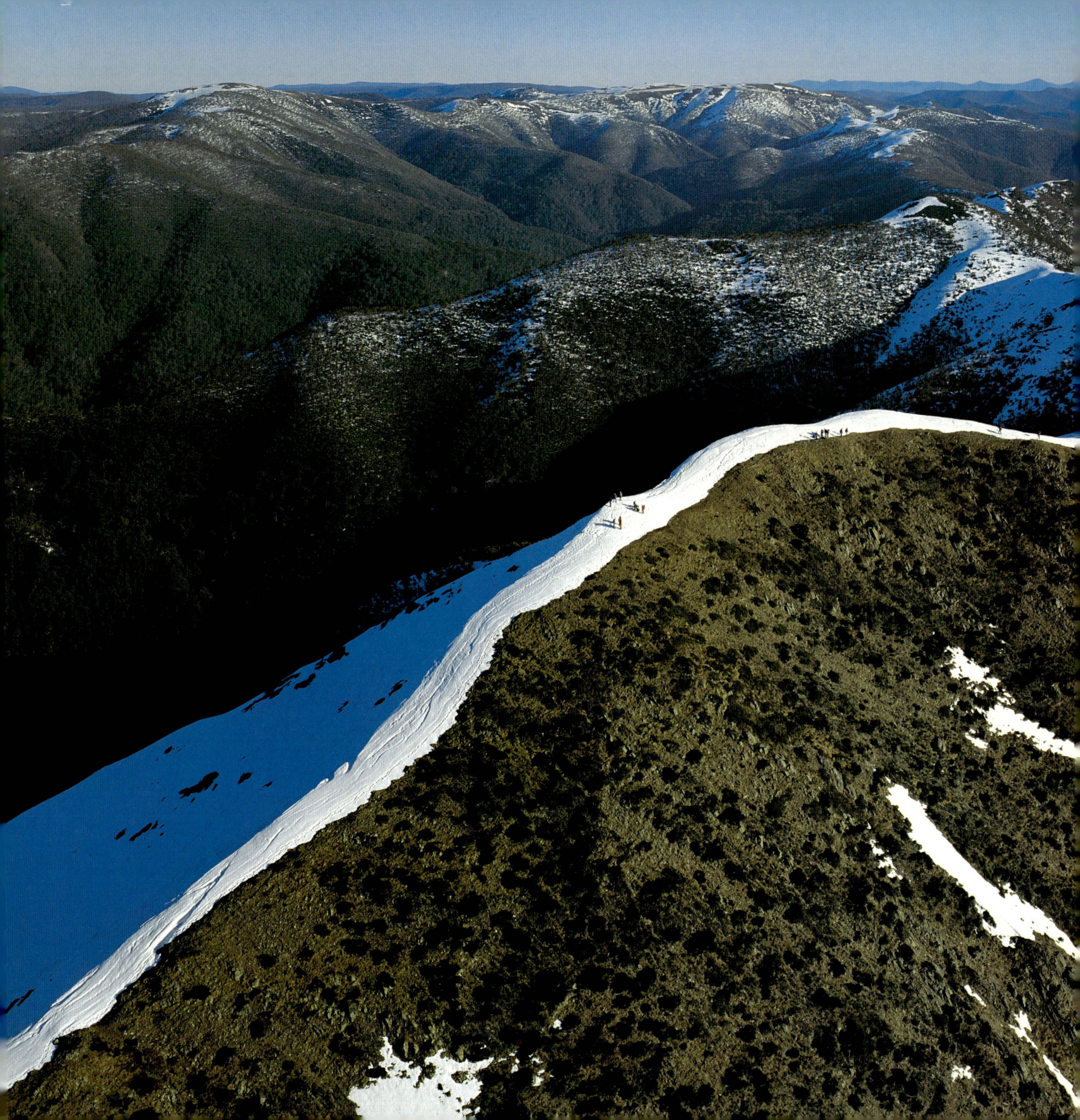

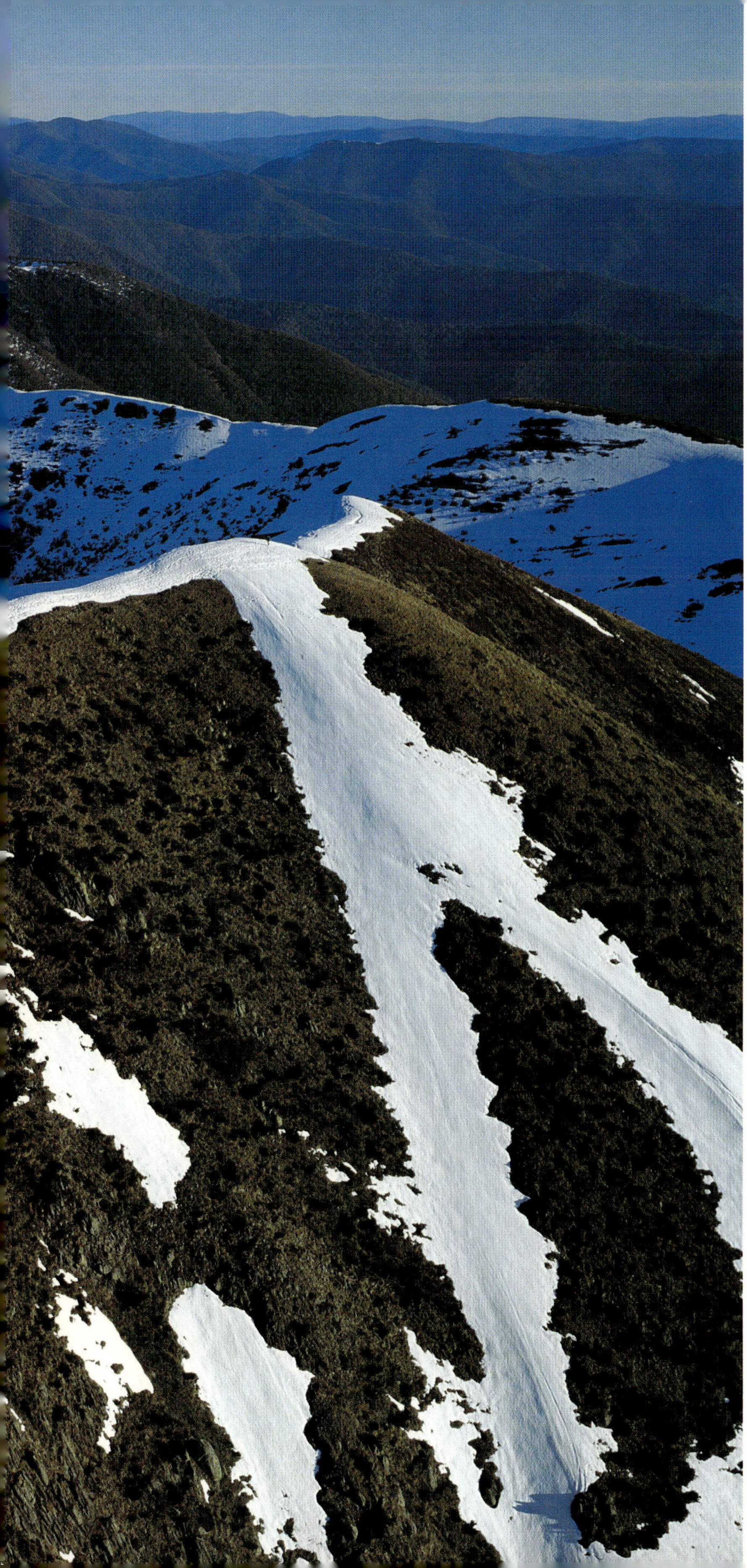

The Alpine National Park

The happy way to Victoria's spectacular High Country lies along the Hume Freeway. The lovely towns of Bright and Myrtleford, just over 300 kilometres from Melbourne, signal the beginning of an alpine adventure which can include the peaks of Mt Bogong, Victoria's highest at 1986 metres, Mt Hotham (1862 metres) and Mt Feathertop (1922 metres).

Alpine National Park, Victoria's largest reserve, was declared in 1989 and extends over 646 000 hectares of magnificent mountainous country. Next largest, at 31 000 hectares, is Mt Buffalo National Park, and both are popular with downhill and cross-country skiers in winter and rock-climbers in summer. There are also well marked bushwalking tracks and camping areas. The skiing season officially opens in June and closes in October, but the High Country is a place for adventure all year round.

Left: Mt Feathertop, capped with snow.
Following pages: The view from Mt Hotham.

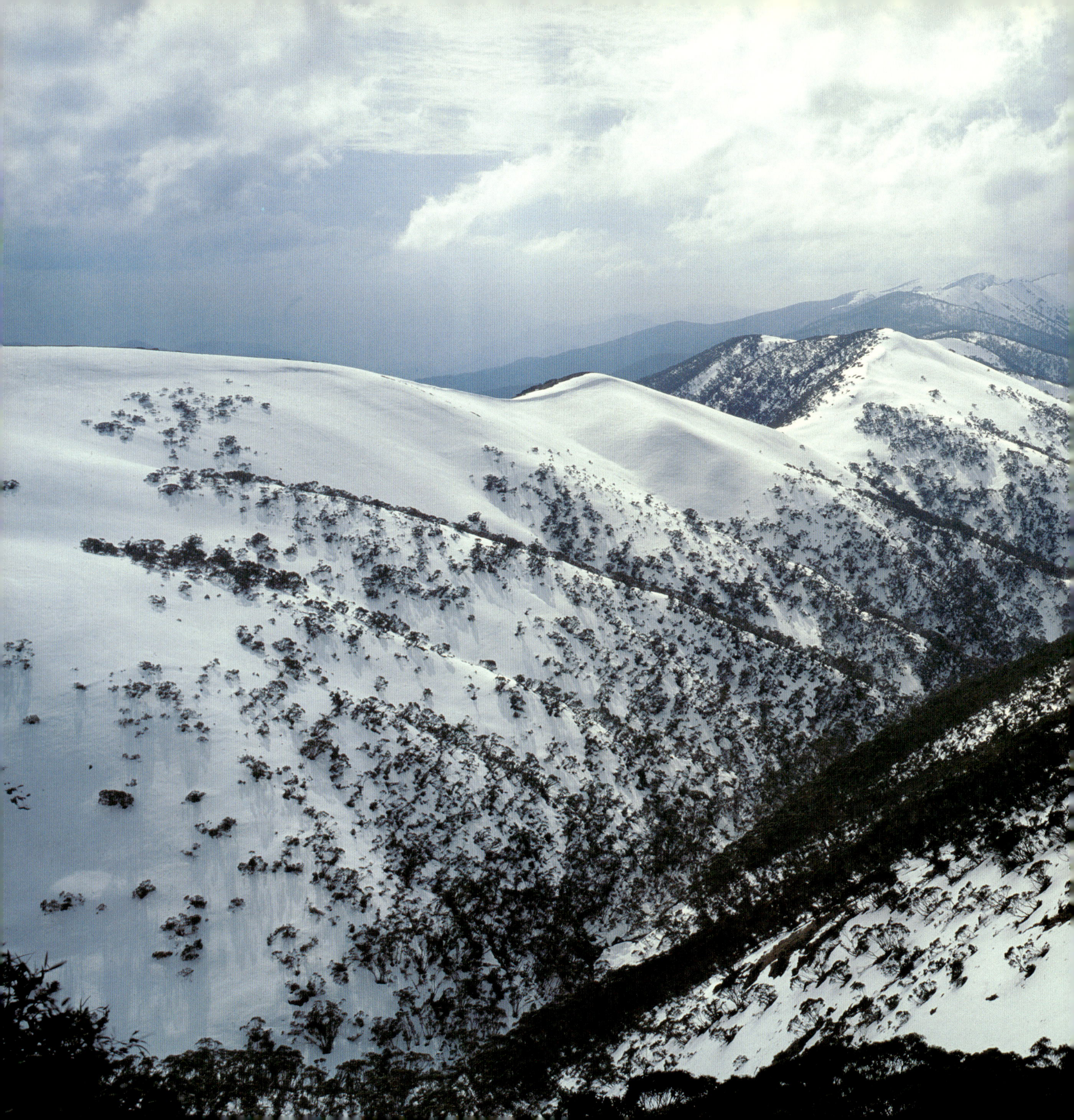

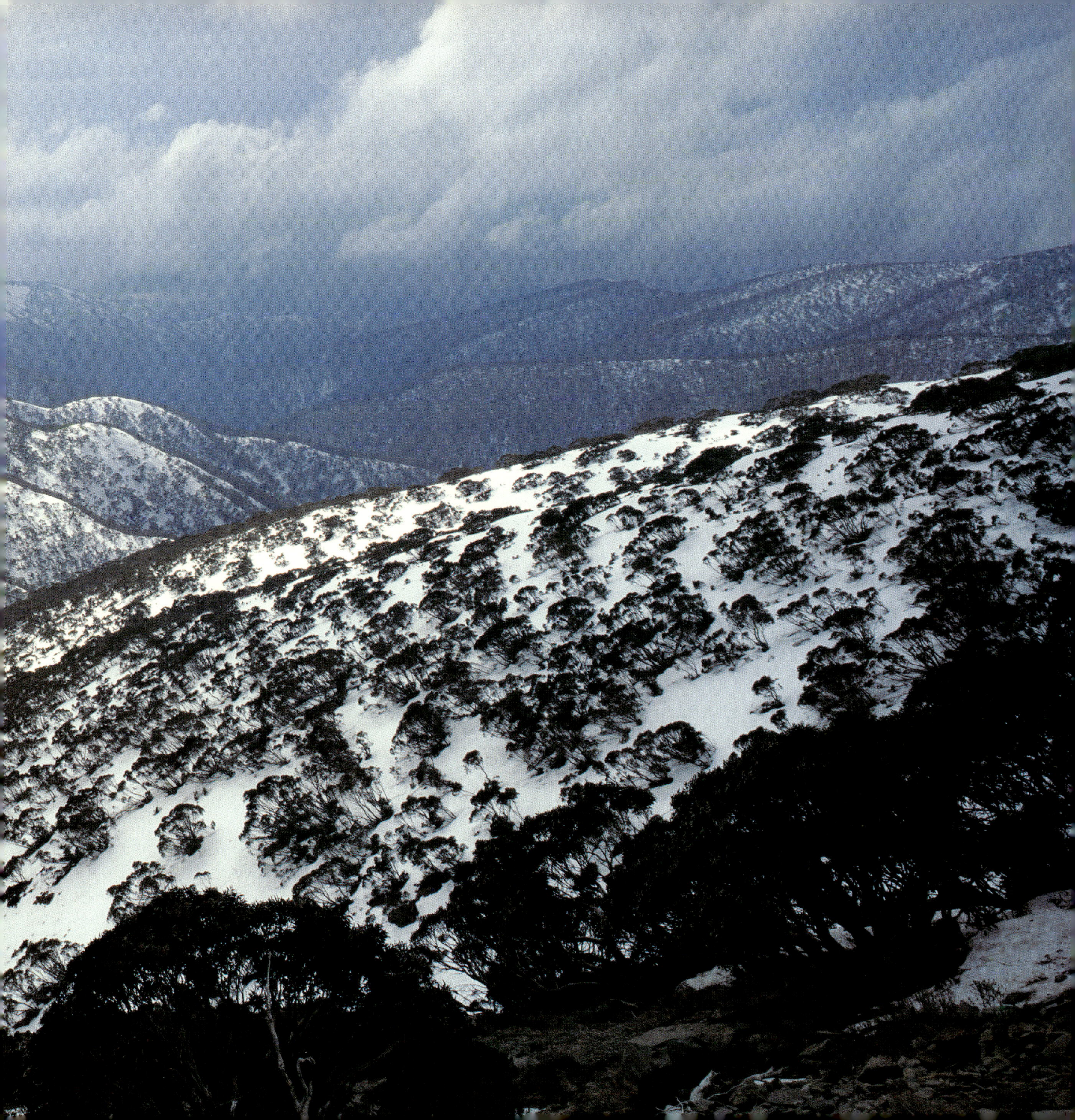

Two faces of the High Country

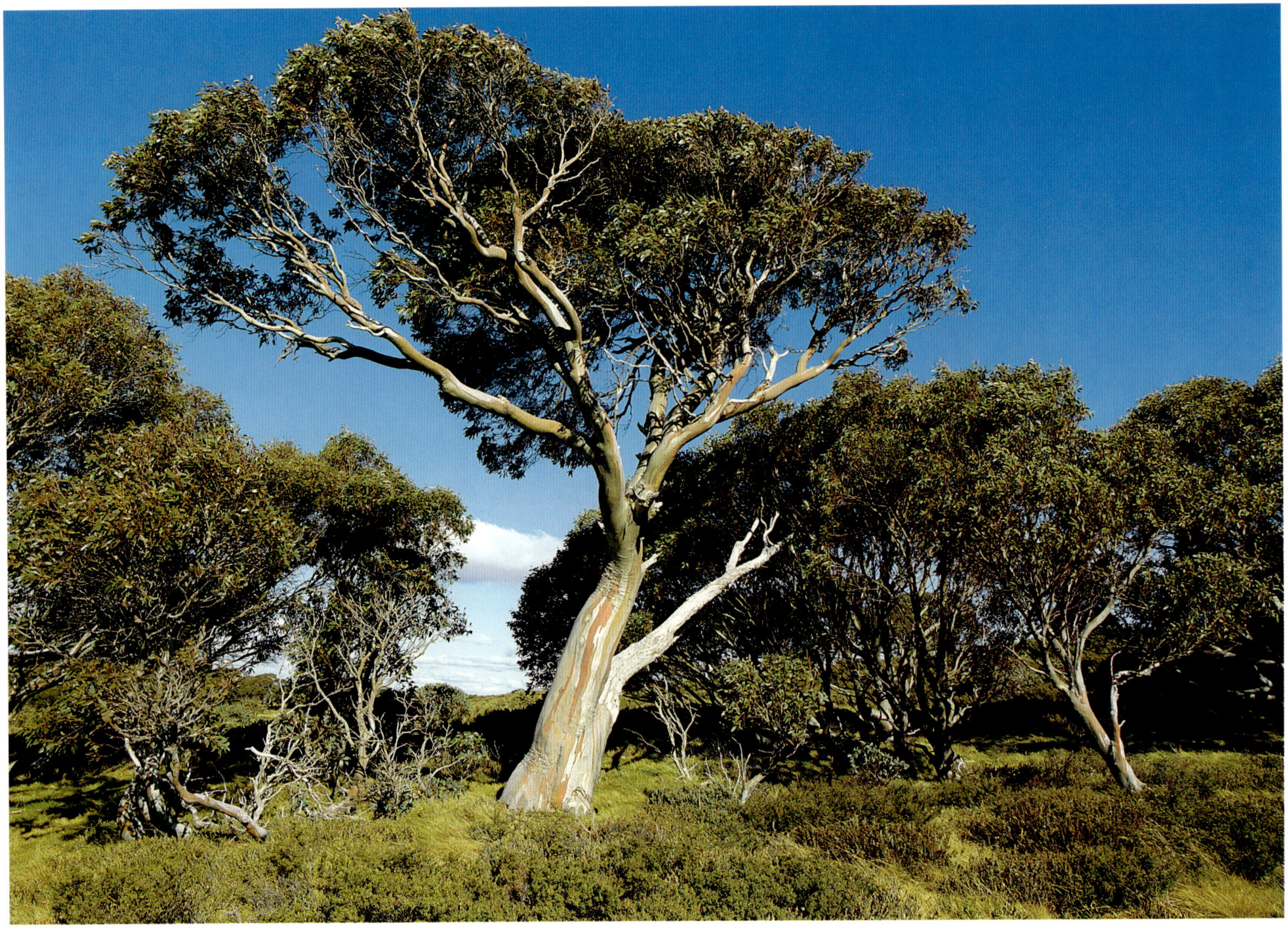

A leaning Snow Gum dominates a summer alpine landscape.

Victoria's High Country has two faces. One is worn in spring and summer, when snow melts, new growth appears and wildflowers surround the burnished trunks of the Snow Gums. This is the time for bushwalking, fishing, canoeing, birdwatching, picnicking and camping amidst some of Victoria's most dramatic scenery.

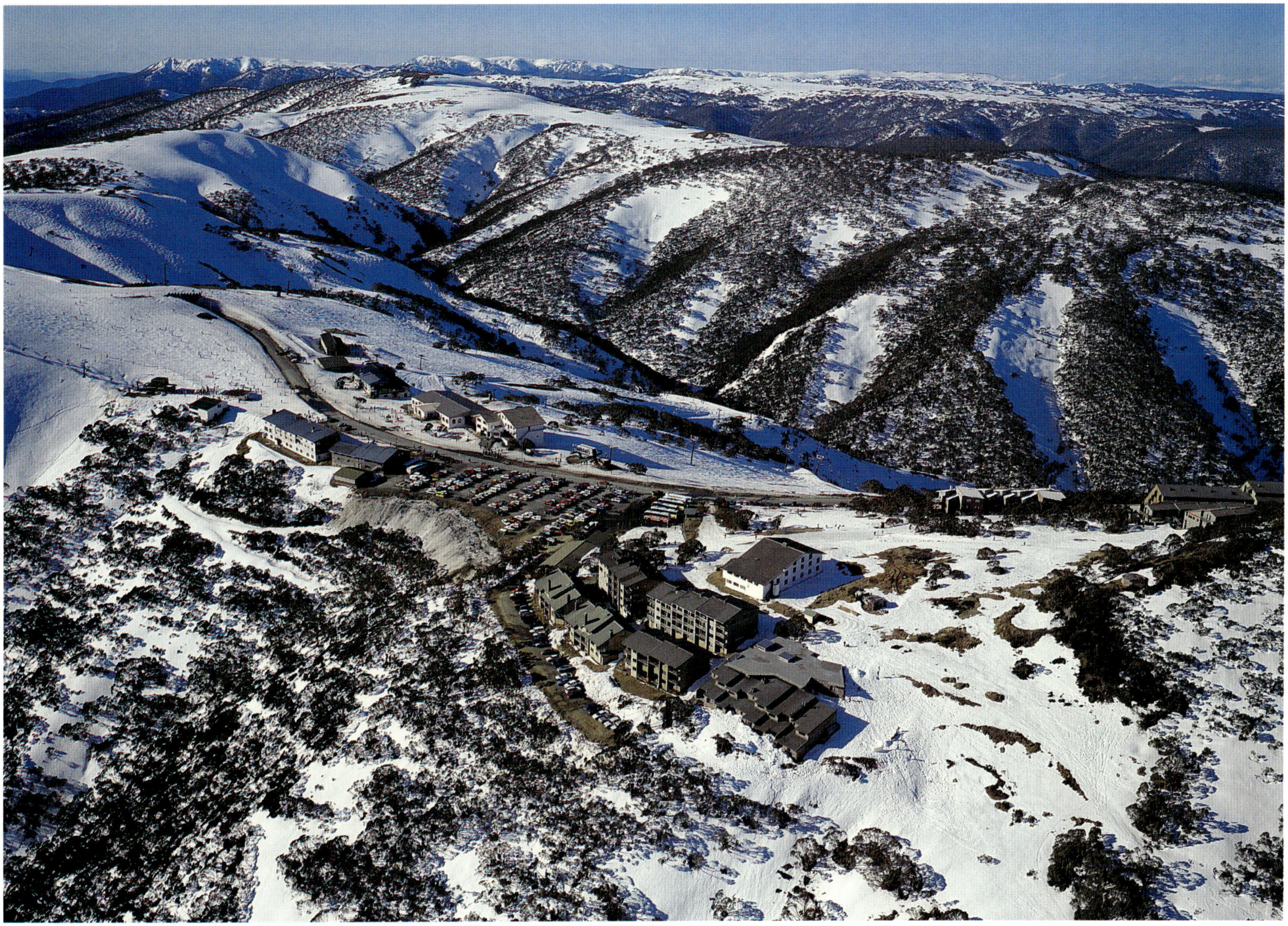

The alpine resort at Mt Hotham.

The first snowfall of the season frosts the alpine landscape with silver powder. Crystals cling to crystals and deep white snowbanks surround granite outcrops. The Snow Gums stand proud under canopies of snow, and the High Country's resorts become home to holiday-makers who ski all day and party for most of the night.

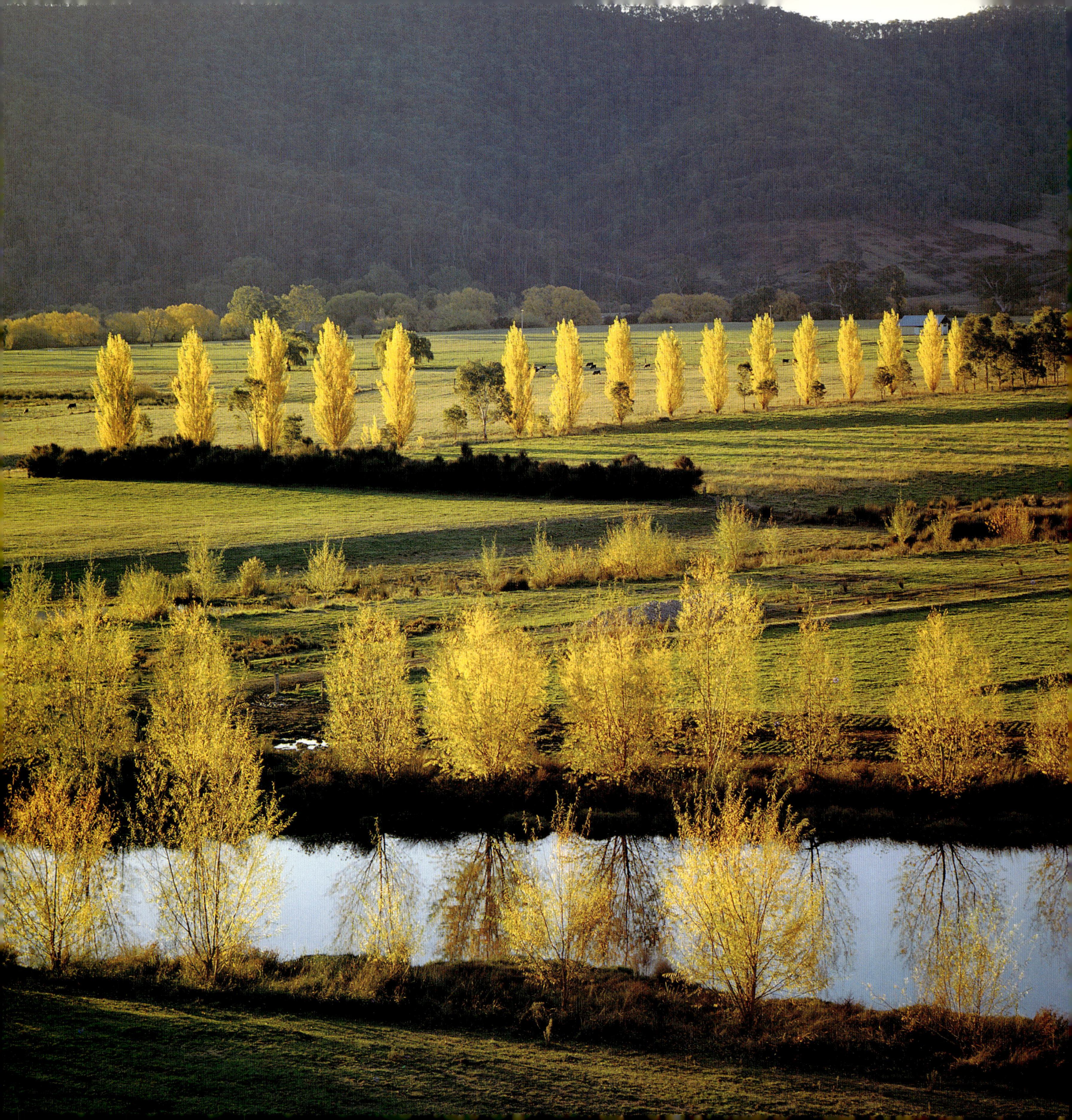

Autumn colours

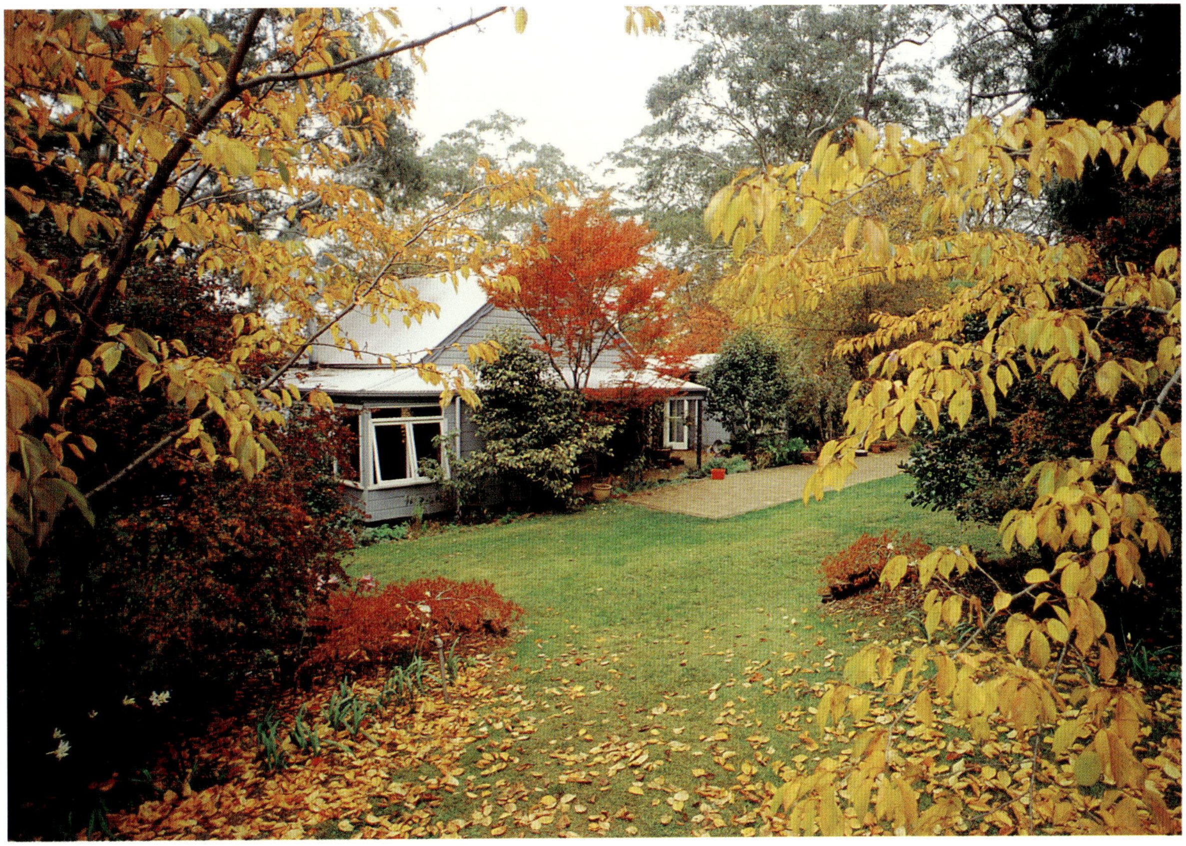

Above: The beauty of an autumn garden, Bright.

As summer withdraws, the first frosts of autumn tell the deciduous trees which have been planted so lavishly across the farmlands and in the gardens of north-eastern Victoria that it is time to sleep. Leaves change from their vibrant summer hues to warmer shades, ranging from palest gold through bronze to deepest russets and tawnies. They tremble in the chilly breezes, then fall to carpet the ground in splendour. Bare branches remain, ready to bud again in a thousand shades of green with the coming of springtime.

Opposite: In the foothills of the Victorian Alps, poplars in their autumn foliage march across the paddocks.
Following pages: The town of Bright, which has been extensively planted with deciduous trees and shrubs, in autumn.

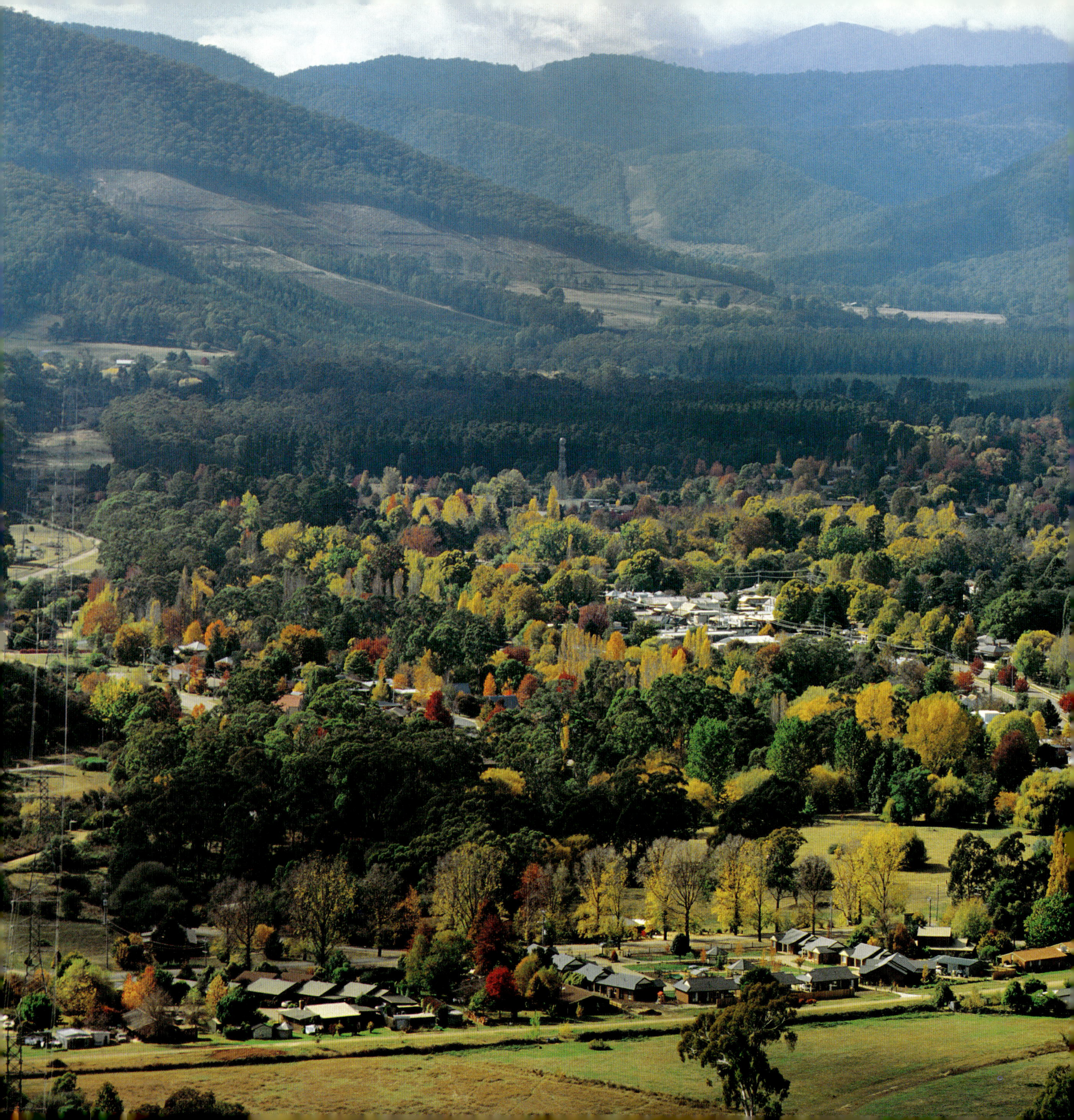

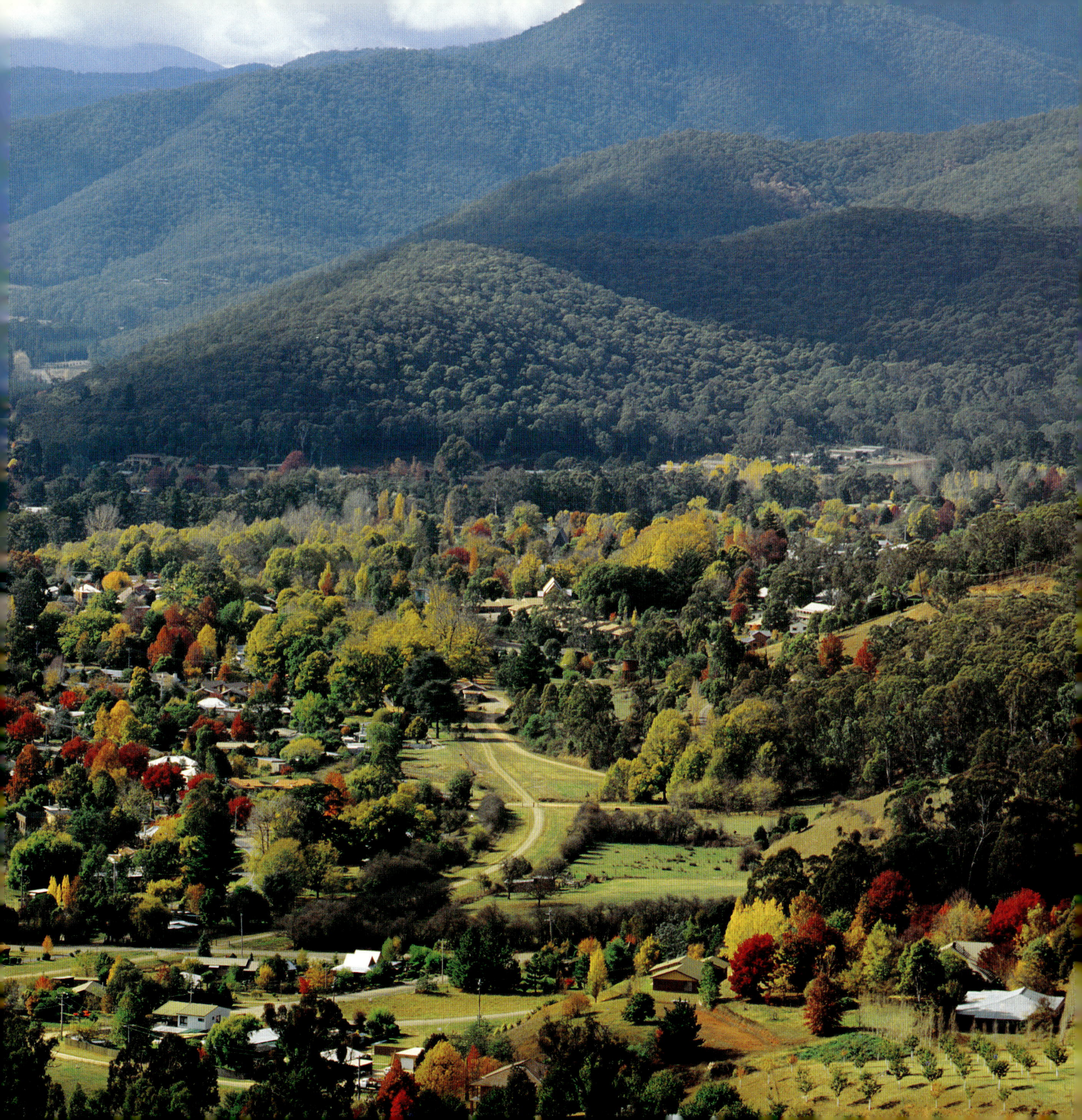

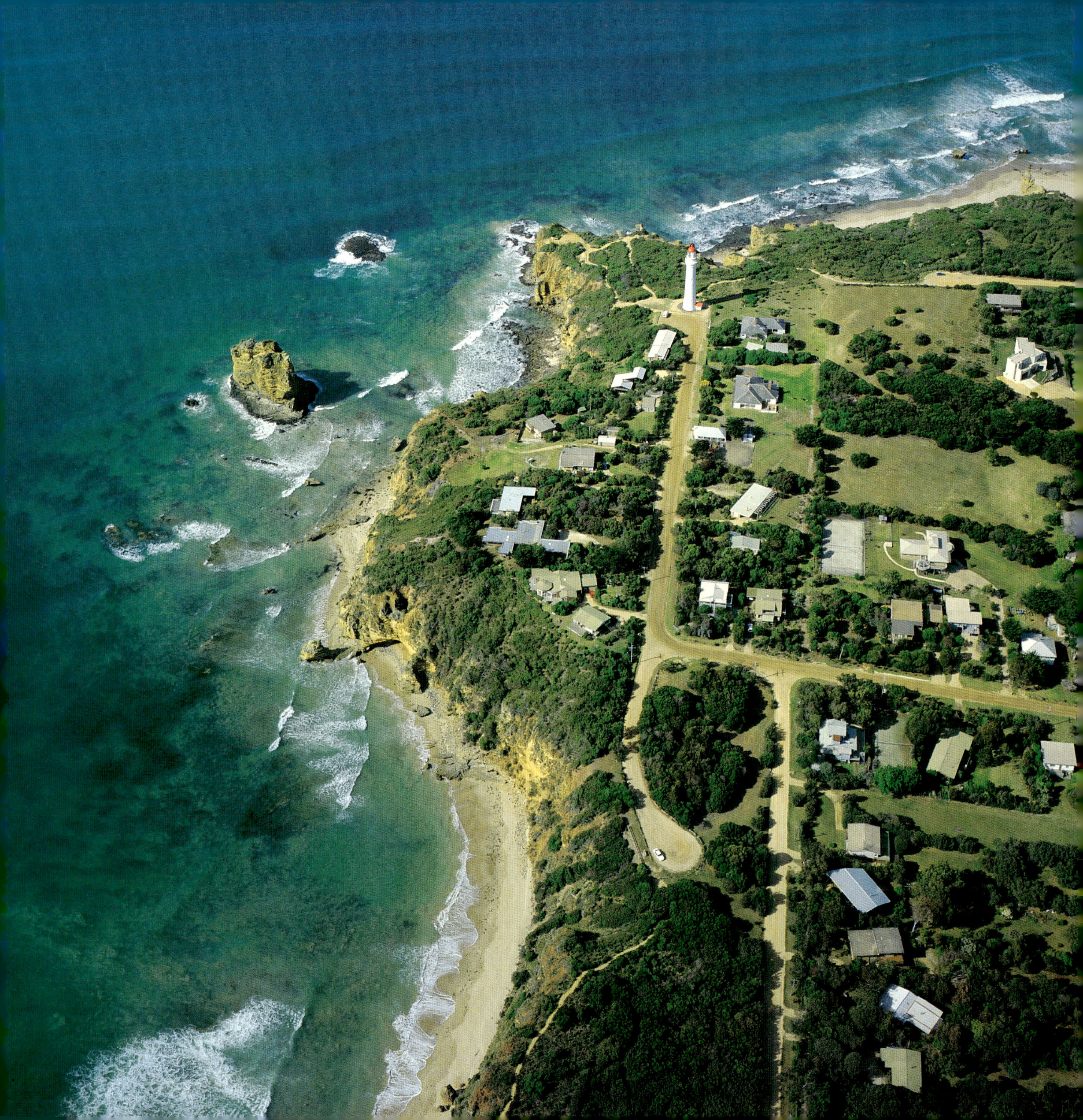

The Great Ocean Road

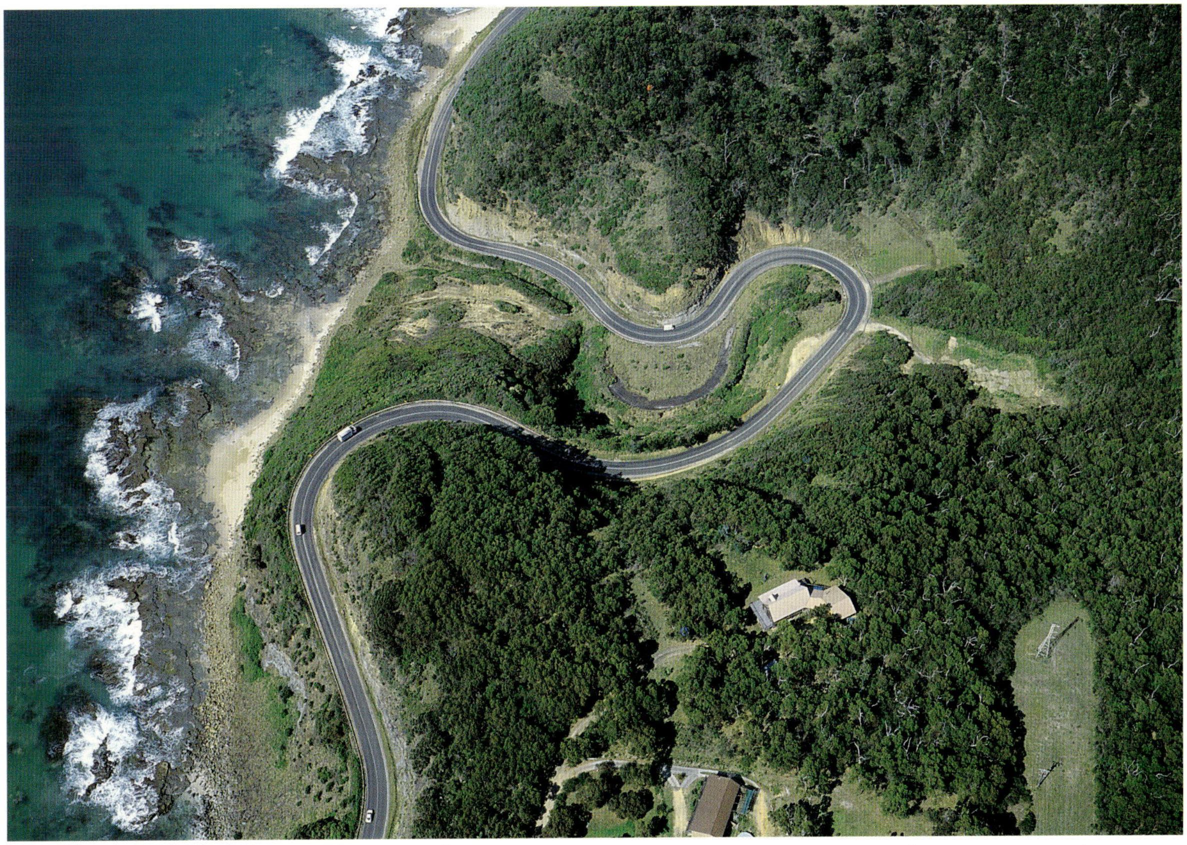

Opposite: An aerial view of Aireys Inlet. Split Point and its lighthouse, built in 1891, are at top left. *Above:* The winding Great Ocean Road near Lorne.

The Great Ocean Road, which skirts the shores of Victoria west of Melbourne from Geelong to the South Australian border, is a pathway to the magic of some of Australia's best-known and most scenic coastline. The road from Anglesea to Apollo Bay was begun in 1919. Using picks, shovels and horse-drawn vehicles, returned World War I soldiers carved the road out of the limestone cliffs. It was completed in 1932 and provided a land link for coastal towns which before depended on shipping to bring them supplies. Today, the much improved and extended Great Ocean Road opens the way to such scenic splendours as the Shipwreck Coast and the Otway National Park.

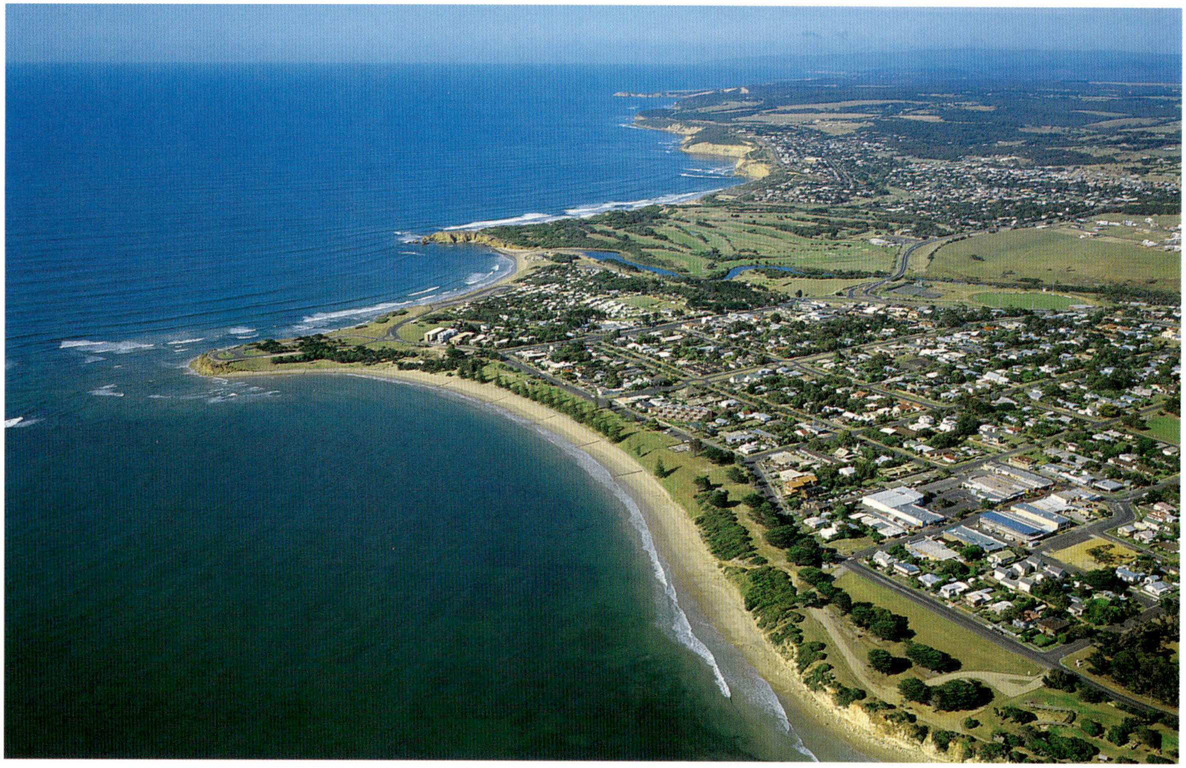

Torquay, Australia's "surfing capital". The Rip Curl Pro is held at nearby Bells Beach.

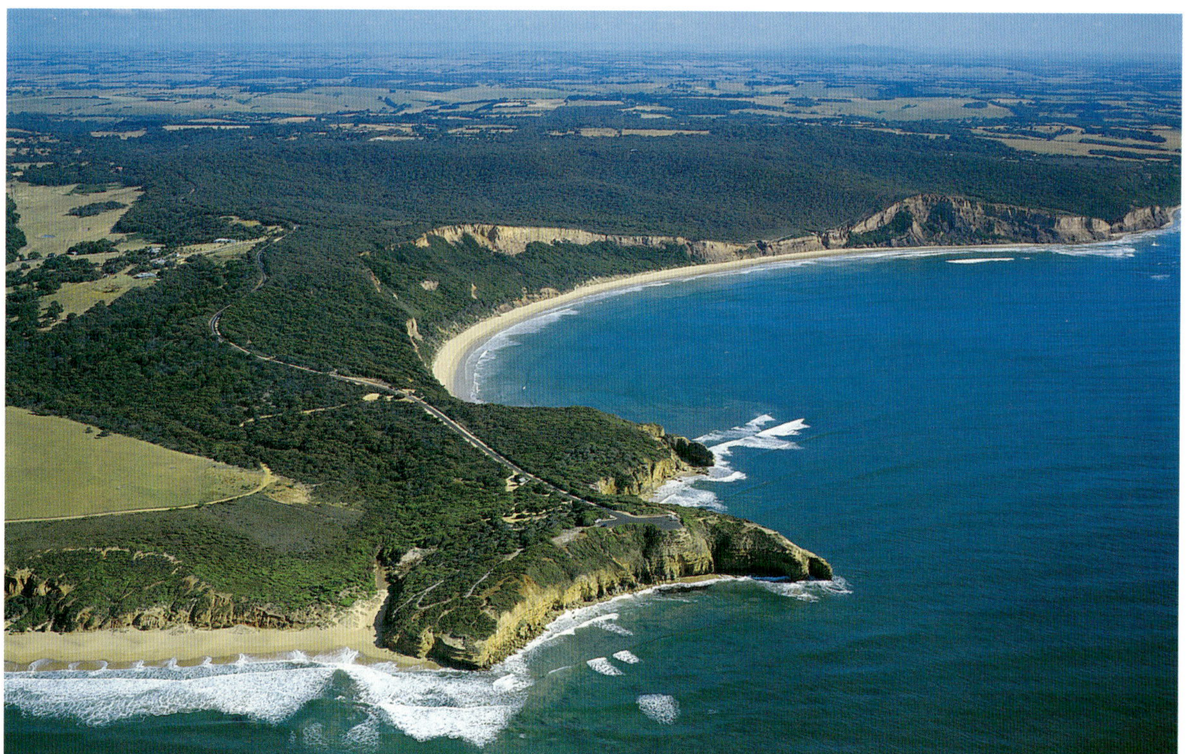

Point Addis, to the west of Bells Beach.

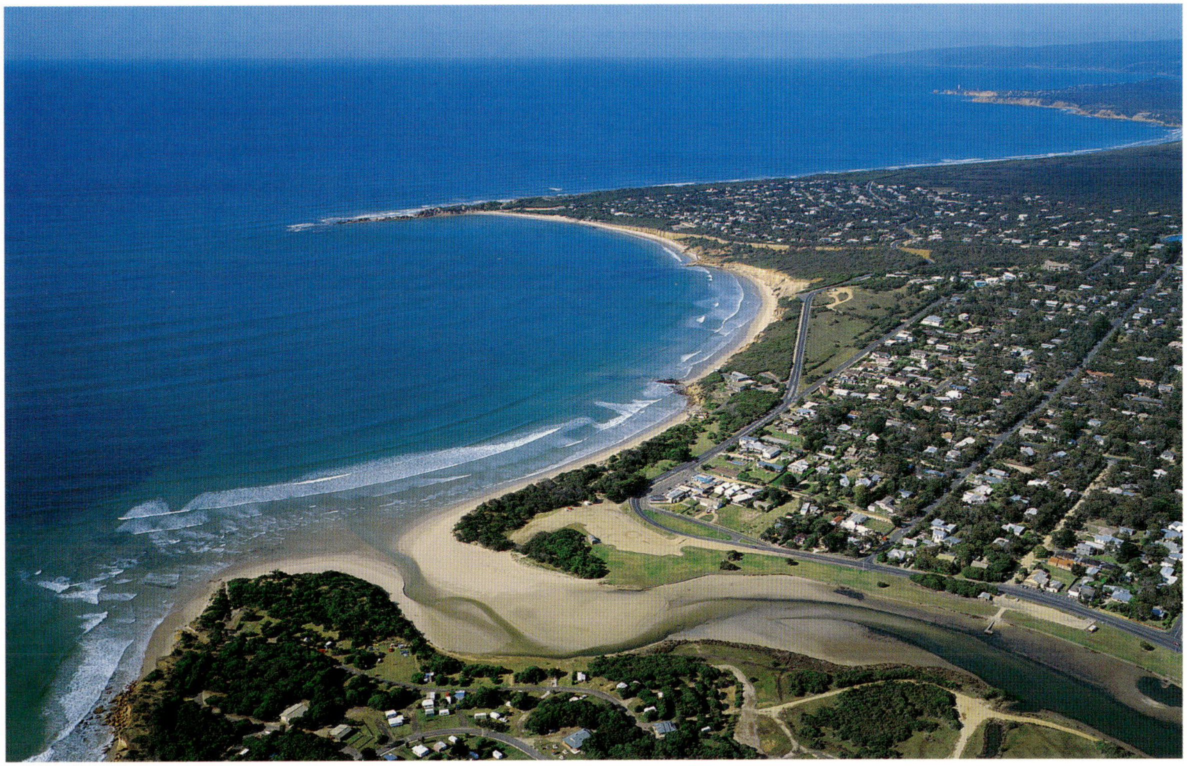

Anglesea is popular with holidaying families and near to Angahook-Lorne State Park.

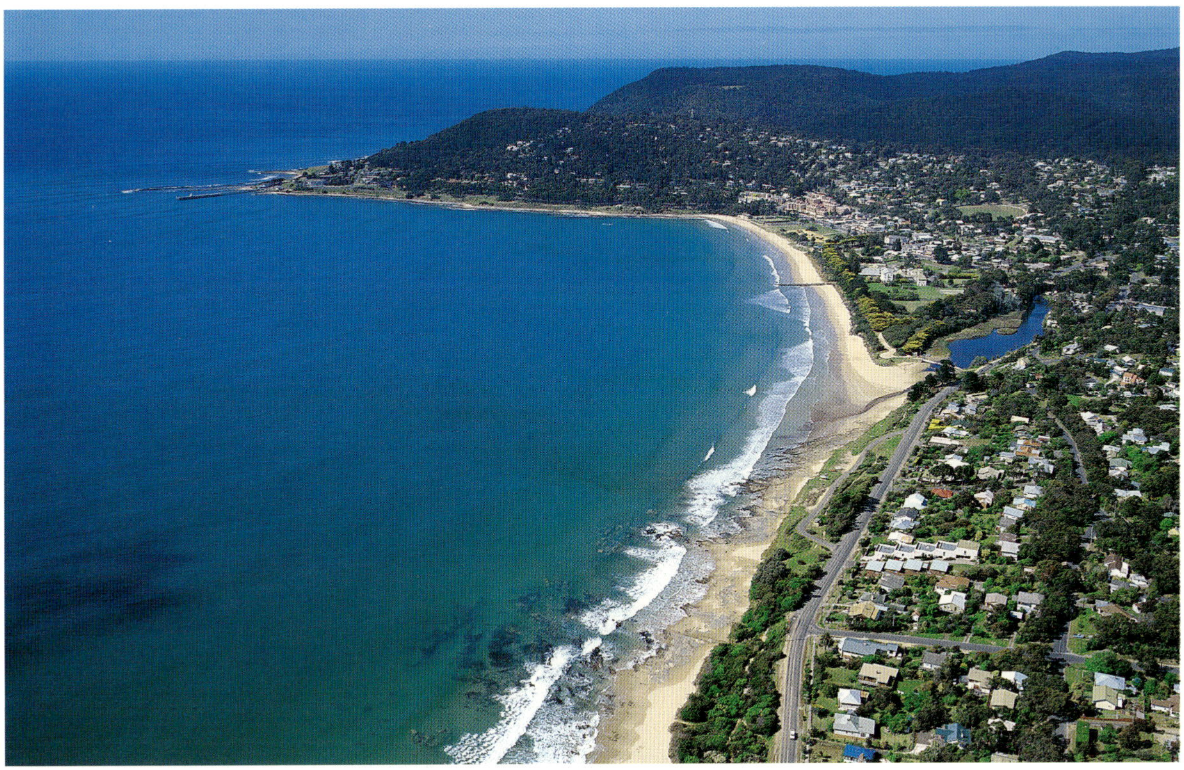

Lorne, set between the sea and the Otway forests.

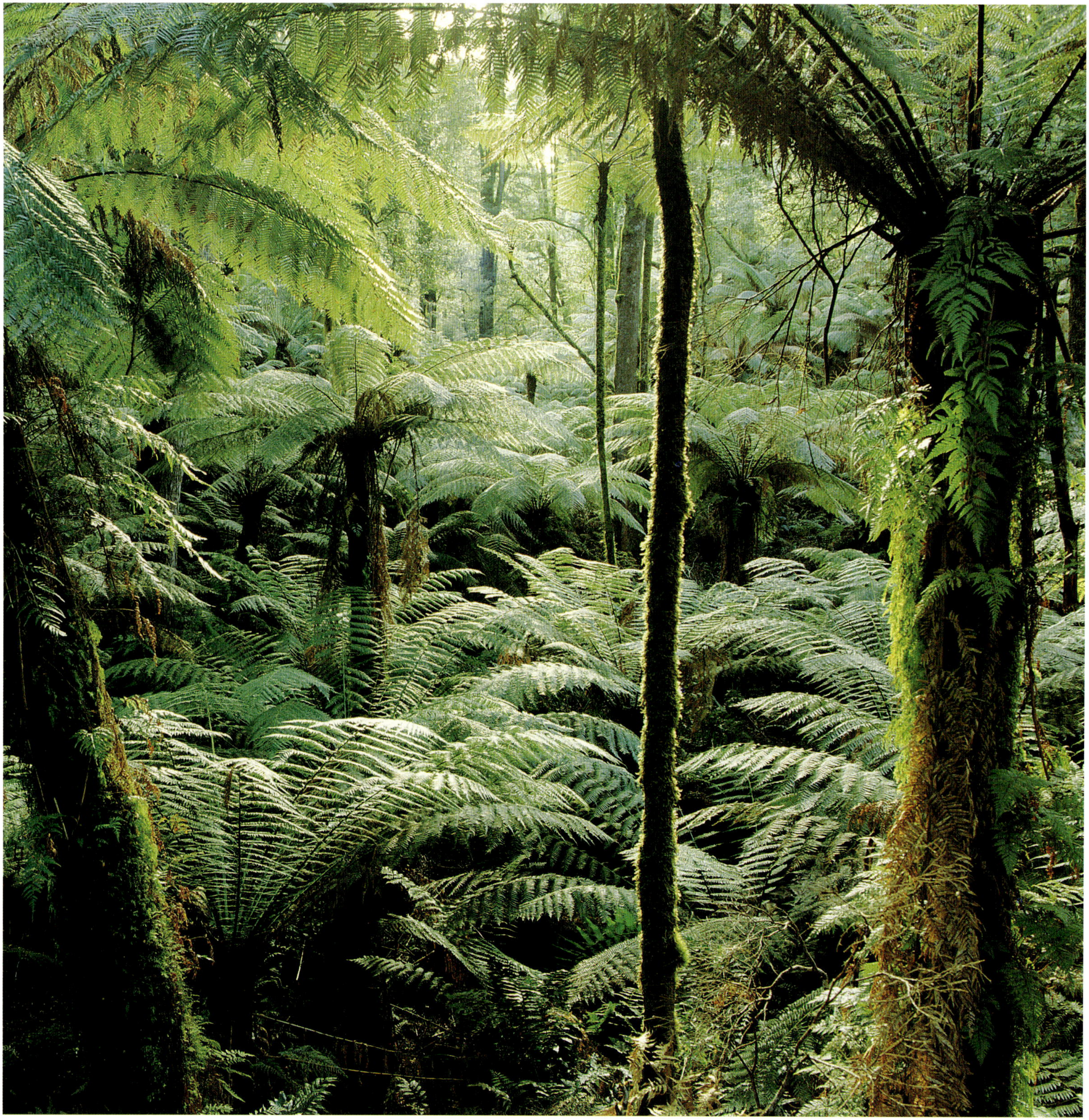

A fern gully in the Otway National Park.

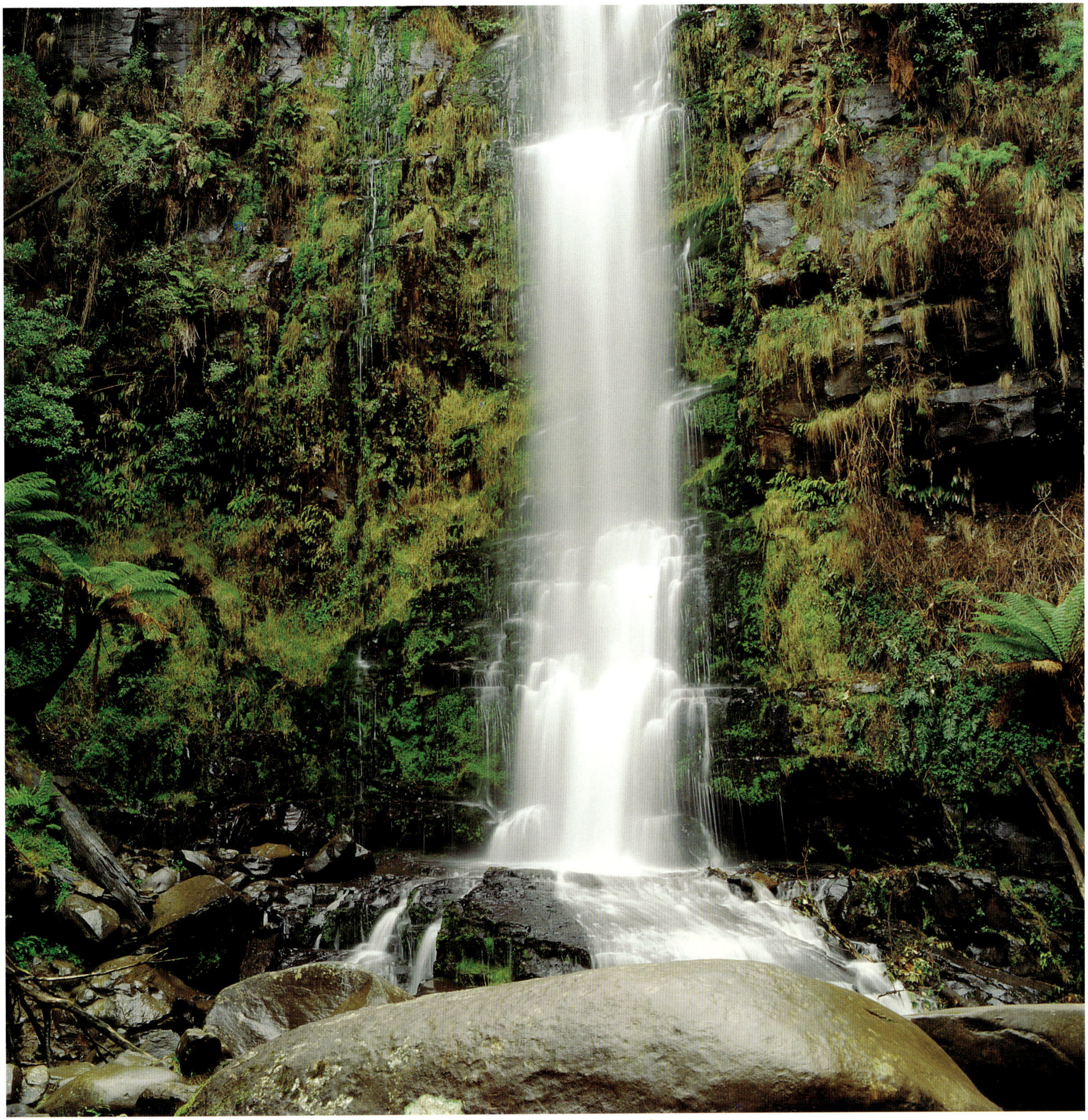
Erskine Falls, Angahook-Lorne State Park.

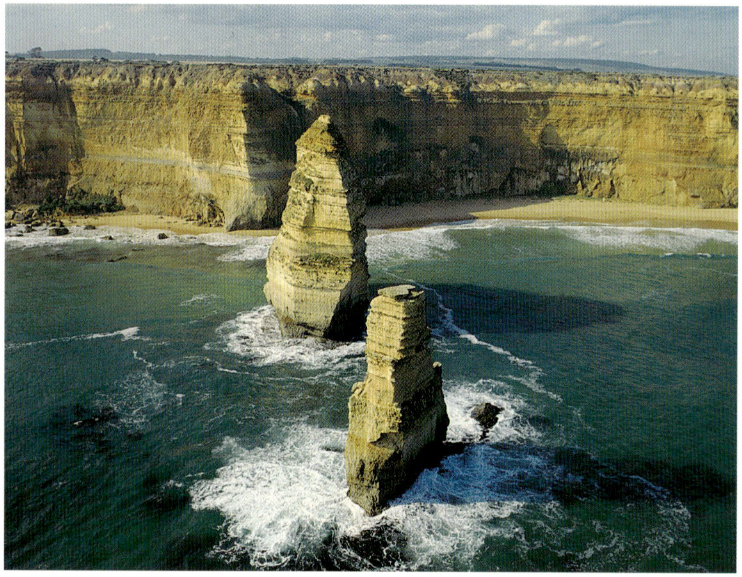

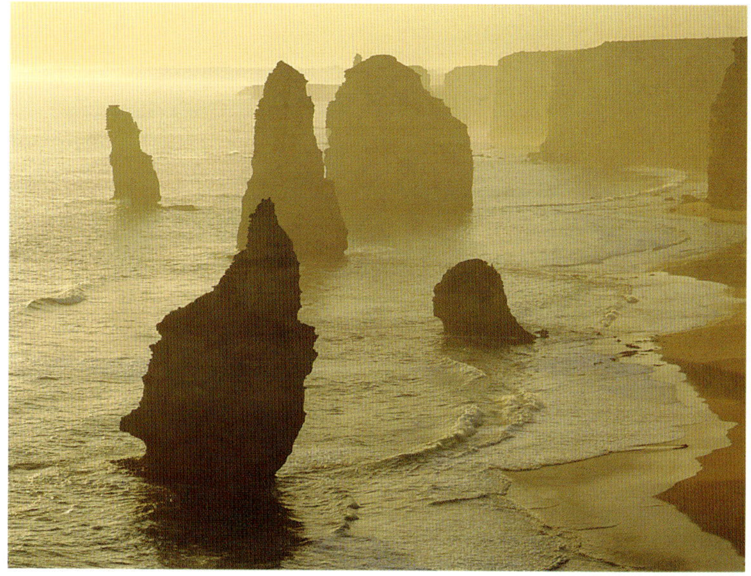

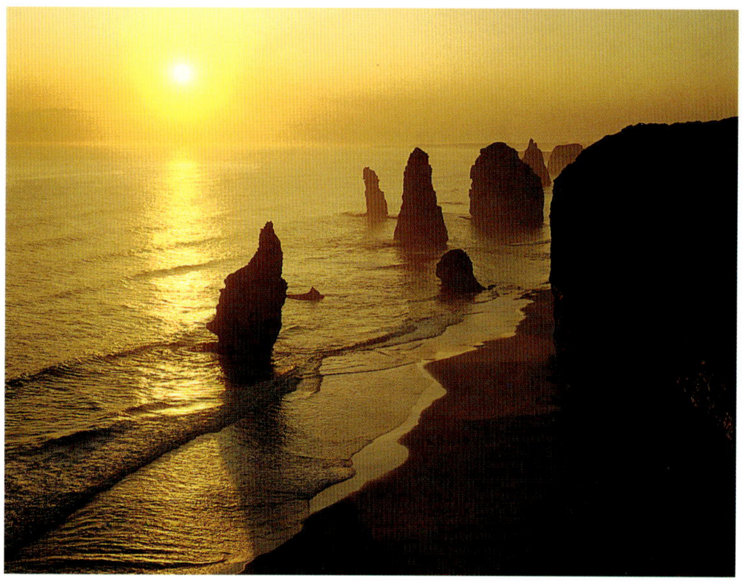

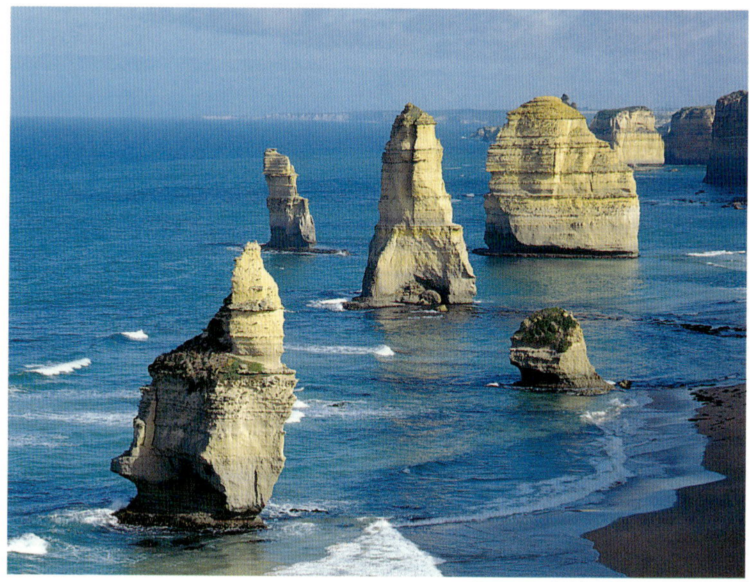

Some of the many moods of the Twelve Apostles.

Port Campbell National Park

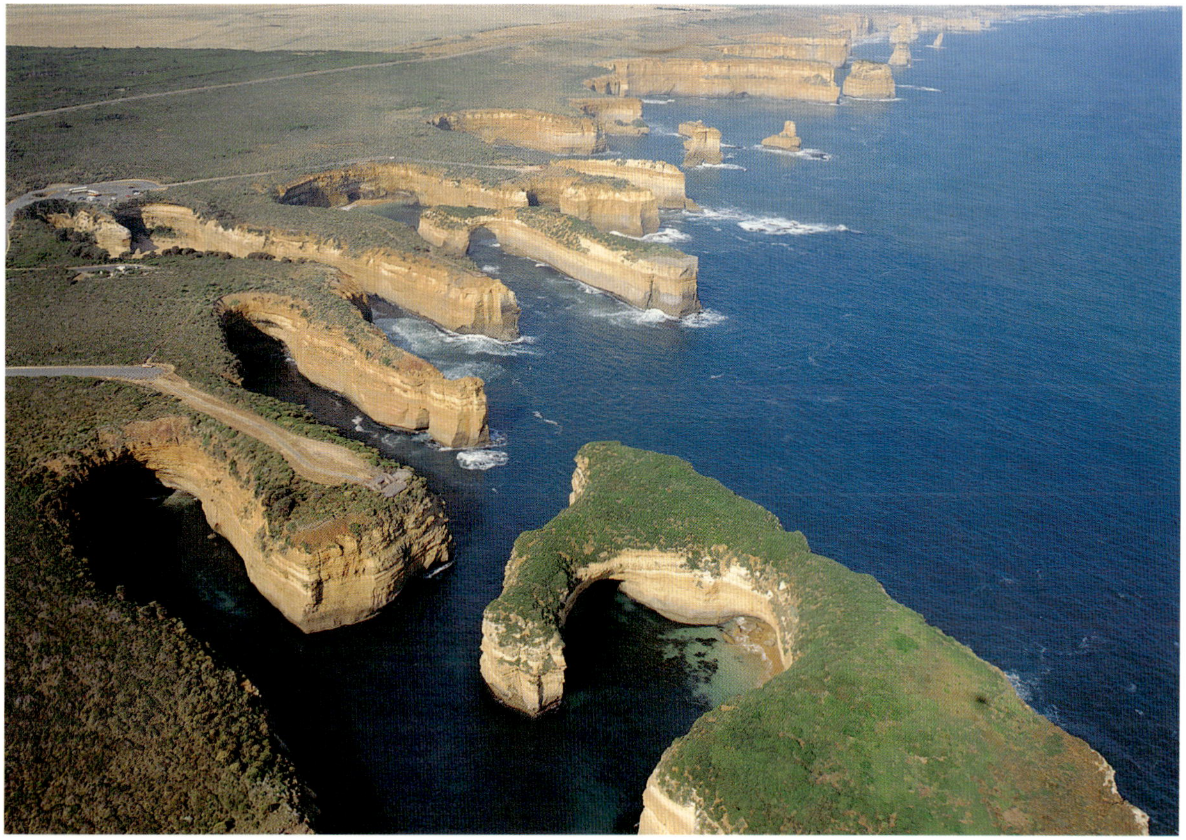

The indented coast of Port Campbell National Park.

The Historic Shipwreck Trail signposts twenty-five places where the wild waves of the Southern Ocean brought vessels to disaster on the rocks of the coastline which now is Port Campbell National Park. Most infamous of these disasters was the wreck of the *Loch Ard*, which claimed fifty-two lives. The Shipwreck Coast, so glorious in good weather, so terrifying in heavy seas, lists amongst its scenic attractions the Twelve Apostles, the Blowhole, London Bridge, the Bay of Martyrs and the Bay of Islands.

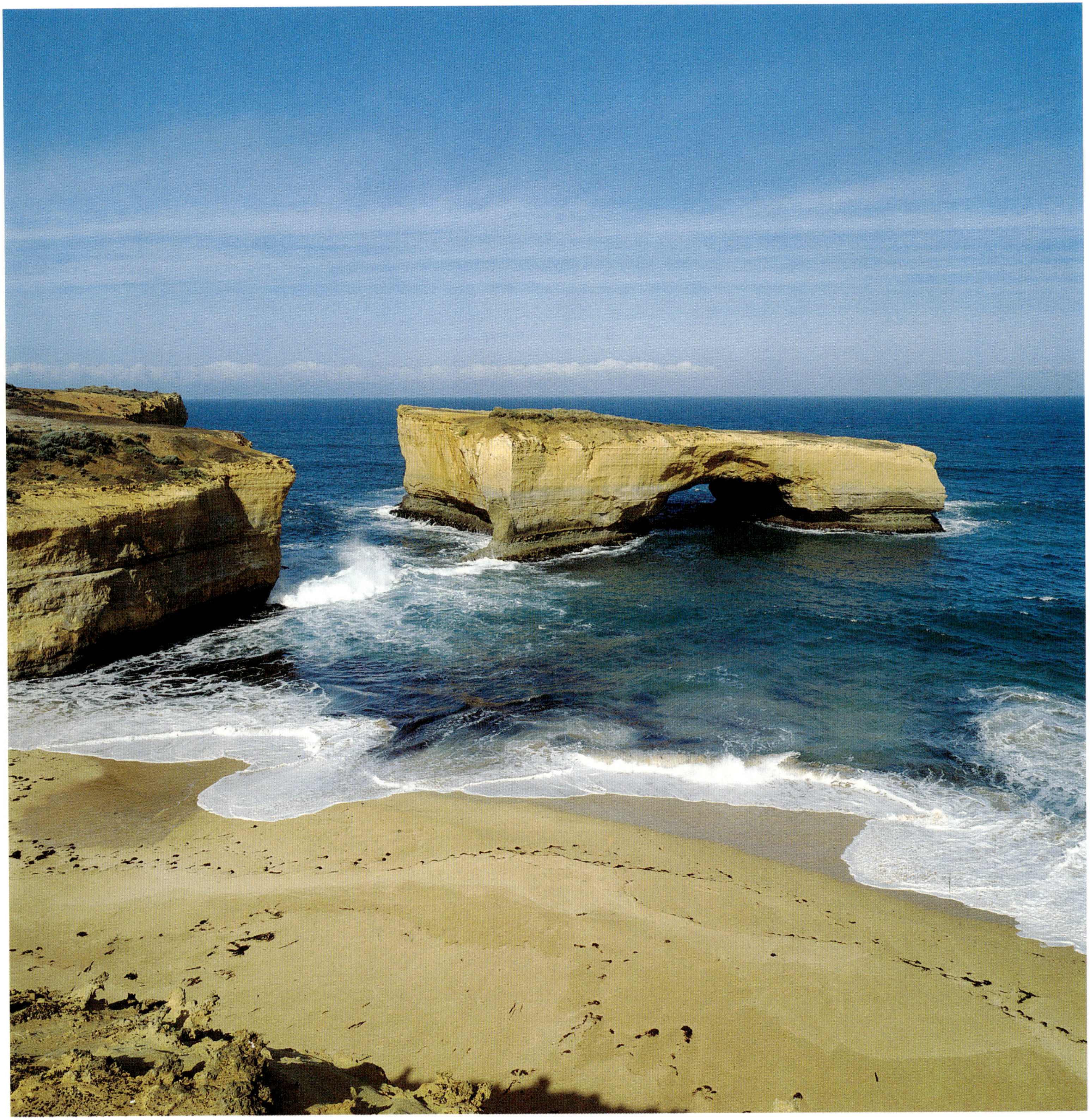
London Bridge after its landward arch collapsed into the sea. Eventually, it will stand as stacks like the Twelve Apostles.

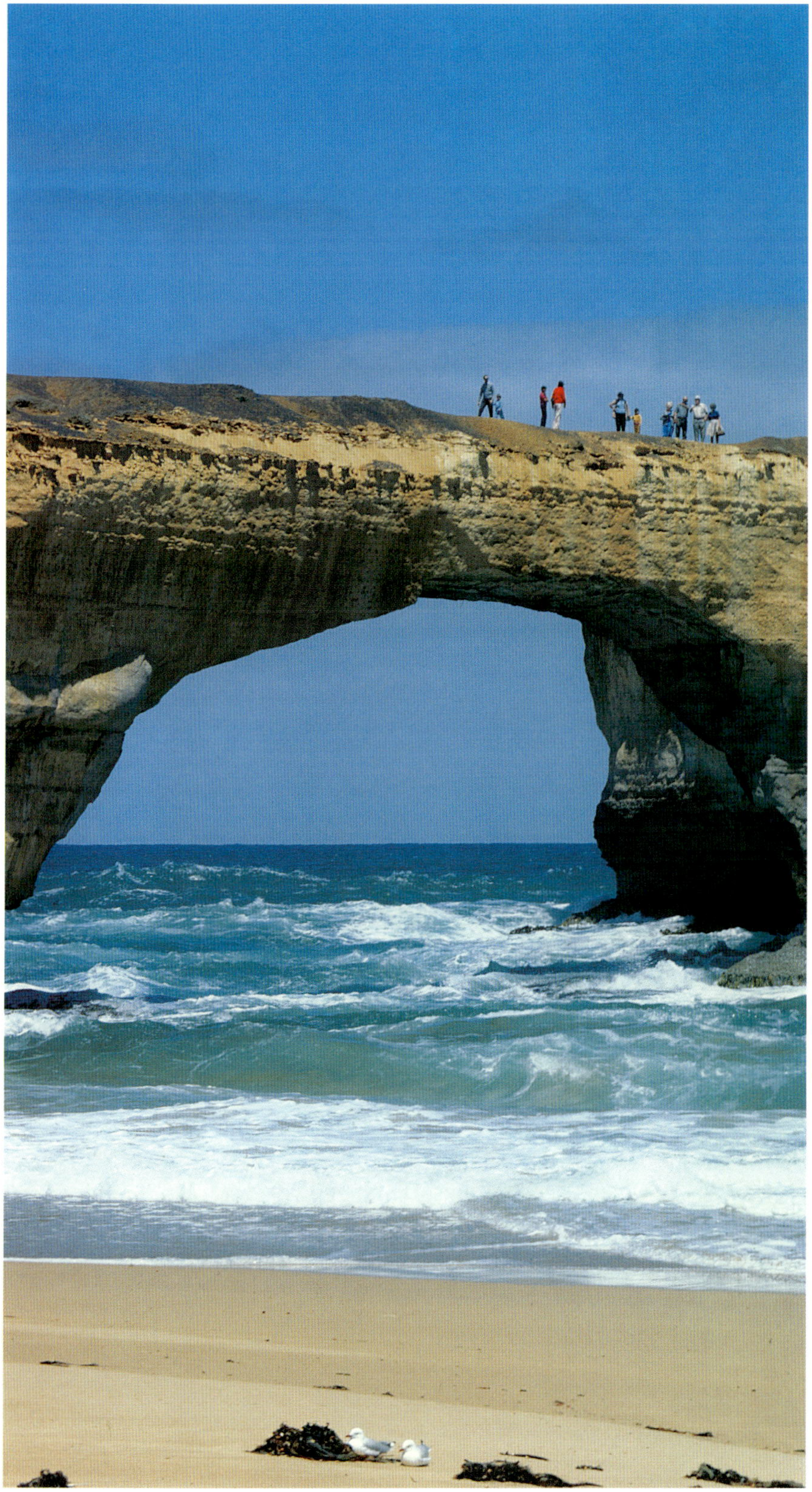

London Bridge, three days before it collapsed.

London Bridge has fallen down

One moment, the massive spur of limestone jutting from the mainland stood solidly while a group of sightseers admired the view from its windy top. The next, with a thunderous crash and terrifying explosion of foam, the landward arch collapsed into the ocean.

A helicopter rescued the marooned holiday-makers, alarmed but uninjured. London Bridge, so called because of its two sea-cut arches, had lost its connection with Victoria and today stands isolated, arching above the water. The waves continue their work, steadily undermining its supports. Eventually, it will stand as two stacks, and finally they will vanish beneath the sea.

Westwards past Warrnambool

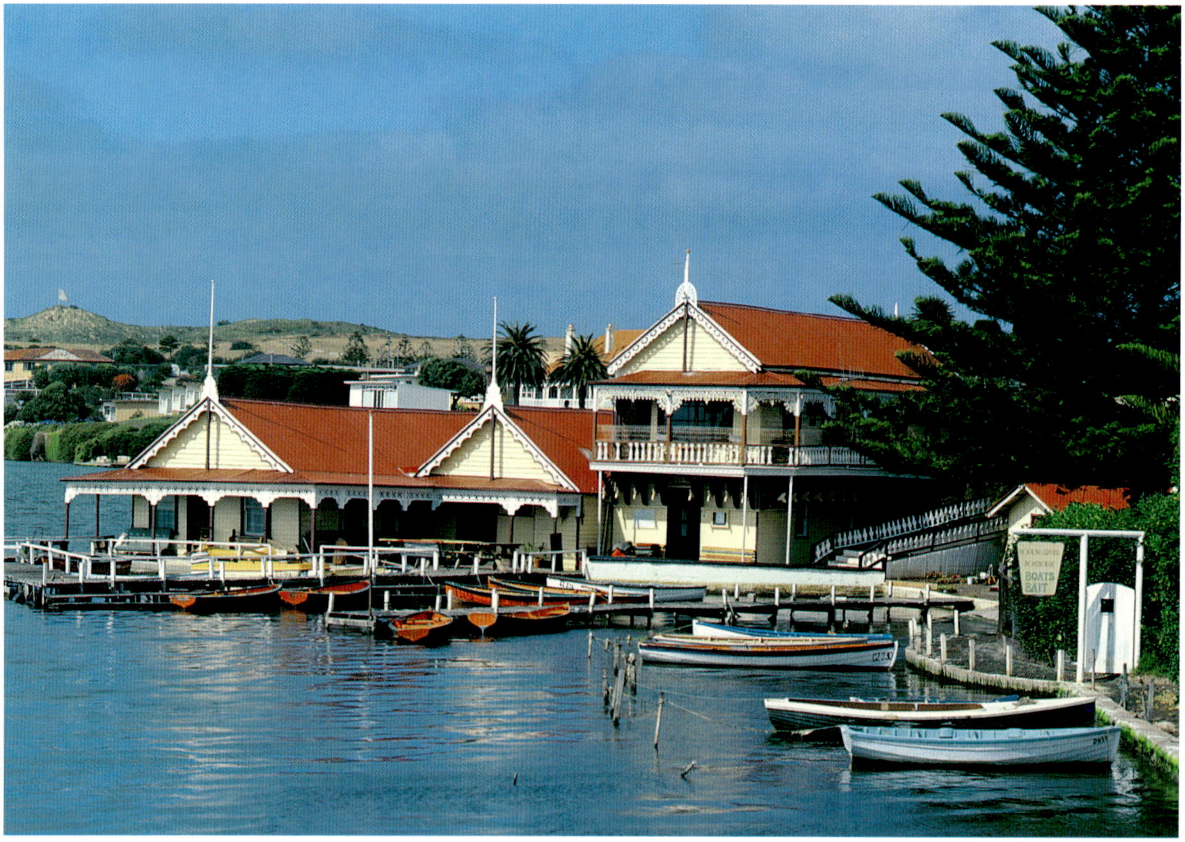

Proudfoots Boathouse, restored to Victorian elegance, stands on the Hopkins River at Warrnambool.

Warrnambool, the main centre for the Shipwreck Coast, is an excellent base for whale-watchers who gather to see the Southern Right Whales which arrive to give birth off the coast around May and remain until October. Flagstaff Hill Maritime Museum and Proudfoots Boathouse are only two of Warrnambool's many attractions.

Port Fairy, west along Princes Highway, was once a whalers' base: today it contains more than fifty National Trust classified properties. This charming town is famous for its three annual music festivals – the Folk Music Festival held in March, the classical/jazz Spring Music Festival in October, and Rhapsody in June which has something for all musical tastes.

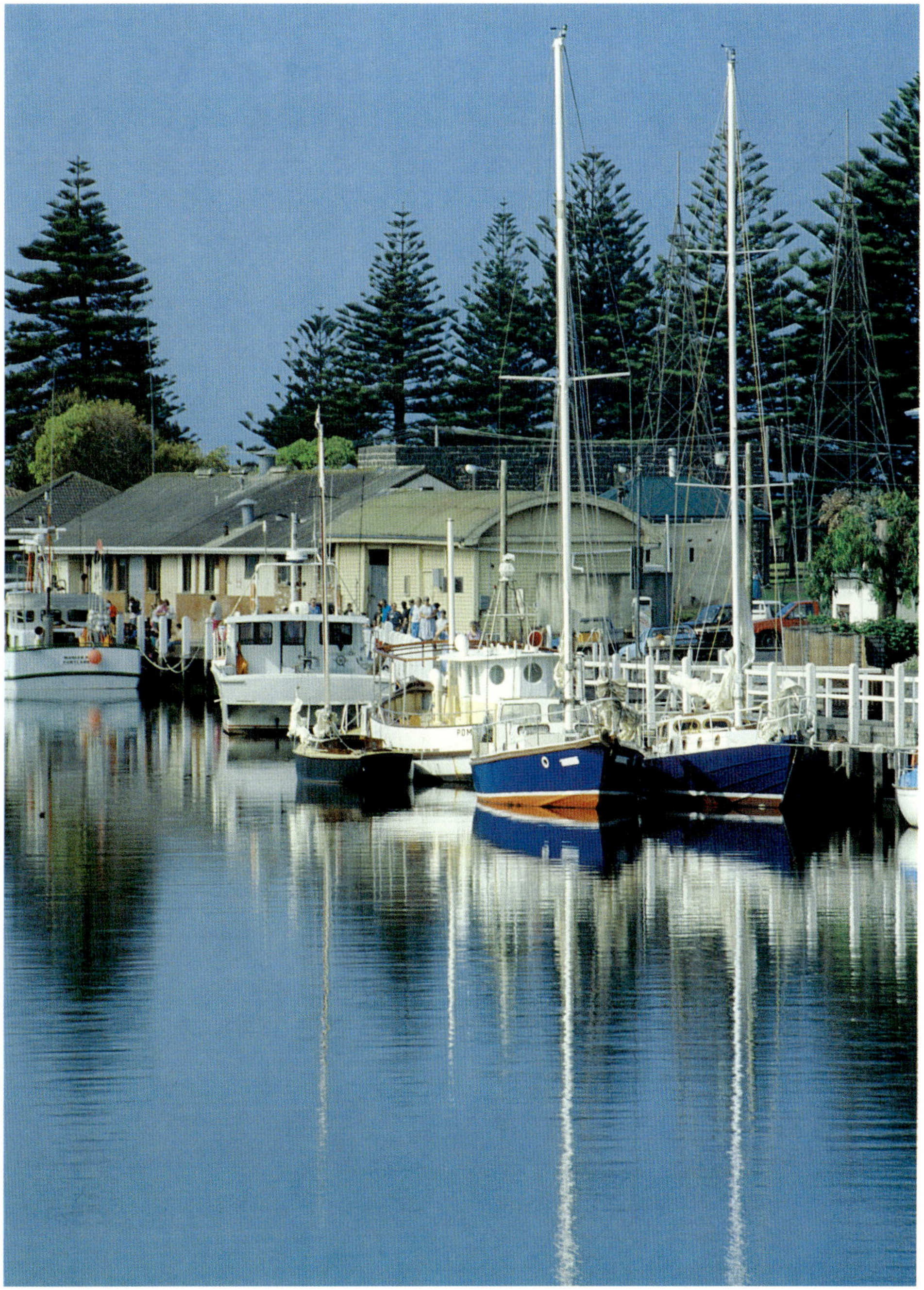
Fishing and pleasure craft at Port Fairy.

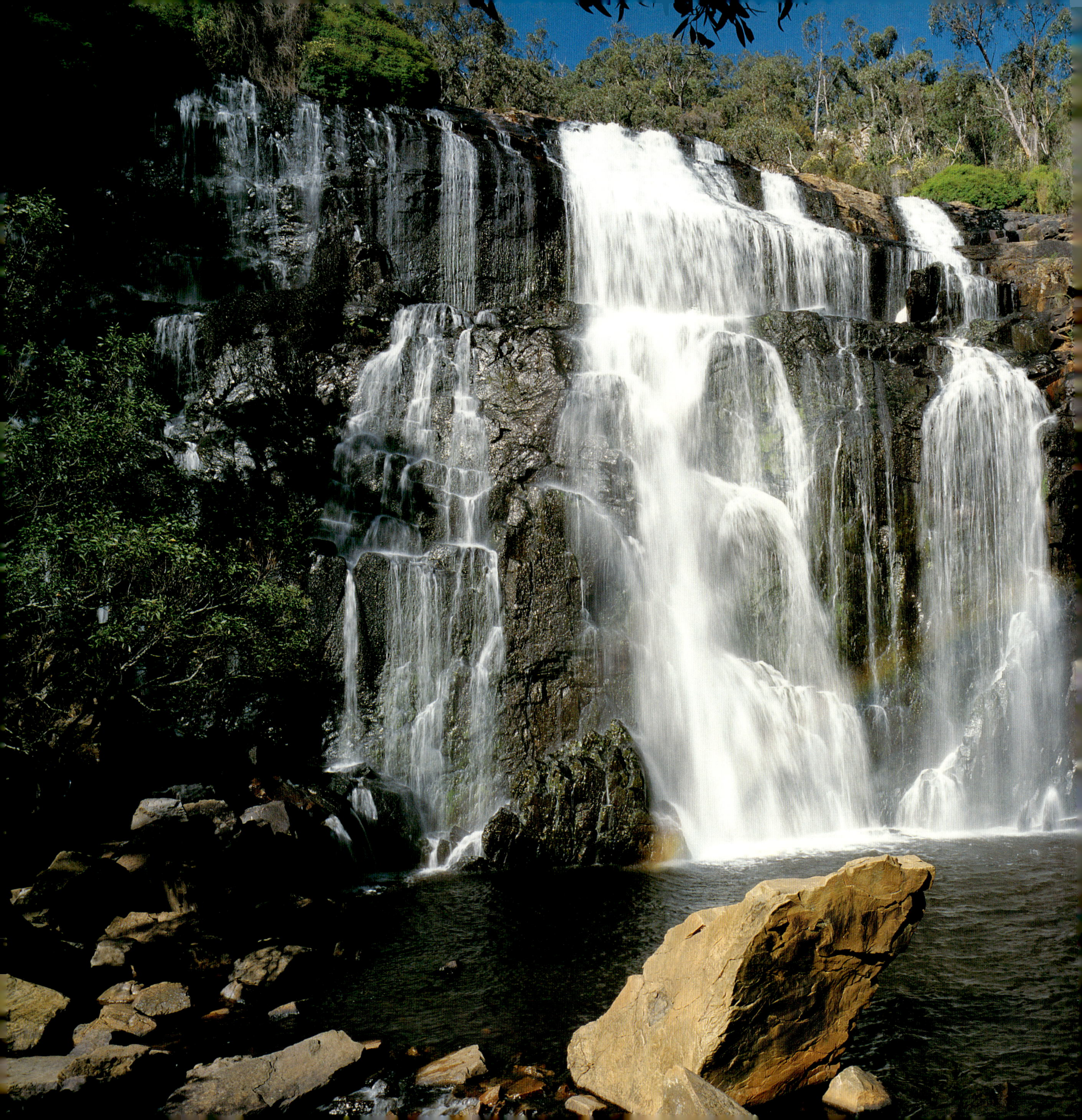

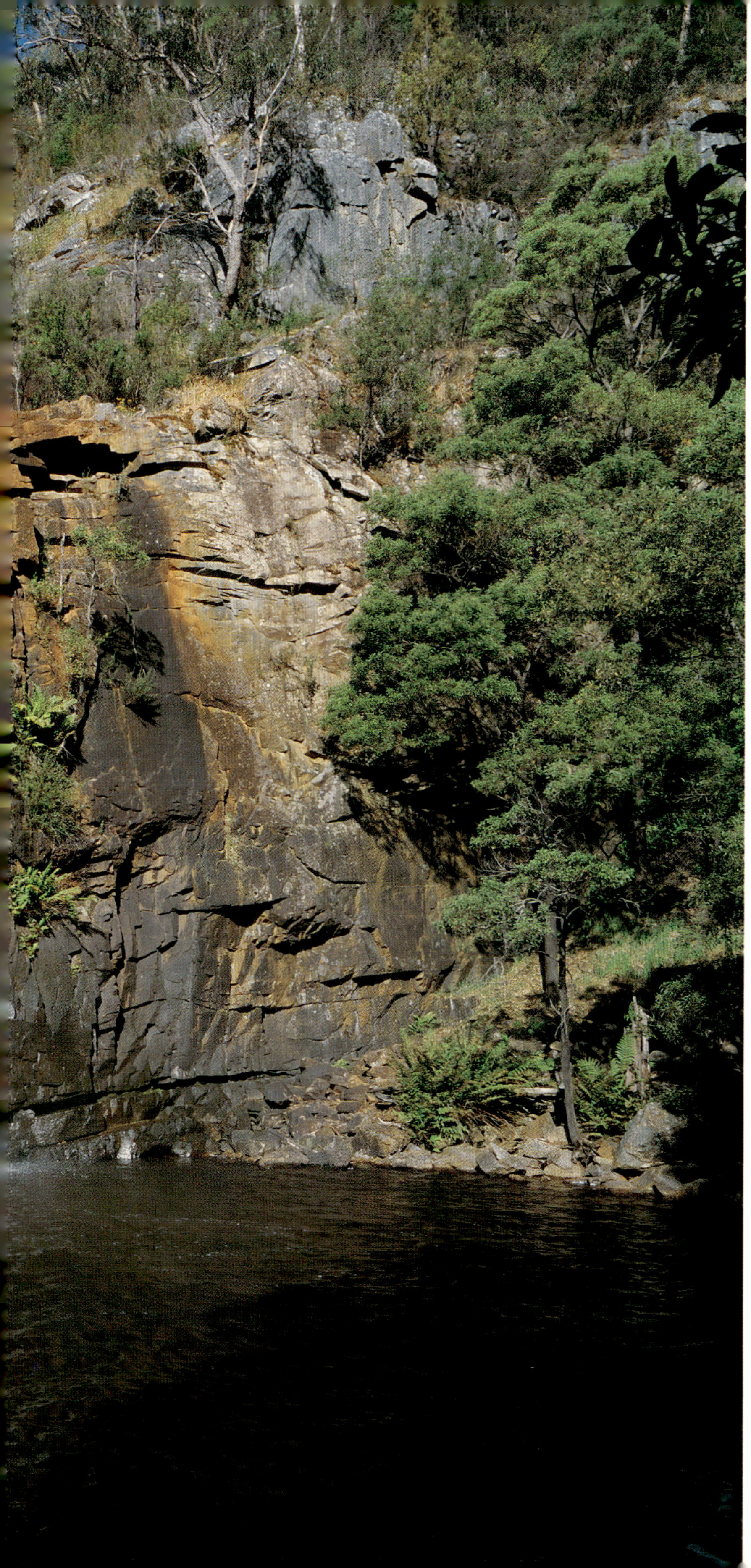

The Grampians

The Grampians stand in monumental grandeur on the Western Plains of Victoria, about 300 kilometres from Melbourne. Their highest peak, Mt William, is just over 1160 metres high, but they have a scenic appeal which does not depend on height alone. Their four major sandstone range systems run roughly north and south: on the west, each slopes gently to the plain, but the eastern aspect is marked by cliffs and jagged rock faces. Four watercourses, the Mackenzie, Glenelg and Wannon Rivers and Fyans Creek, are fed by the water which runs from the Grampians.

After the farming lands of the Western Districts, the green gullies and waterfalls of the Grampians offer a very different world. In springtime, forests and heathlands are paradises of wildflowers, which attract honeyeaters, lorikeets and other nectar-feeding birds. Halls Gap, gateway to the Grampians, holds a wildflower exhibition each October.

Close to Halls Gap is the memorable Wonderland area, with weathered sandstone slopes and cliffs and picturesque rock formations. The Pinnacle Lookout is a popular viewing place. Further west, the Balconies form a vantage point to admire Victoria Valley and the Serra Range. Mt William offers magnificent views and, at the right time of year, a bounty of wildflowers.

Left: Mackenzie Falls, one of the Grampians' loveliest landmarks.

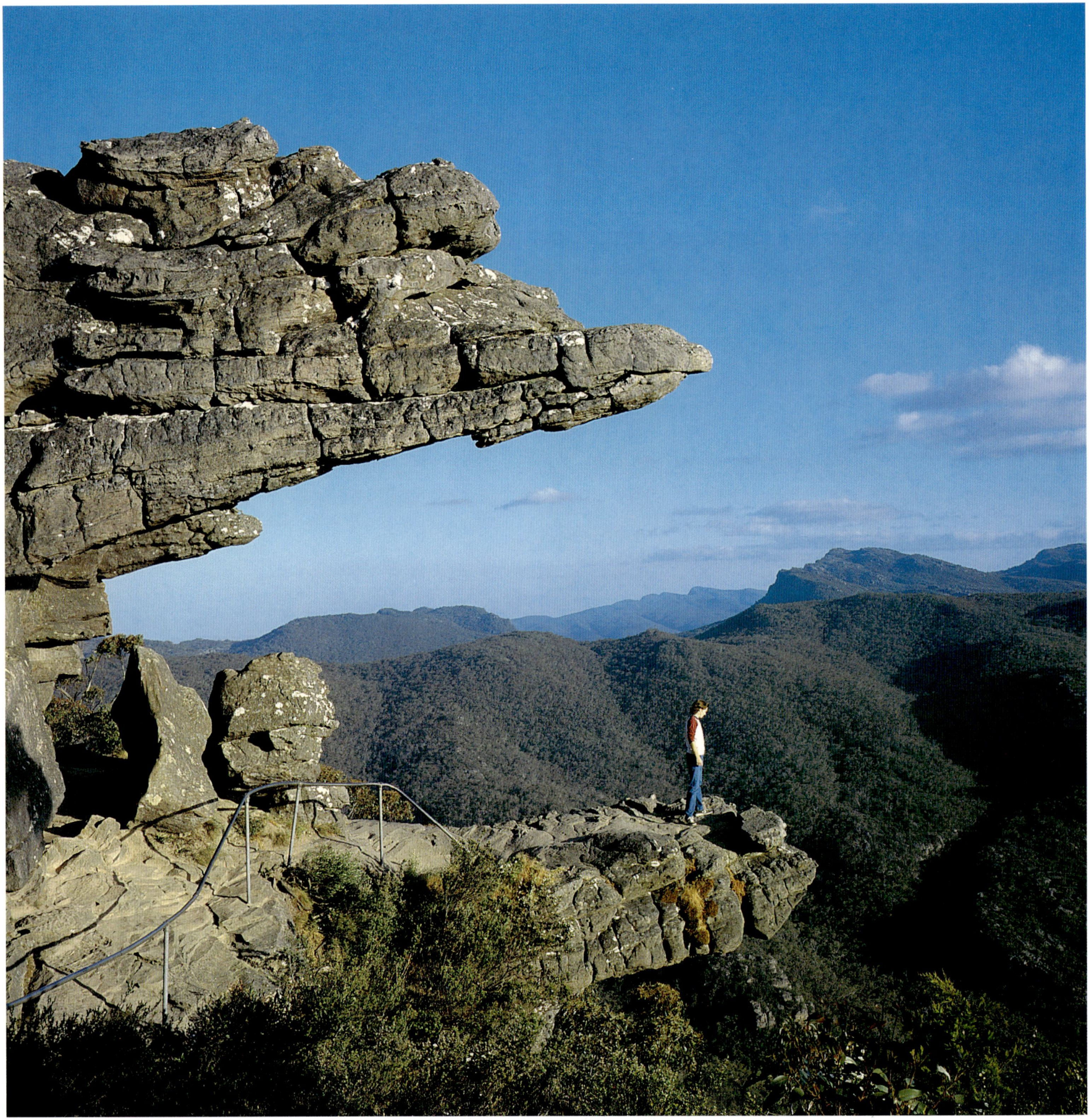

Overlooking the ranges from The Balconies.

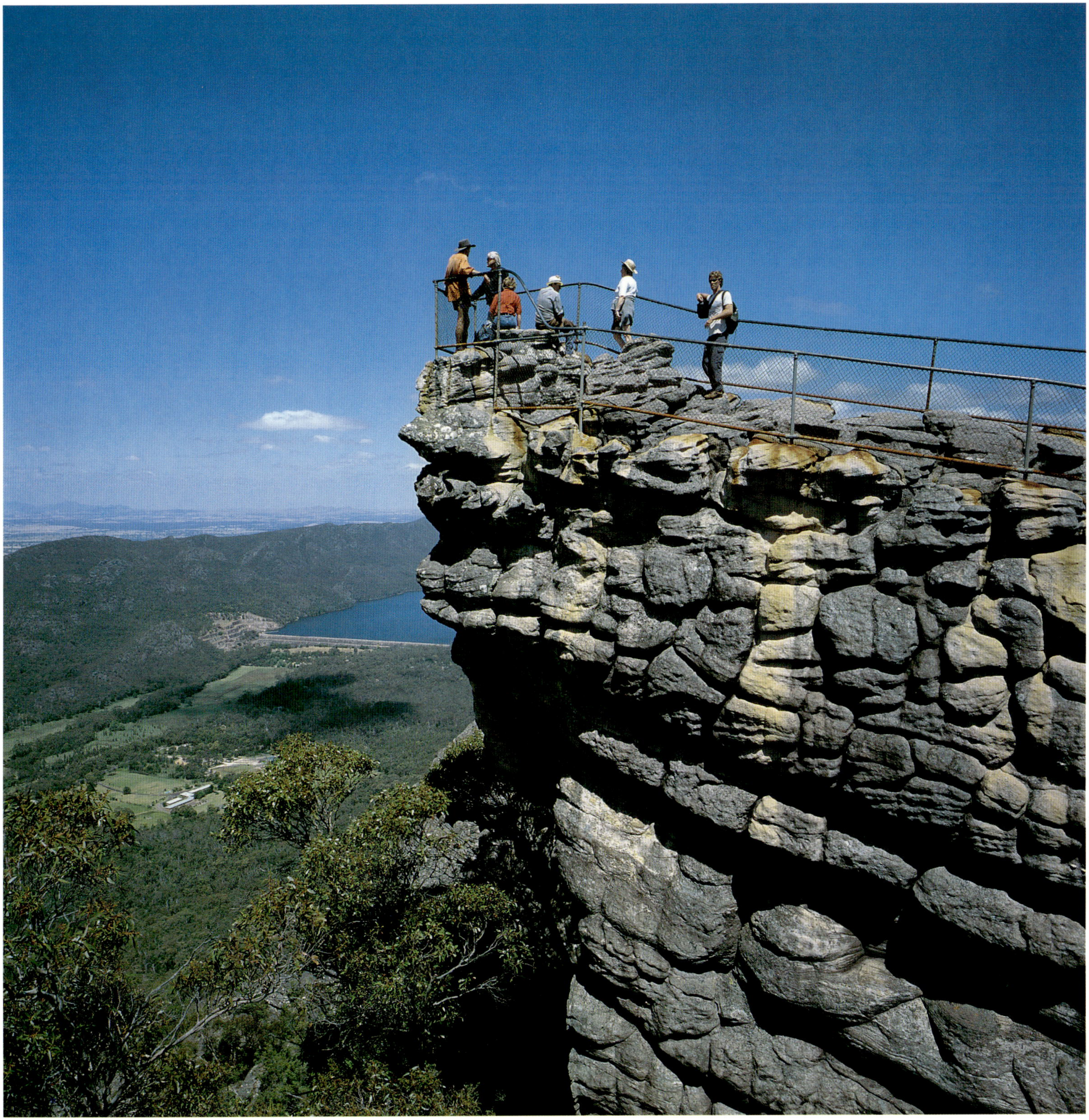

Above: The Pinnacle is a popular vantage point.

Following pages: The formation of the sandstone ranges is clearly seen from Mt William.

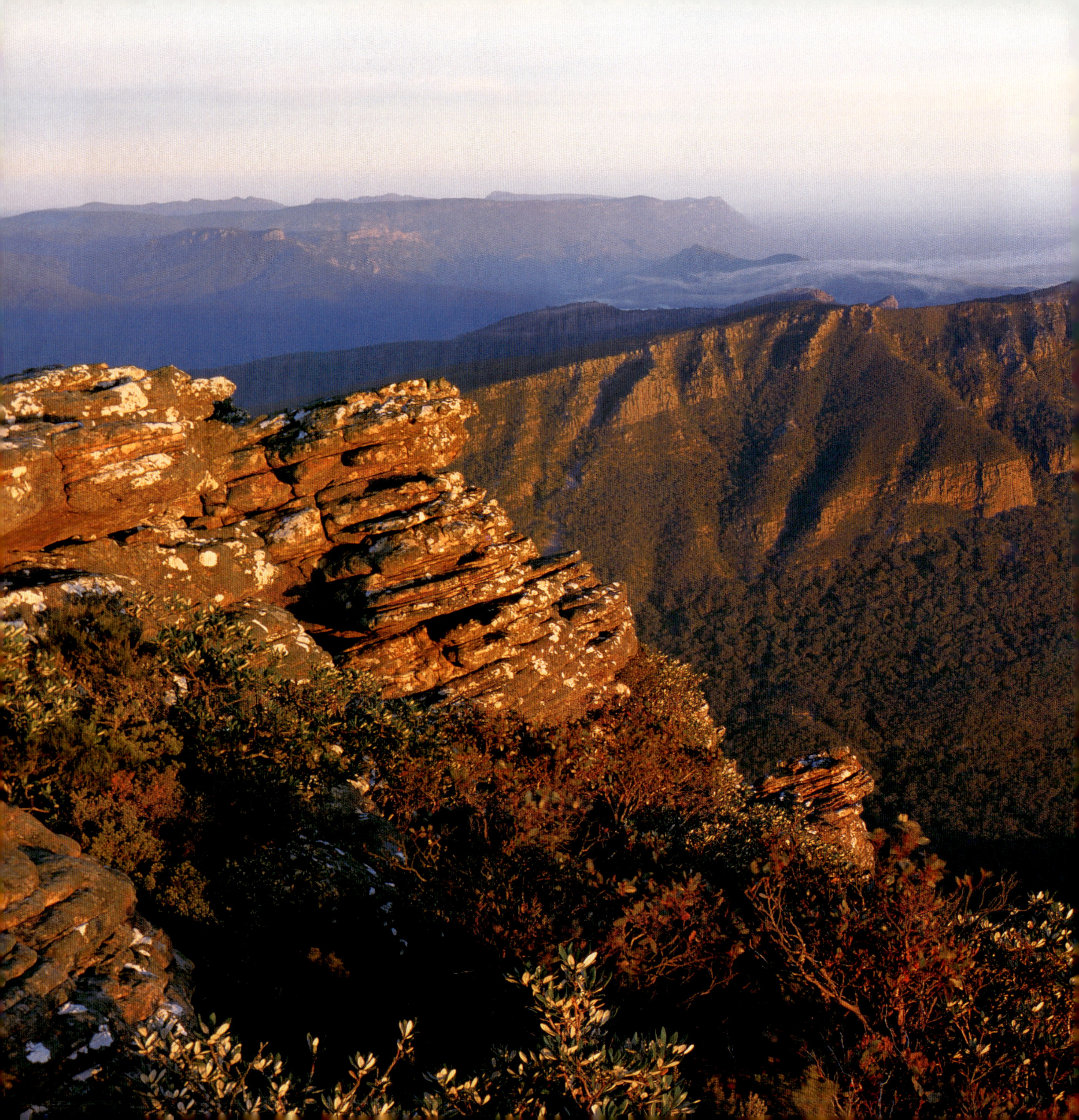

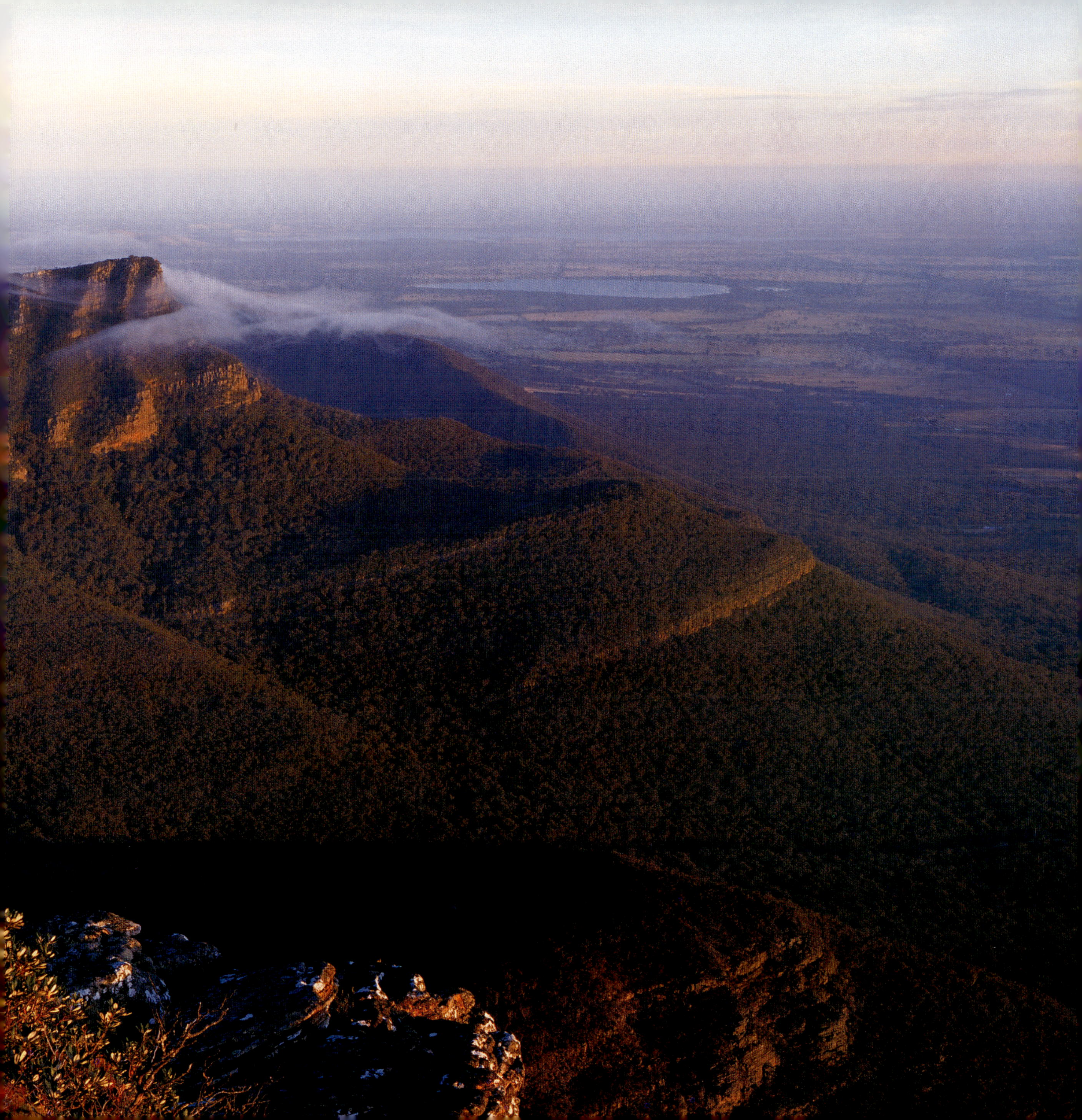

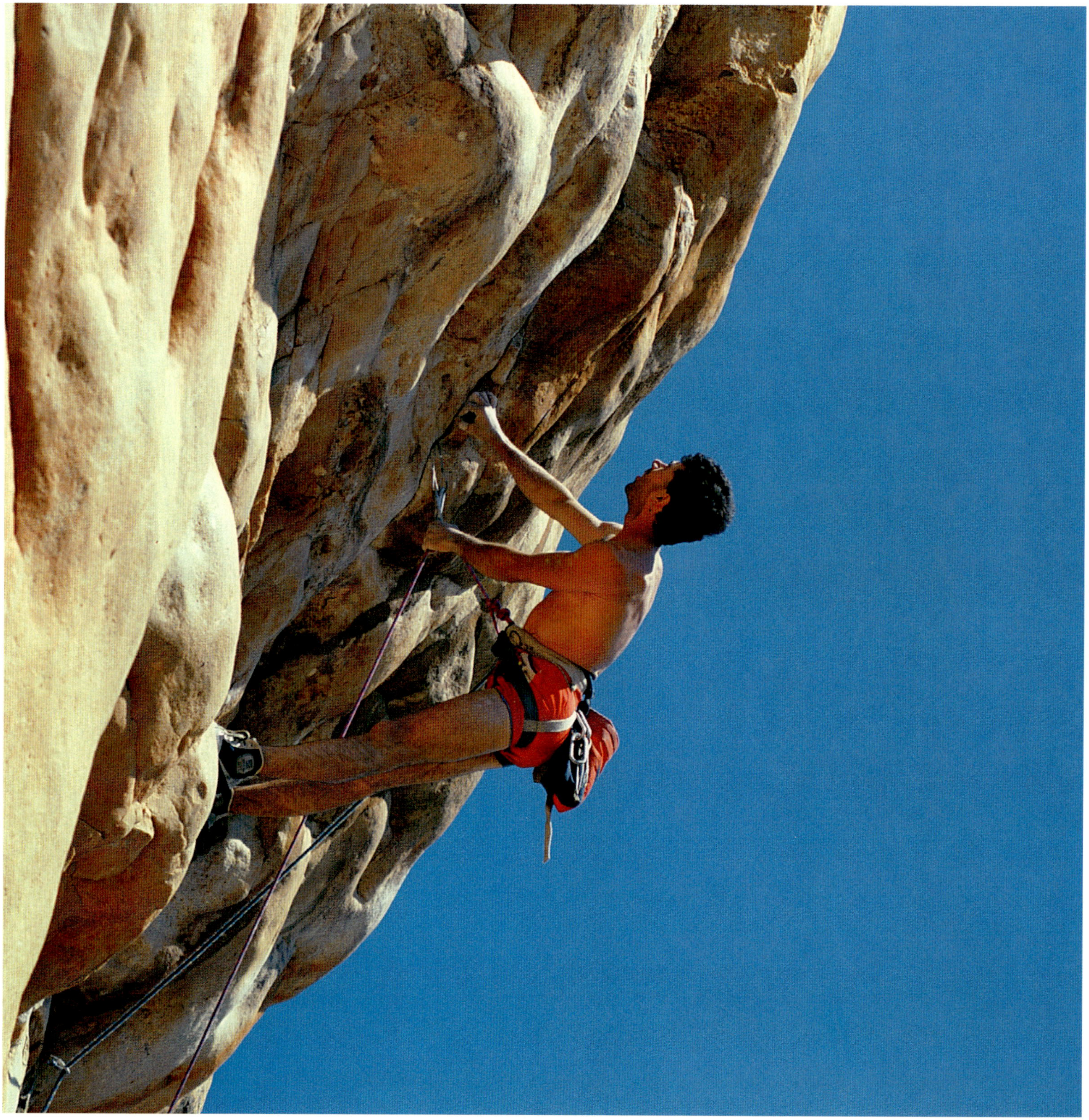

The sandstone of Mt Arapiles forms a firm and reliable climbing surface.

Mt Arapiles

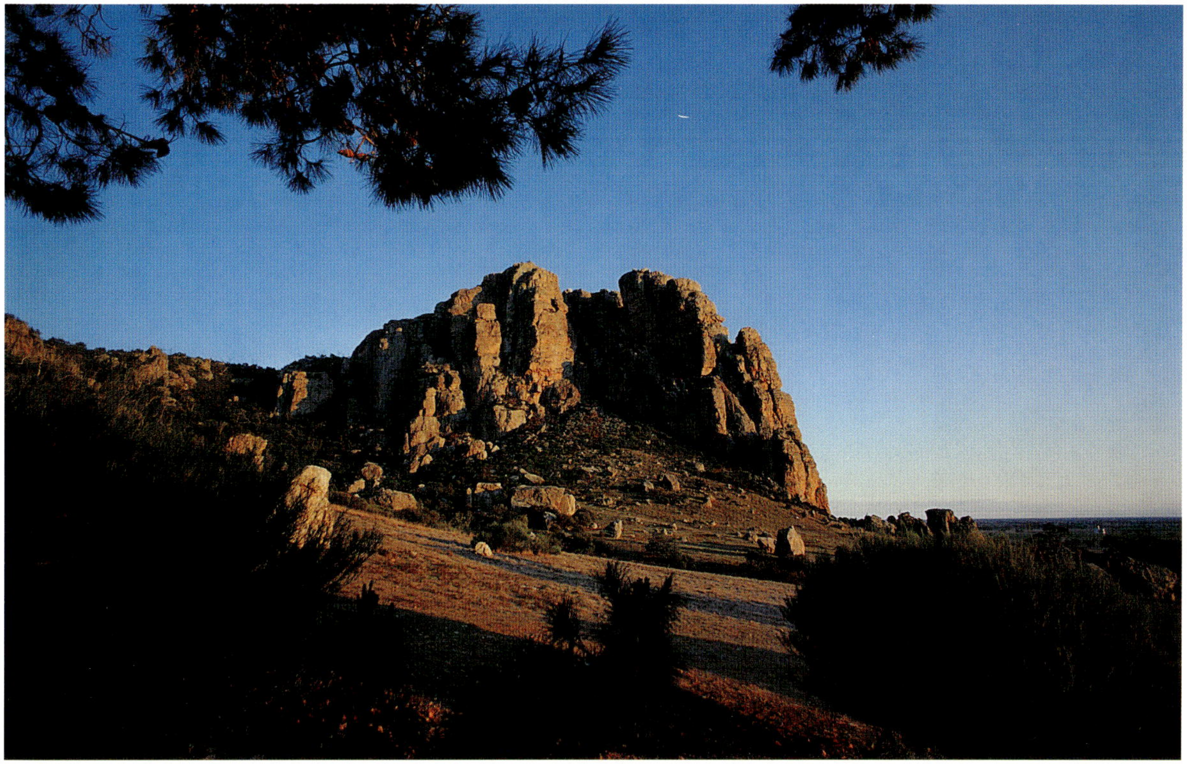

Mt Arapiles rises abruptly from the surrounding plain.

Mt Arapiles-Tooan State Park is 320 kilometres west of Melbourne. With the Grampians, this stark pile of rock offers some of the best and most varied sandstone climbing to be found anywhere in the world. Climbers come from everywhere, and more than 2000 routes have been pioneered up its faces, gully walls and pinnacles.

The surrounding Tooan area is woodland and heathland, noted for its rich and varied plant life. Around 500 species grow here and in springtime the floral display, which includes ground orchids, and birdlife are remarkable.

English explorer Major Mitchell climbed Mt Arapiles in 1836 and named the formation after a landmark near the Spanish battleground, Salamanca. In the 1880s, the bushranger Captain Melville camped in a cave on Mt Arapiles.

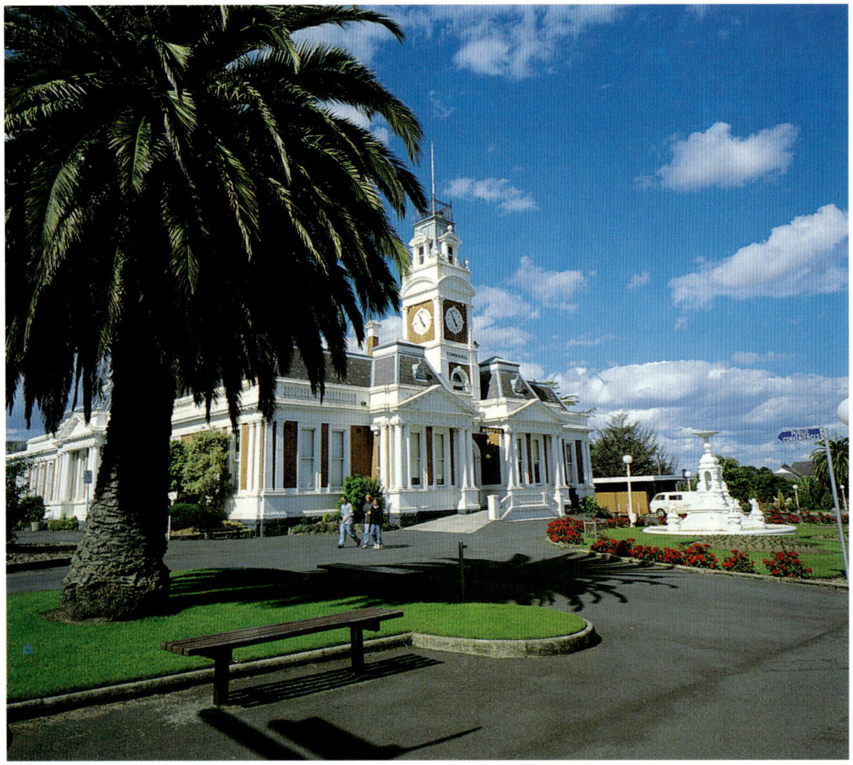

Above: The Town Hall in Ararat, near the Grampians. Ararat has many buildings dating to gold rush days.

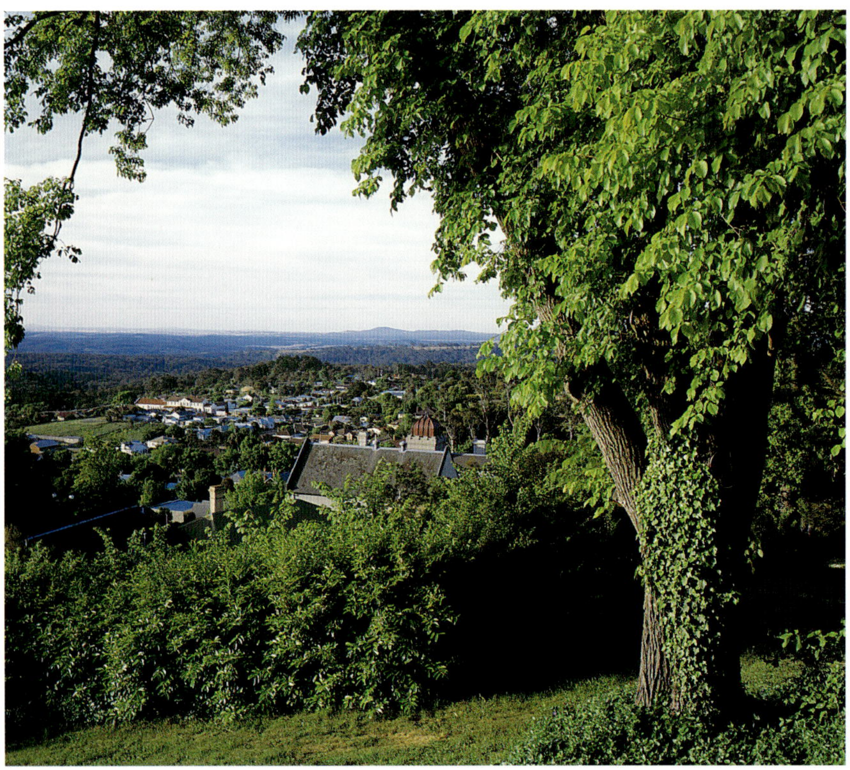

Above: Daylesford, once known as Wombat, stands in an area where gold was discovered in 1851.

Gold rush towns

The discovery of gold in the 1850s changed the face of Victoria. Small country settlements, linked to Melbourne by roads which were merely rutted tracks, found themselves swamped by gold-seekers from all over the world. The bush was denuded for pit-props, firewood and shanty frames, creek banks were scarred by gold-panning, creek flats turned into ant beds of mine shafts and miners. Bushrangers preyed on anyone they could find on the road to rob. Officialdom tried to impose a structure on the miners, a police force was created to enforce regulations, rebellion simmered and erupted and legends were born.

Today, Victoria's old gold-mining towns proudly display their heritage in grand civic buildings and statues, museums and re-creations of gold rush events.

Opposite: Ballarat's magnificent Town Hall.

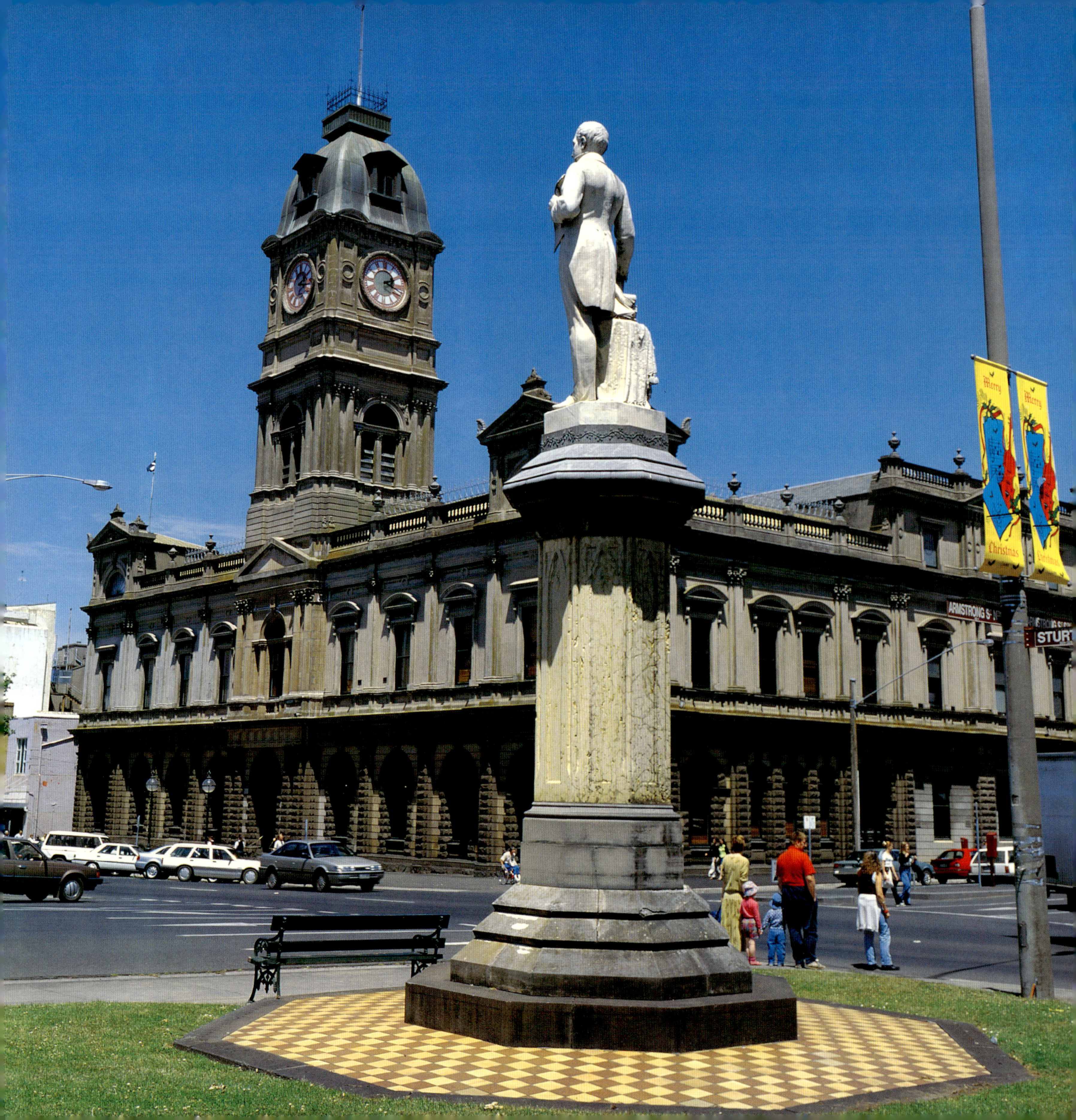
Merry
Christmas
Merry
ARMSTRONG St
STURT

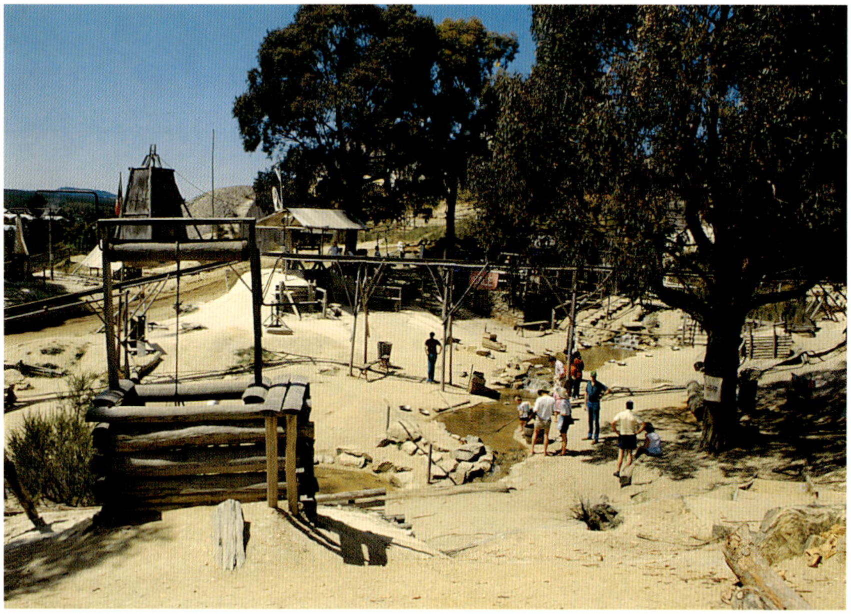

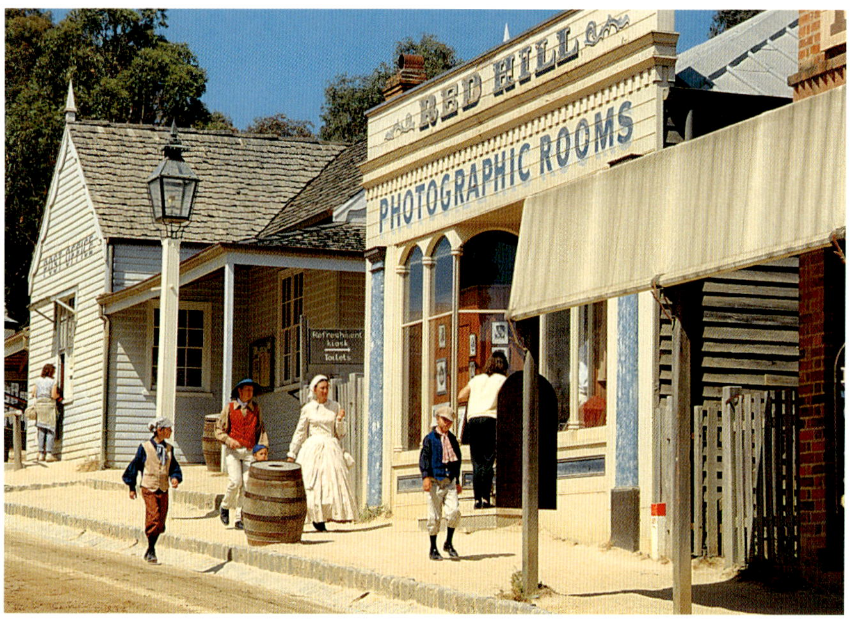

Above, top and *opposite:* Scenes re-creating life in the gold rush days at Sovereign Hill.

Sovereign Hill

Gold was discovered at Buninyong and Poverty Point, near Sovereign Hill, Ballarat, in 1851. Eureka Stockade, the miners' armed rebellion against the way the goldfields were governed, took place in 1854. Sovereign Hill re-creates in meticulous detail the Ballarat of the gold rush days, and offers an exciting re-enactment of the Eureka Stockade.

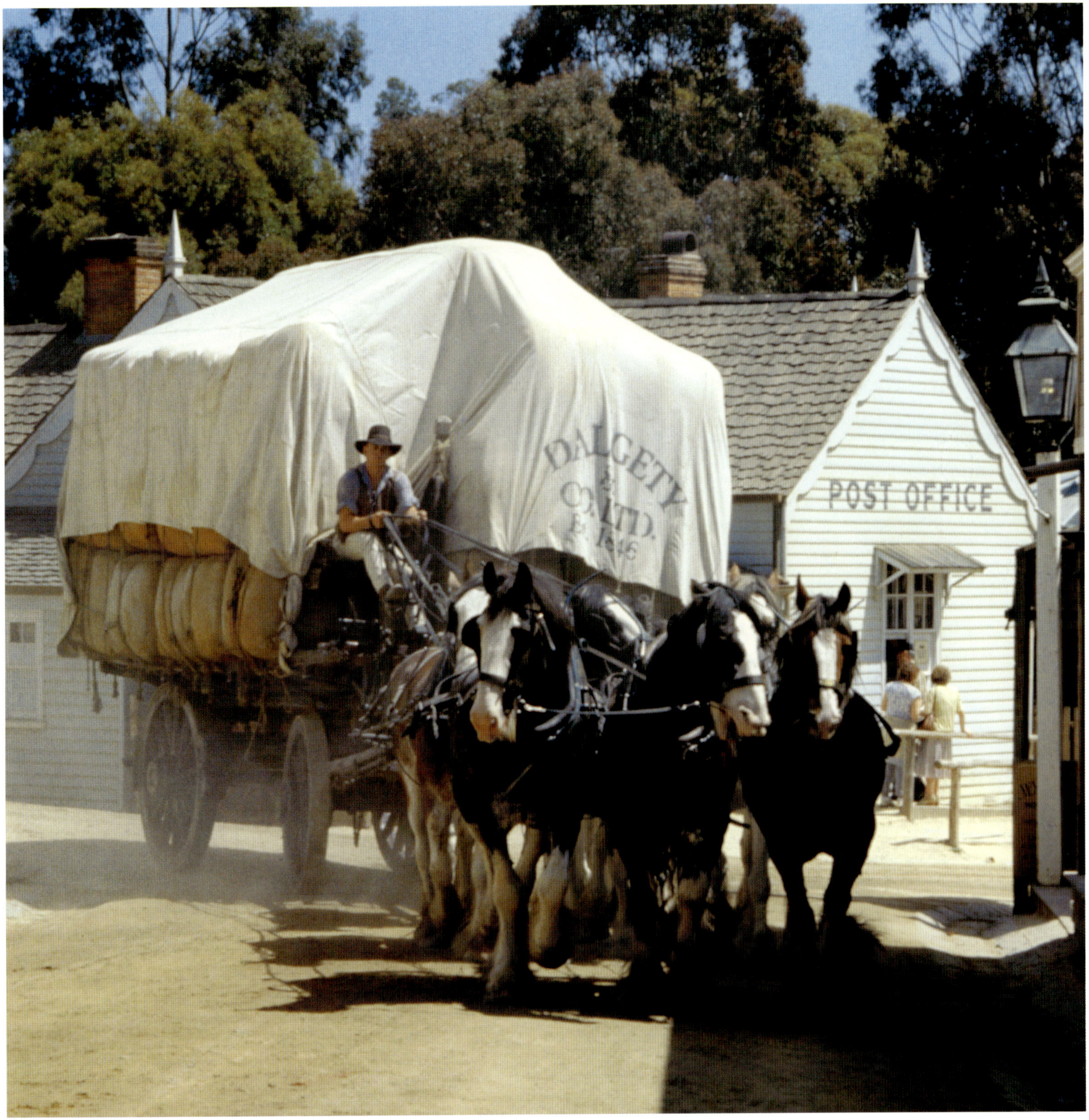
DALGETY
& CO. LTD.
POST OFFICE

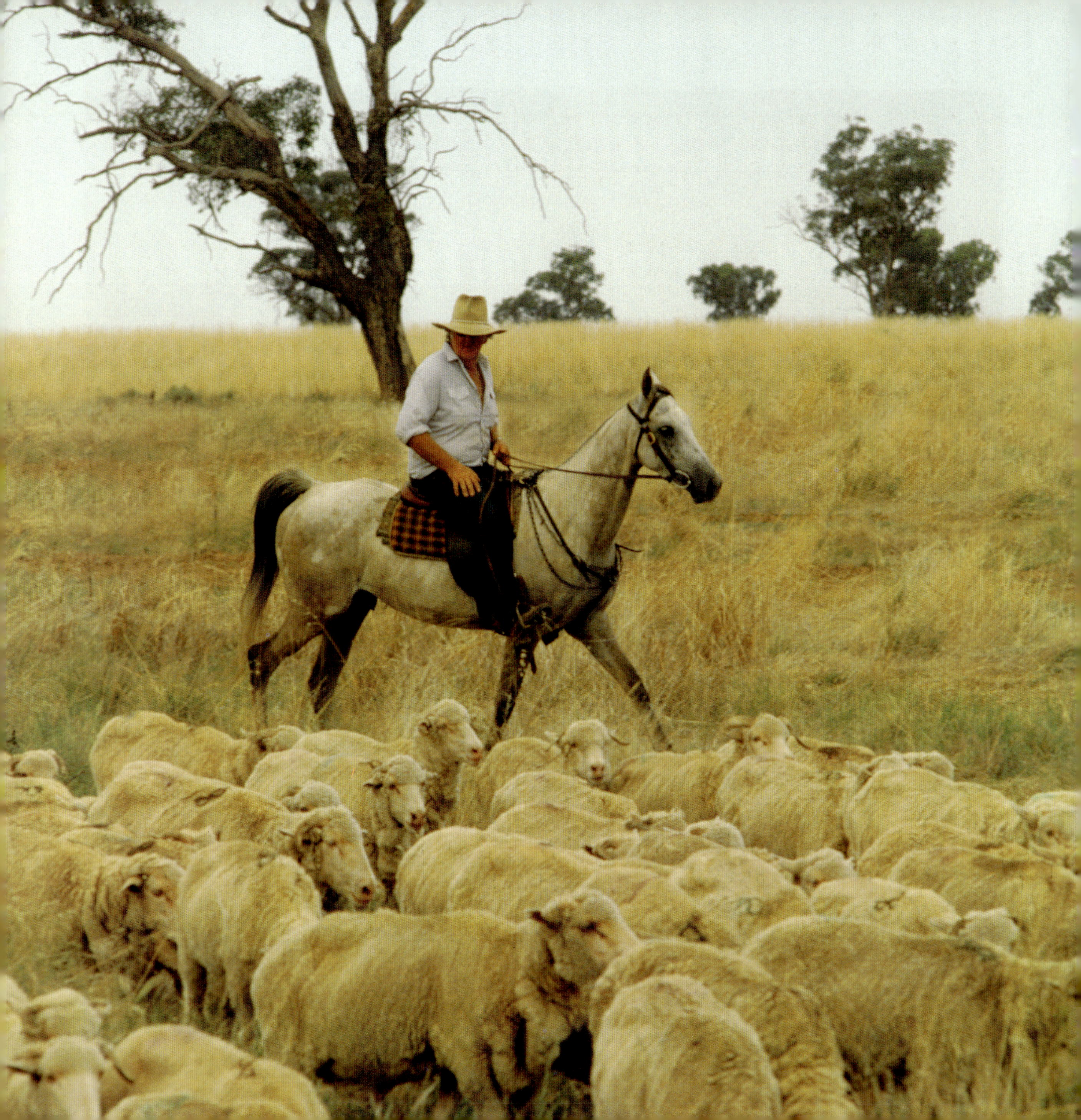

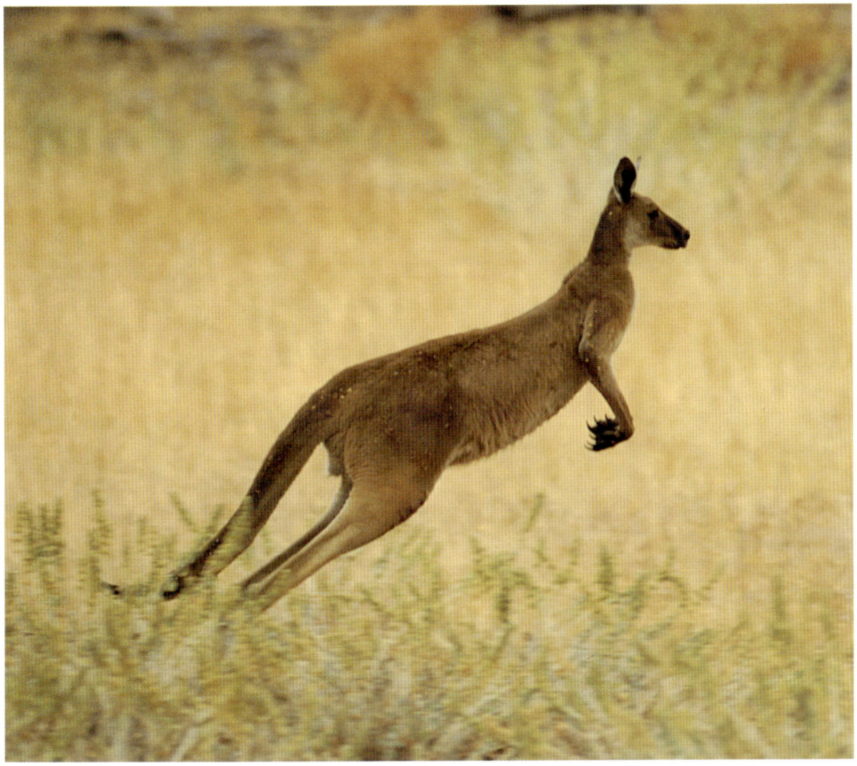

Above: A kangaroo bounds across the plains of the Mallee.

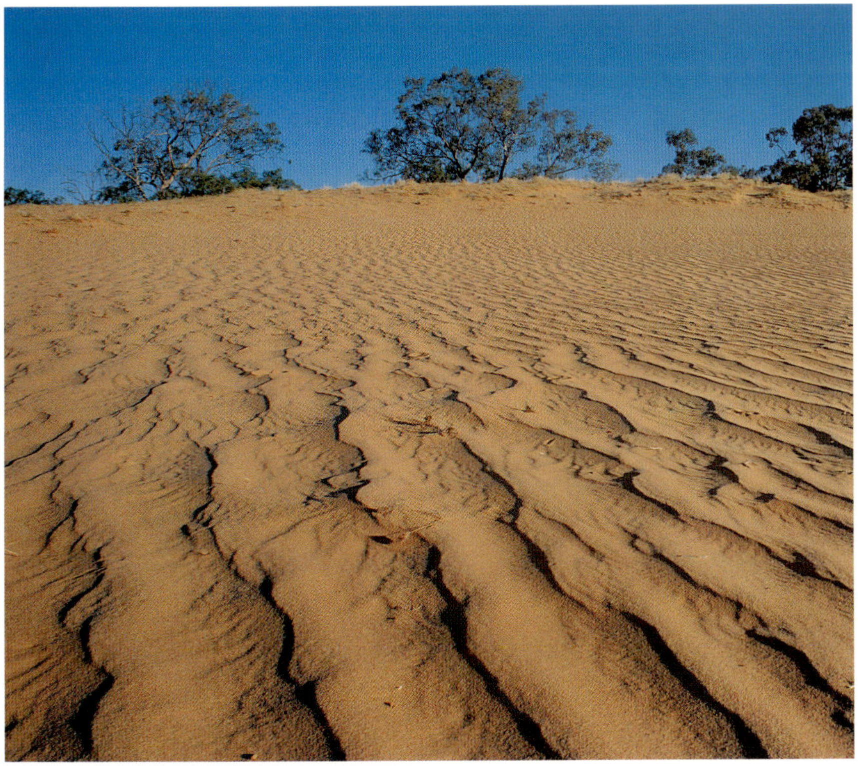

Above: When the rains come, dams will fill and creeks overflow their banks.

Sunset country – Victoria's north-west

Much of the north-western corner of Victoria is known as the Mallee, named after the tough little trees which send many trunks up from roots which quest through the sandy soil in search of any available drop of moisture.

This is country of wide open spaces, of sand dunes and sandy plains, of spectacular sunsets and night skies spangled with stars. It is fragile country, whose native plants and animals are well adapted to surviving periods of drought then breeding after rainfall brings the land to life.

To explore Wyperfeld, Little Desert, Big Desert, Hattah-Kulkyne and Murray-Sunset National Parks, take plenty of water, identification guides to birds and plants, and marvel at the delicacy with which the lives of all living things are interwoven in this arid wonderland. If you are fortunate enough to visit the Mallee after rainfall, be prepared for an explosion of wildflowers and birds nesting everywhere.

Opposite: Large pastoral holdings are typical of Victoria's north-west.

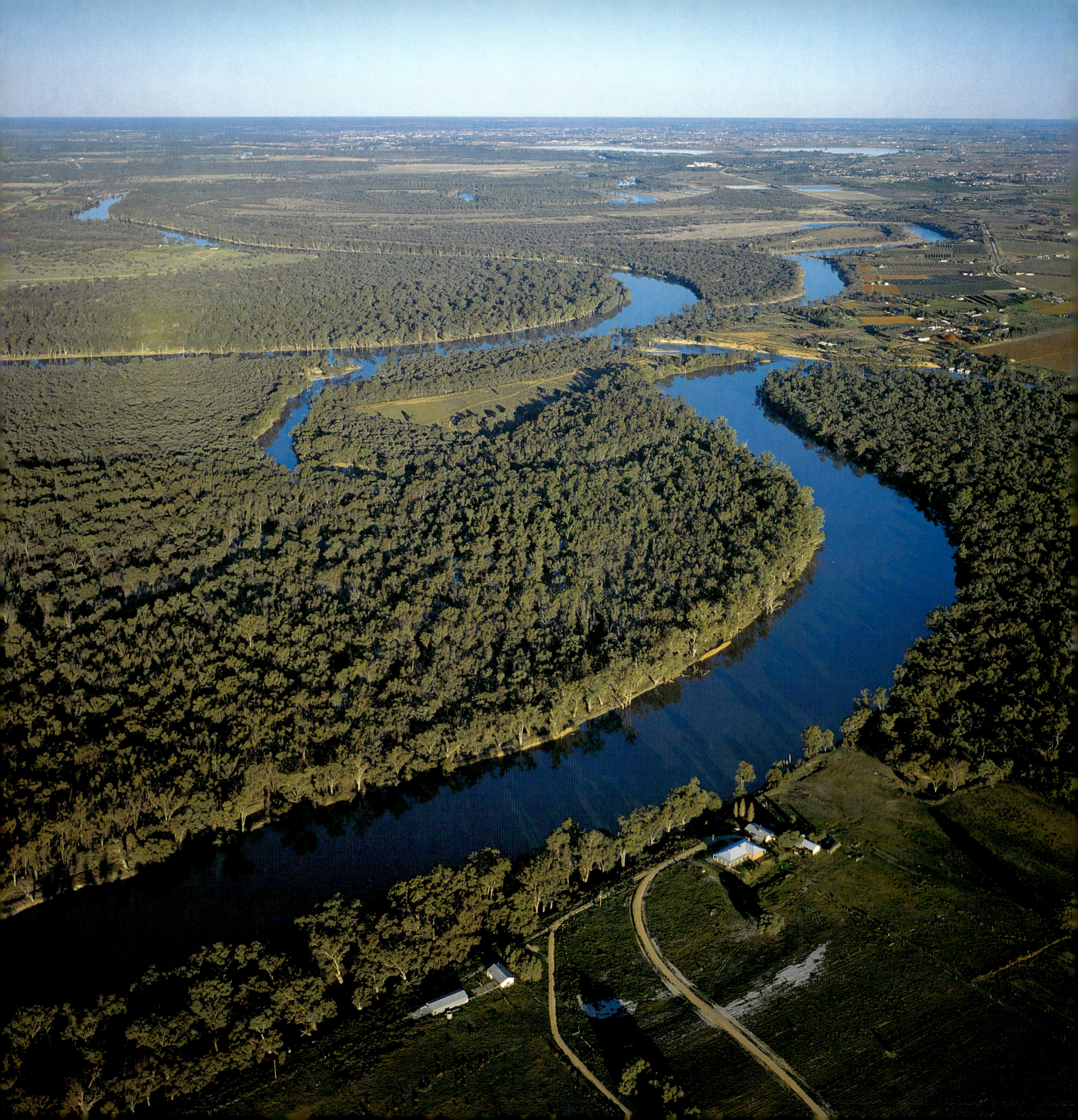

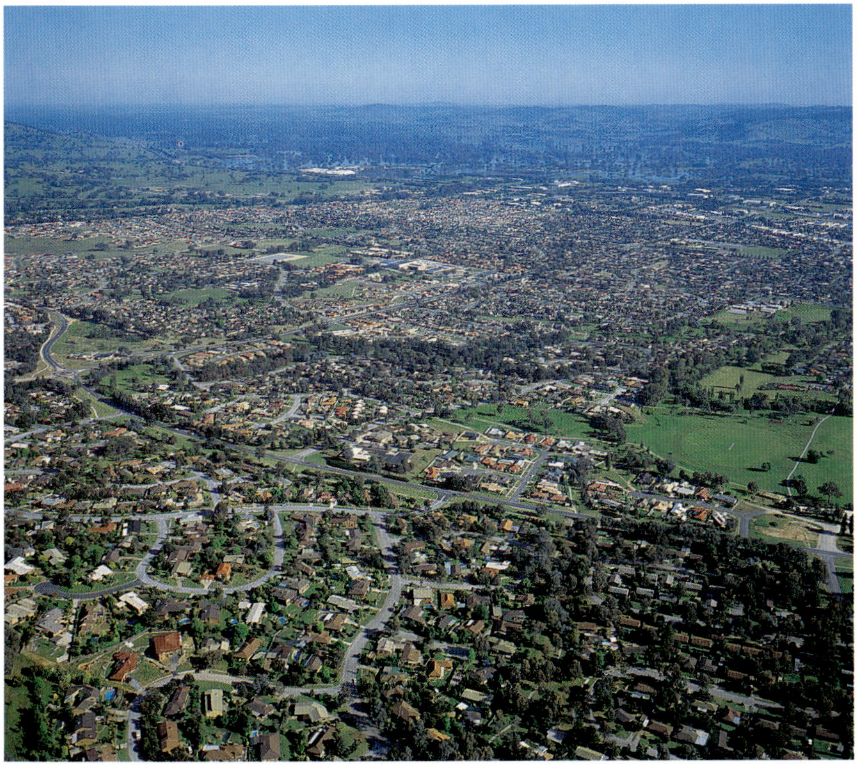

Above: An aerial view of Wodonga.

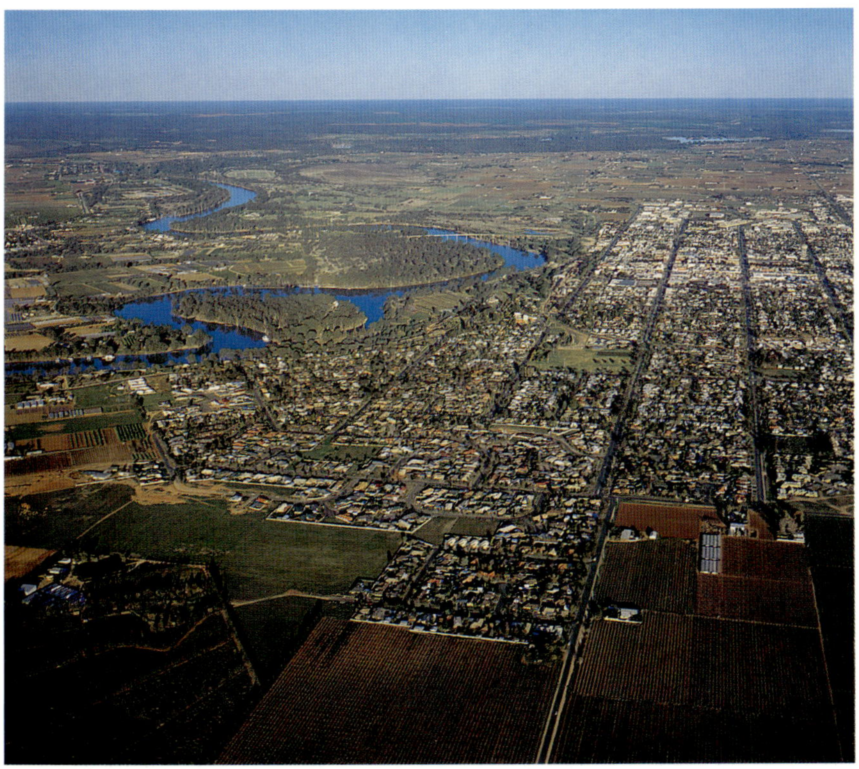

Above: Mildura, heart of the Sunraysia district, with the Murray River at top left.

The mighty Murray

As it flows westwards to form the border of north-western Victoria, many kilometres after its source in the Australian Alps, the mighty Murray River creates a long line of green across the Mallee. Orchards, vineyards and lush pastures are all possible here because of the Murray's bounty.

For much of the nineteenth century, the Murray was a busy commercial waterway. Eventually, railways and roads took over the transport of cargo and passengers: today the roaring days of the river are commemorated in museums, historic displays, and the paddlewheelers which transport their enthralled passengers back to a more gracious age.

At least half a million people annually holiday on the Murray near Mildura, on its banks or on houseboats, where highlights include Red Cliffs Scenic Reserve, Kings Billabong and Karadoc Beaches.

Opposite: The Murray River, a lazy giant, flows placidly past Mildura towards the South Australian border.
Following pages: A paddlewheeler on the Murray River.

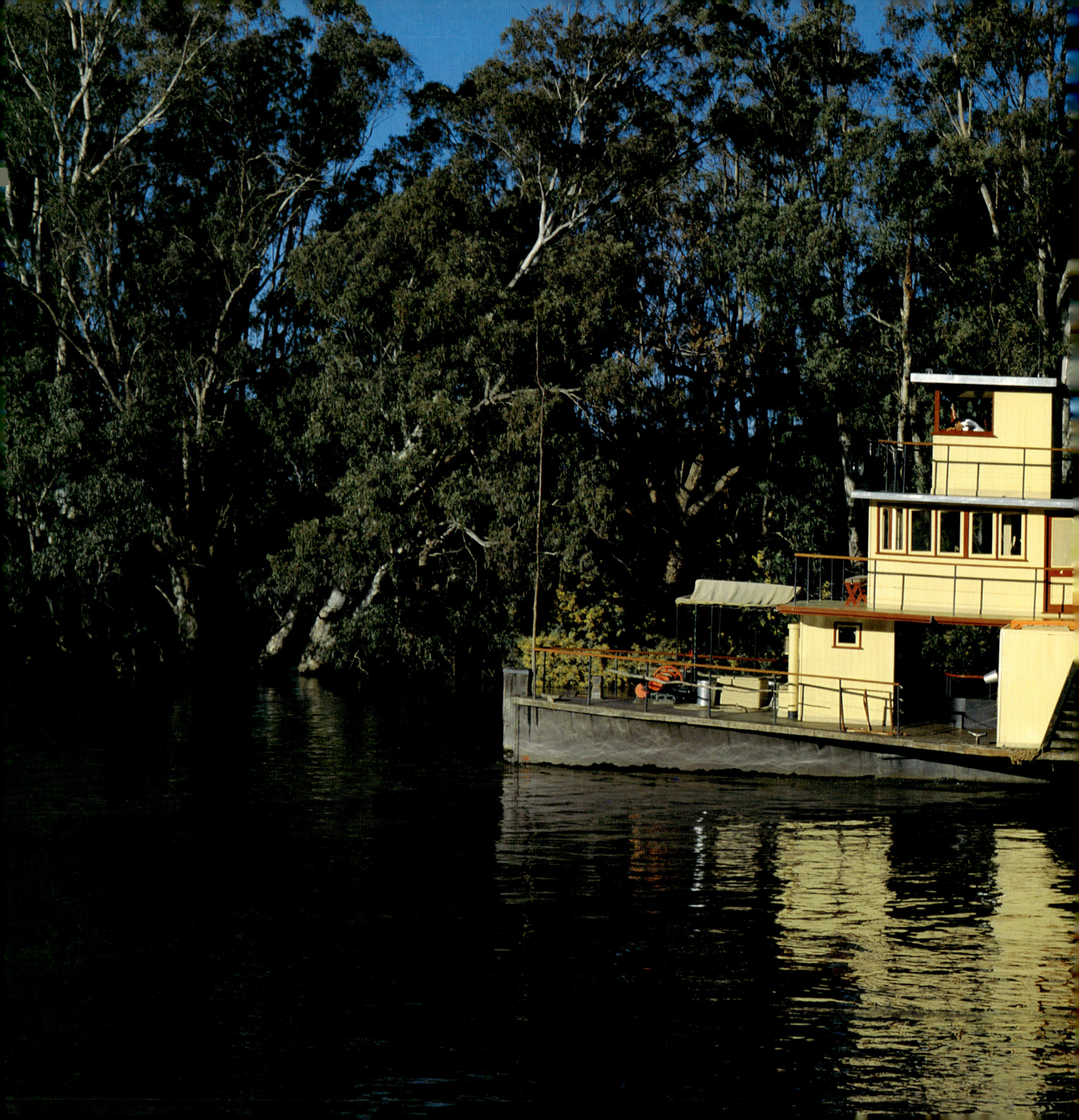

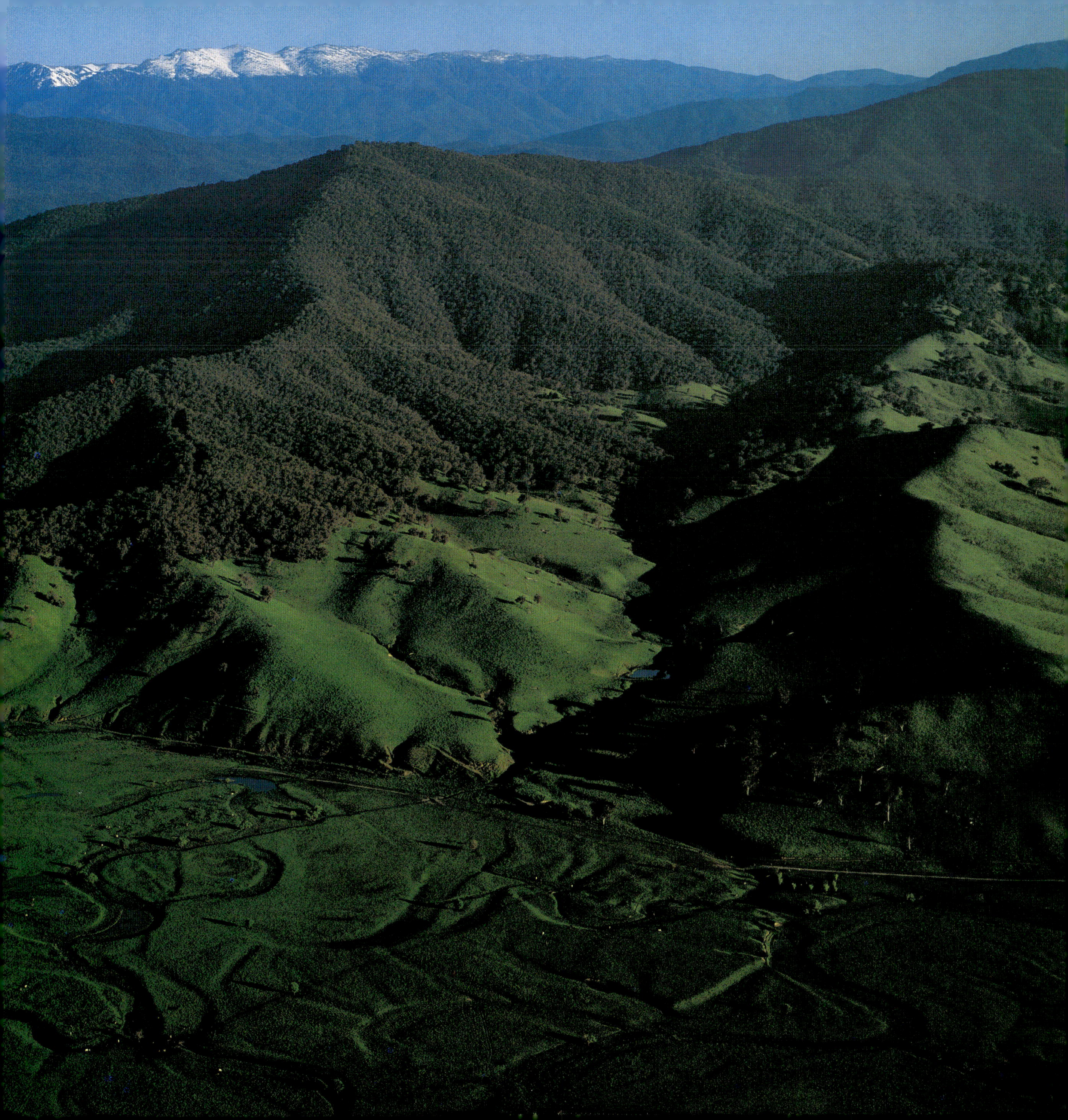

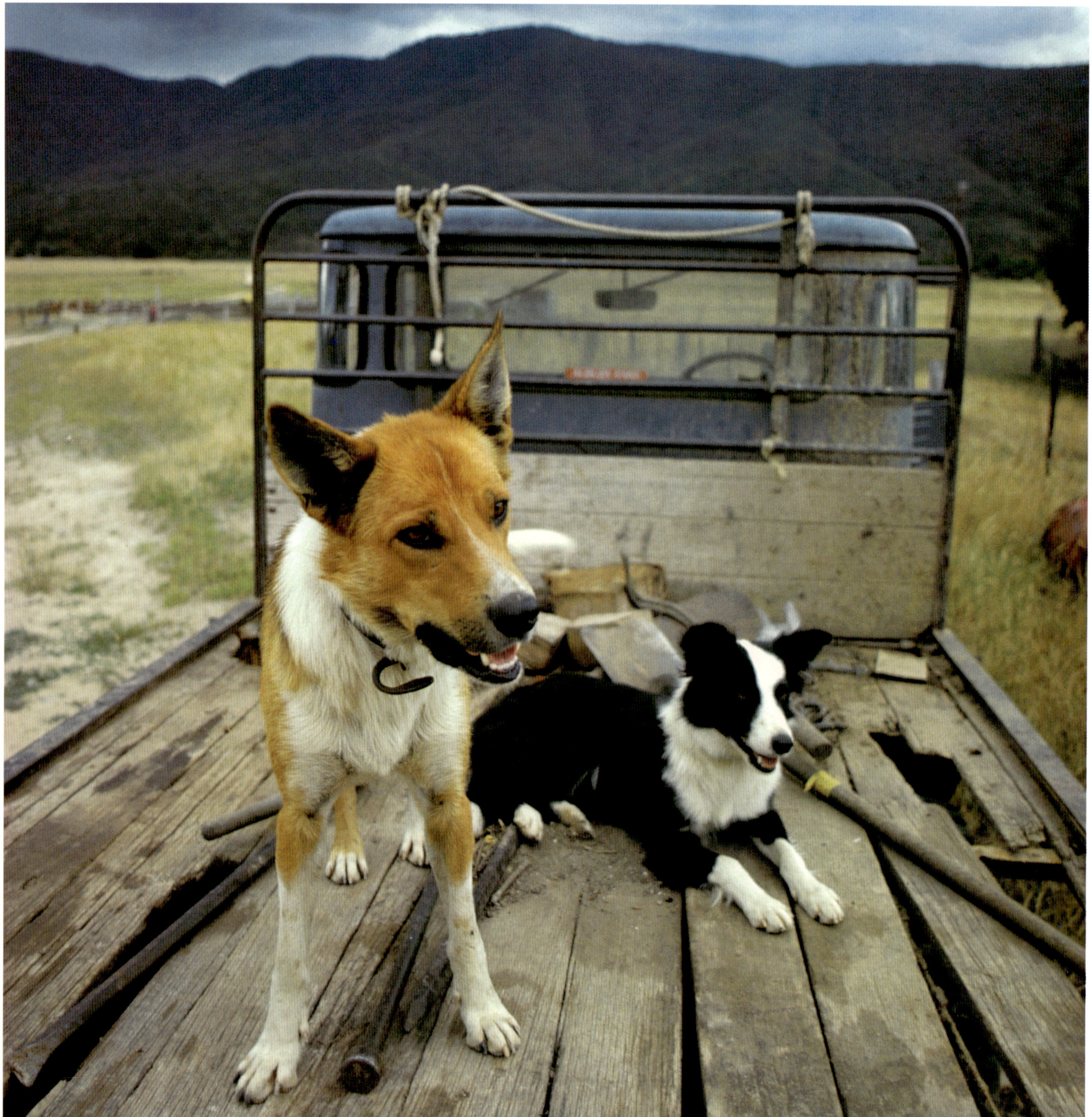

Australian working dogs are bred for intelligence and obedience. In the rugged mountains of the Murray River headwaters, these two are taking a break from mustering stock.

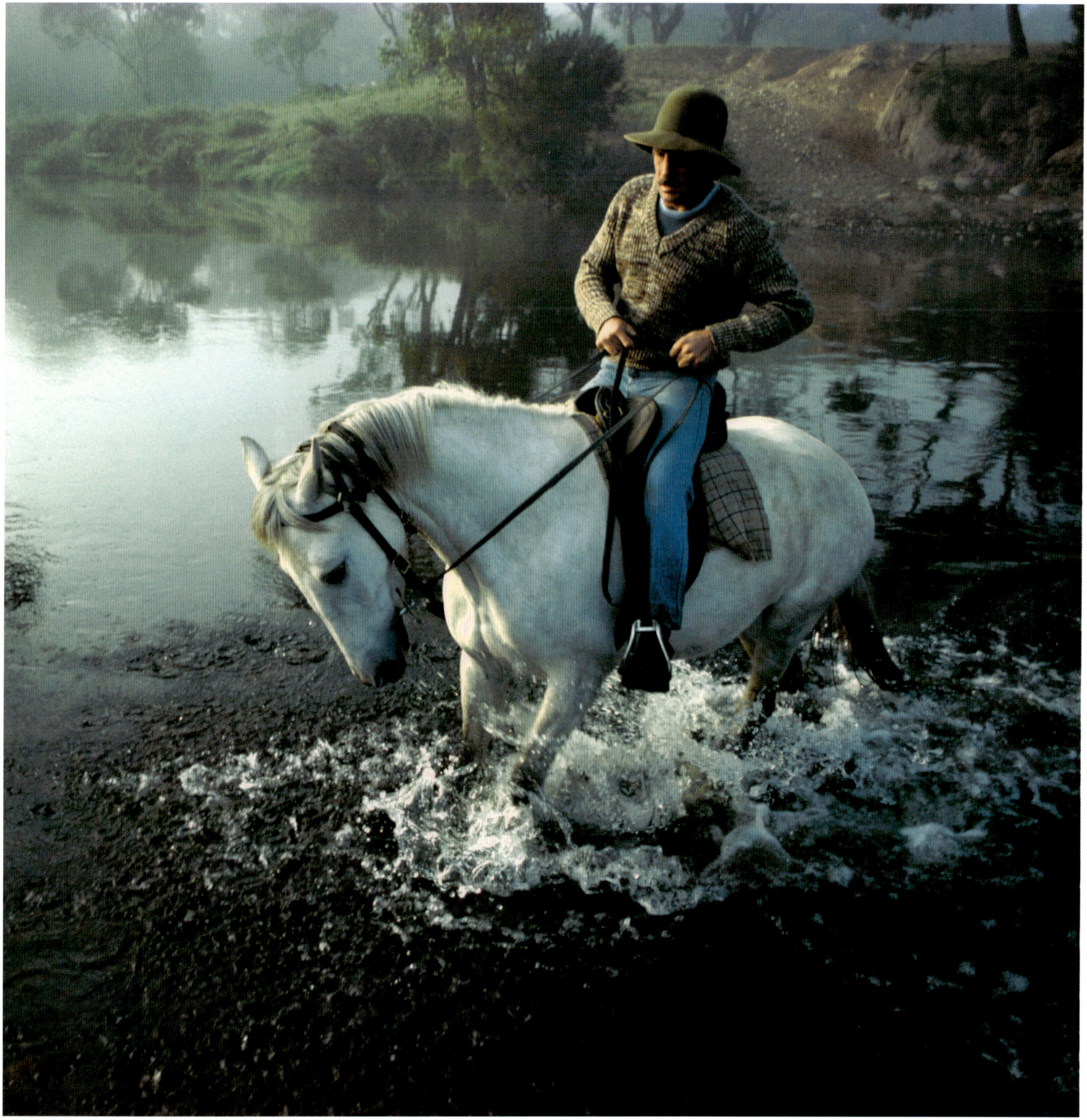

This is Man from Snowy River country.

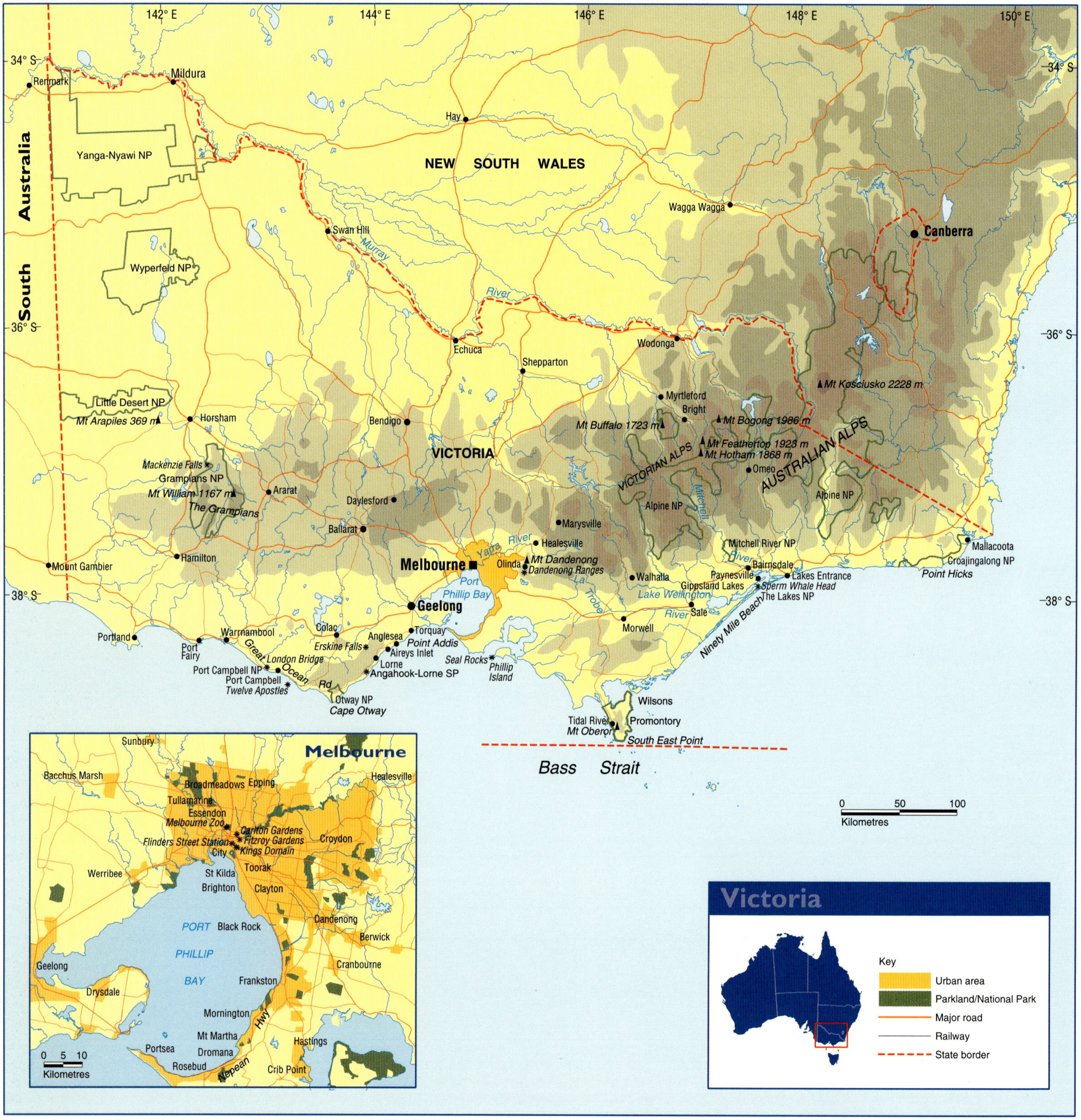
Victoria
142° E
144° E
146° E
148° E
150° E
34° S
36° S
38° S
South Australia
NEW SOUTH WALES
VICTORIA
Renmark
Mildura
Yanga-Nyawi NP
Hay
Wagga Wagga
Canberra
Swan Hill
Murray River
Wyperfeld NP
Echuca
Wodonga
Shepparton
Mt Kosciusko 2228 m
Myrtleford
Bright
Mt Bogong 1986 m
Mt Buffalo 1723 m
Mt Feathertop 1923 m
Mt Hotham 1868 m
VICTORIAN ALPS
AUSTRALIAN ALPS
Omeo
Alpine NP
Mitchell
Little Desert NP
Mt Arapiles 369 m
Horsham
Bendigo
Mackenzie Falls
Grampians NP
Mt William 1167 m
The Grampians
Ararat
Daylesford
Ballarat
Marysville
Healesville
Yarra River
Melbourne
Olinda
Mt Dandenong
Dandenong Ranges
Mitchell River NP
Mallacoota
Croajingalong NP
Point Hicks
Bairnsdale
Lakes Entrance
Paynesville
Gippsland Lakes
Sperm Whale Head
The Lakes NP
Walhalla
La Trobe River
Lake Wellington
Sale
Morwell
Ninety Mile Beach
Mount Gambier
Hamilton
Port Phillip Bay
Geelong
Portland
Port Fairy
Warrnambool
Colac
Anglesea
Torquay
Point Addis
Erskine Falls
Aireys Inlet
Lorne
Great Ocean Rd
London Bridge
Port Campbell NP
Port Campbell
Twelve Apostles
Angahook-Lorne SP
Seal Rocks
Phillip Island
Otway NP
Cape Otway
Wilsons Promontory
Tidal River
Mt Oberon
South East Point
Bass Strait
0 50 100
Kilometres
Melbourne
Sunbury
Bacchus Marsh
Broadmeadows
Epping
Healesville
Tullamarine
Essendon
Melbourne Zoo
Carlton Gardens
Fitzroy Gardens
Flinders Street Station
Kings Domain
City
Croydon
Toorak
Werribee
St Kilda
Brighton
Clayton
Black Rock
Dandenong
Berwick
PORT PHILLIP BAY
Geelong
Cranbourne
Frankston
Drysdale
Mornington
Nepean Hwy
Mt Martha
Dromana
Portsea
Rosebud
Hastings
Crib Point
0 5 10
Kilometres
Key
Urban area
Parkland/National Park
Major road
Railway
State border

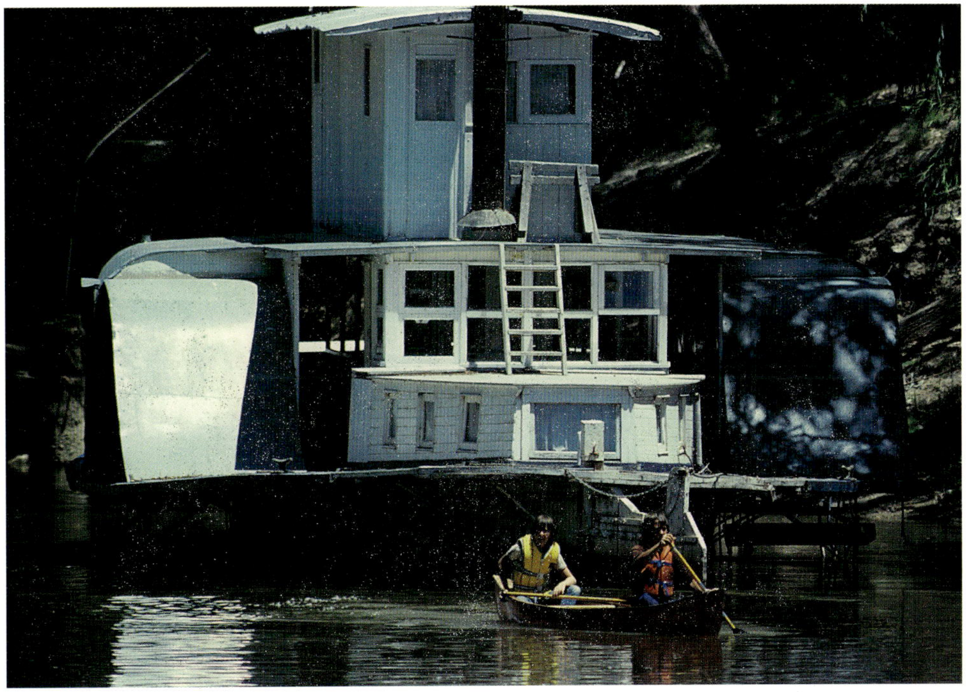

Exploring Victoria

There are three very practical advantages to exploring Victoria. First is the comparatively small size of the State – Croajingolong National Park, in the extreme north-east, is 500 kilometres from Melbourne, while the Big Desert Wilderness Park, in the north-western corner, is 480 kilometres from the capital. The second advantage is the excellent quality of Victoria's road system. The third is the wide variety of experiences possible and the almost limitless variety of scenic beauty to be appreciated.

For the thrill of snow sports, go to the Victorian Alps. To be steeped in history, try the Gold Fields Heritage Trail. Along the Great Ocean Road is coastal grandeur; in East Gippsland or the Grampians are majestic mountains; in the Gippsland Lakes are fishing and water sports; while all over the State the wildlife and plant life are fascinating.

And of course there is always Melbourne, one of the world's great cities, offering Victorian elegance, modern sophistication, a wealth of culture and friendly hospitality.

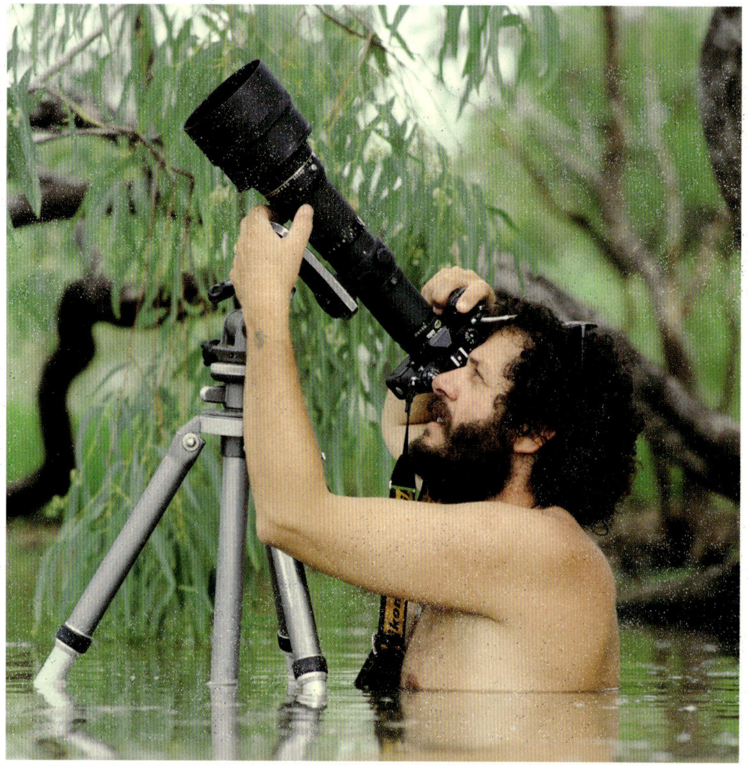

Steve Parish

World-famous photographer Steve Parish began his remarkable career by recording marine life off Australia's coasts. After discovering the fascinations of the rainforest and its wild creatures, he has spent much of his life journeying around Australia photographing the landscapes, plants, animals and the people of the land. Of recent years, he has extended the range of his subjects to include Australia's cities and towns.

The magnificent library of images which has resulted has become the heart of Steve Parish Publishing Pty Ltd. Through the firm's publications, Steve and his wife and partner Jan are realising their dream of sharing Australia with the world.

Celebrating Australia is a collection of titles which present the incomparable beauty of the southern continent in superb photographs and text. As Steve comments: "After a lifetime of travel and asking questions, I have only just begun to discover how much there is to learn about Australia. I hope these books arouse in others a desire like mine to explore and to appreciate this wonderful country."

Index

First published by Steve Parish Publishing Pty Ltd, 1997
PO Box 2160, Fortitude Valley BC, Queensland 4006, Australia

ISBN 1 875932 95 X

Photography: Steve Parish
Text: Pat Slater, Steve Parish Publishing, Australia

Map supplied by MAPgraphics
Additional photos supplied by Hans and Judy Beste, p. 56 top
Editing, design: Steve Parish Publishing, Australia
Printed in Hong Kong
Colour separations by Steve Parish Publishing, Australia